CONSERVATIVE

ESSAYS

LEGAL AND POLITICAL.

BY

S. S. NICHOLAS,

OF LOUISVILLE, KENTUCKY.

SECOND SERIES.

PHILADELPHIA:

J. B. LIPPINCOTT & CO

1865.

CONTENTS.

CHAPTER IV.

CHAPTER V.

CHAPTER VI.

CHAPTER VII.

CHAPTER VIII.

CHAPTER IX.

CHAPTER X.

CHAPTER XI.

CHAPTER XII.

CHAPTER XIII.

CHAPTER XIV.

CHAPTER XV.

CHAPTER XVI.

CHAPTER XVII.

CHAPTER XVIII.

CHAPTER XIX.

CHAPTER XX.

DEDICATION.

TO THE

HON. JOHN STUART MILL,

OF ENGLAND,

AUTHOR OF TREATISES ON "LIBERTY" AND "REPRESENTATIVE GOVERNMENT."

In affording myself the gratification of making you the small compliment of this dedication, it is not merely as a tribute of respect to the profoundest, most enlightened political thinker of Europe, but as a mode of acknowledging the great gratification received from finding such singular coincidence of thought between us as to great essentials, though differing much as to minor matters.

This coincidence has also struck others who are acquainted with my political writings of the last twenty-five years, and serves to show that difference of country and education does not necessarily cause difference of opinion as to the fundamentals of good government. Sincere thinkers have long agreed that *a government of law* is the *desideratum*, and the true method of best securing such government was the great *problem* to be solved. We Americans confidently believed and arrogantly boasted that our institutions, as developed in their practical working, were a most successful solution of the problem. The more intelligent and considerate among us no longer make that boast. The dear-bought experience of the last four years has undeceived us. Nothing is more common than for intelligent Americans frankly to recant the cherished delusion of a lifetime, and avow their opinions that all the great essentials of liberty are better secured in England than in this country; that is, hers is a much nearer approach than ours to a true, practical government of law, giving better security to all personal private rights, and affording much the better chance for wise, uncorrupt administration of the government. This is a most mortifying confession for an American to make to an Englishman, and to no one of my fellow-citizens can it be more acutely so than to myself. No one participated more largely in the almost universal marvel among even the thinking, informed men here, that with the light of our successful experiment on a Representative Republic the intelligence of England could so patiently endure hereditary rule. While the inconsiderate are exulting with unstinted joy over our military success over the detestable rebellion, most of our worth and intelligence are moaning over the probable permanent destruction of constitution-secured liberty.

The coincidence of opinion between us extends even to the extreme point of giving suffrage to women. This has been a cherished creed with me for more than fifteen years. It has, however, resulted from no latitudinary democracy. Though a born child and educated son of that school, and still believing that every white person in a Republic who pays a tax, however small, ought to have a right to vote, yet I have long been convinced that we were very wrong in having no restriction to the right and in conferring it so recklessly upon unprepared foreigners. This, however, is past remedy and cannot now be changed. In seeking a counteracting check to the evil, the conservative element of woman's suffrage occurred to me, as it probably did to you, as the only practical, because the only attainable remedy. It seems to look like a mere extension of the democratic principle, and therefore may obtain popular assent, while it will never be given to any other remedy that I can devise. That it would prove highly conservative, there can be no doubt. Women generally are lovers of order and quiet. As a class they are on the average much more moral than men, and much more under the influence of religion—that great conservative element of our society. The objection that it would practically give two votes to married men has no proper validity, for it would not be an alteration for the worse to require every voter to be either a husband or a father. Society has a right to demand at least that amount of *prima facie* evidence of conservatism, and it would be much less obnoxious to popular prejudice and ultra democracy than a property qualification.

If you took the trouble of looking into the first volume of my Essays, which was sent you, the title of the chapter in which the coincidence of our opinions is most apparent will probably have caused it to escape your notice. It is the chapter on "The New Constitution of Kentucky." The subject caused an attempted theoretical development of some of the main fundamentals of republican government, and the discussion of topics that have since been handled with so much ability by yourself.

But, sir, the true motive for the obtrusion of these remarks is the desire I have felt to give a public expression of my congratulations to you and other workers of England in the conservative cause of liberty, for your bold, novel plan of electing members of Parliament, the better to insure a practical protection and representation to minorities. That protection was the main idea upon which our written Constitutions were made. But, as Madison foresaw, the want of some such practical power of self-protection, some extraneous power to cause the Constitution to be obeyed, has caused its supposed ample security to prove a mere delusion in the very hour of its utmost need. Our dear-bought experience of the last four years has fully proved that you cannot well do too much in that direction; that is, you cannot be too solicitous about bridling and curbing the arbitrary will of your majorities. This is all the more essential for you, as your judiciary have no veto power over the omnipotence of your Parliament. Such omnipotence anywhere in terrestrial government is what we Americans have been taught to view with abhorrence. If you will excuse me for saying so, we contemplate your nation as in the unenviable position of enjoying freedom only by the permission of its own servants. To enjoy it as we shall have to do in all the long future only by the permission of the majority, or rather of the majority party, is a degradation of the same character, only somewhat less perhaps in degree. To every enlightened lover of true civil liberty either is sufficiently degrading to the manhood of those who make the proud boast of being freemen.

That such is our present degraded condition is a most melancholy fact. All the guarantees of our Constitution in favor of liberty, free speech, free press, free ballot, jury trial, *habeas cor-*

pus, exemption of private property from arbitrary seizure and confiscation, exemption from arbitrary arrest and imprisonment, secret trial and punishment, exemption of private contracts from tender laws, exemption of the people from Federal conscription, exemption from *ex post facto* laws and bills of attainder, the supremacy of civil over military power, have all been trodden into nonentity by a willing soldiery, at the needless silly bidding of a vengeful political party, whose most honest members are to be found among those of them who are sincere fanatics. That it was silly as well as wicked to resort to the unfounded pretext of necessity as a justification for these acts of tyranny, is now apparent. The final development of the feebleness of the South and of the vastly superior strength of the North in numbers and military resources, shows that there never was the slightest need for a resort to such means, and that they only served to prejudice instead of aiding the Union cause, their only real effect having been to cause division and dissension at the North. But neither silliness nor timidity alone caused the resort to those measures. They were prompted by party hate, in pursuit of party vengeance. So I repeat, do what you can to bridle and curb party power. That is the enemy to your liberties most to be feared, as it is also to ours. Nor is this the worst. The late Presidential election gave the irreversible sanction of the nation to all these tyrannical usurpations and abuses of power, and they are to stand as unimpeachable precedents for all that any political party may want to do toward wreaking their vengeance upon their opponents. How we are ever to be relieved from this degradation, how the Constitution is to be reinstated in its intended needful supremacy, no man can tell me. My own reflections point to only one remedy. That is, perhaps a revival at some distant future of the appreciation of liberty, and a manly effort to regain it by a rebellion against the then usurping party, causing another severe civil war, which, if resulting in favor of the rebellion, will reinstate the Constitution by the voice and power of the people, and cause it to be respected for a long time. Bad as this is, it is our only chance. It would appear to be an ever-enduring part of the destiny of the Anglo-Saxon race to win their freedom by rebellion and to preserve it by rebellion.

We were told that these usurpations were war measures, justified by State necessity, and that when peace returned they would all instantly cease. But we do not find it so. For some six weeks or more there has not been an armed rebel anywhere in the field from the Potomac to the Rio Grande; yet these usurpations have by no means ceased. Military commissions still usurp the power to try and punish private citizens outside the rebel States and in loyal States where the civil courts are in full, unimpeded operation. Notwithstanding the express prohibition of the Constitution, the ruling power continues to perpetrate other similar enormities.

We had thought that the improper dominance of a political party through the Federal Government was amply guarded against by a written Constitution carefully defining its power, also by a subdivision of its powers between a Congressional, Judicial, and Executive Departments, and by a large reservation of power to be exclusively exercised by the separate State Governments. But all this has proved illusory. The practical working has proved it to be throughout the Government of a political party. The President, the members of Congress and of the State Governments all belong to the dominant party, work in its interest as a paramount duty, far above all others of a political character, and instead of acting as a counterpoise or check, serve as a great aid to the arbitrary domination of the party. This suicidal vice in our institutions was seen long ago, and it has been the principal endeavor of my life for more than thirty years to arouse public opinion as to the danger necessarily to ensue from such a state of things. With this view the Essays on the Presidency contained in the first volume were published and republished. It was predicted that the collisions between parties in their contests for power would lead to just such a civil war as we have passed through, and having proved that the power and patronage of the Presidency was the principal occasion of these conflicts, recommended the substitution of some other method than that of a popular election for obtaining our Presidents. With that view the plan you will find in the present volume was carefully prepared and laid before the Senate at its last session, but was not acted upon by that body. The principal motive of this address to you is to invite your attention to that plan, with the hope you will place before our nation your opinion of it, whatever that opinion may be. If you should happen to think that it will successfully rescue the Presidential office from the clutch of political parties, or that it will cause the cessation of parties formed or kept up for the main purpose of obtaining its power and patronage, your recommendation may cause leading minds here to give the subject their serious attention, and perhaps enlist their active service in obtaining popular consent to some such change.

Most respectfully,

Your colaborer in the cause of civil liberty,

S. S. NICHOLAS.

LOUISVILLE, KENTUCKY, June 9, 1865.

CONSERVATIVE ESSAYS.

CHAPTER I.

A PLATFORM ADDRESS.

Introductory.

THE following plan of an Address was prepared for and sent to the Chicago Convention; but, from want of time or from deeming an address inexpedient, it was not acted on by the Committee having the platform in charge.

It is thought by most intelligent men not belonging to the Convention, to have been a great blunder not to have adopted a full, detailed platform, particularizing and denouncing many of the multitudinous crimes and blunders of the dominant party; or at least to have done so in the usual mode of an address to the nation. This omission was a great fault, more or less pernicious in its effect on the election. The insufficient, timidly tame thing adopted as a platform, served to give the Abolition party a quasi absolution, which they freely and perhaps successfully claimed, because of the absence of all specification of crimes or faults. It may be that no mode of platform or address could have materially altered the result of the election—still the fault was great. The occasion was appropriate for a proper indictment against that party from such an authoritative, respectable source, representing, as the Convention did, near a half of the loyal part of the nation. It was due to that very large minority that an indictment should have been adopted, setting forth specially many of the multifarious party acts of usurpation, of tyrannical abuse of power, of corruption, and of blundering incompetency. It was due also to the whole nation, to posterity, and to history. It was especially due to all patriots of every denomination who still cherish a hopeful trust or belief in the resuscitation of American liberty. The want of something of the kind will permit those faults and crimes to pass down to posterity as unchallenged precedents. If so, they will eradicate every semblance of the nation's liberty. Ours will forever cease to be a *government of law*, and remain what it has been for the last four years, a consolidated absolutism, under the unrestrained rule of every party majority.

The sudden change of party tactics evinced by this failure of the Convention is incomprehensible. Heretofore, in the prosperous days of the party, when it took the field against an adversary, it was for no gloved conflict, but, under the battle-cry of "war with the knife and the knife to the hilt," its trumpets uttered "no puling strain of the sucking dove," but one "as sonorous as the roaring lion." It boastfully claimed for itself the proud cognomen of "the great unterrified." If it has not lost all pretension to that title, why evade its duty, at so momentous a crisis, by such a specimen of shameful timidity as this pretense of a platform? If that platform gave entire satisfaction to any single member of the Convention, it has had no such success with any intelligent man outside the Convention and the Abolition party. Its timid insufficiency has been freely denounced by all others, not excepting peace Democrats, whose propitiation was the ostensible pretext.

Most of the following plan of an Address was published last October, and its republication now in this form is made from no expectation of serving in the slightest degree to supply the pernicious omission of the Convention, but, as Colonel Benton would have said, "as an aid to history," or as an aid, however small, toward keeping alive the principles of liberty. The materials for attack were so superabundant as to make selection the principal difficulty in its preparation. For the same reason there was no need to strain or mis-glose facts. The principles relied on are those that every one knows, or should know—are the teachings of the fathers of the Republic; and nearly all of them such as were never questioned until within the last four years. Without a boast, the assertion may well be ventured, as to those facts and principles, that, as John Quincy Adams said of his book, "they will abide unshaken the test of human scrutiny, of talents, and of time."

TO THE PEOPLE OF THE UNITED STATES.

The Conservative and Democratic friends of the Union and the Constitution, having met in Convention for the purpose of nominating candidates for President and Vice-President, will set forth their views as to true national policy and those fundamental principles on which it should be based, with some of the reasons for their opposition to the acts and policy of the dominant Abolition party, past, present, and prospective.

The National Situation.

1. We are in the midst of two perilous wars—the war against the Union and the war against the Constitution.

2. The war against the Union is the result of the co-operative aid of bad men North and South, in fomenting sectional jealousy and hate, depreciating the supposed value and weakening the long-cherished love of the Union, and of party strife degenerated into sectional contests for power. This is felicitously expressed in the following resolution, adopted in 1859 by the Legislature of Tennessee when wholly untainted with disunionism:—

"All the evils growing out of intense slavery agitation—all the discord, alienation, and bitter hatred between the North and the South—are the legitimate fruit, not of any necessary or 'irrepressible conflict' between free and slave labor, but of a conflict between rival aspirants in the race of ambition, North and South, urged on by an inordinate greed of official power and plunder."

3. The responsibility for the disunion war rests heavily upon the dominant Abolition party and its President. When, in despite the reiterated earnest warnings of wiser and better men—of all discreet, intelligent men not engaged in their enterprise—they, in the reckless pursuit of political power, availed themselves of the universal prejudice against negro slavery to organize a purely sectional party, whose principal avowed aim was hostility to negro slavery, they enabled the disunionists South to organize an opposing sectional party for protection against that hostility. The inevitable effect of the division of the nation into two such

parties, as foreseen and predicted by all intelligent, disinterested men, was, by their collision, to cause civil war and perhaps disunion. Having disregarded the warning, and by their acts fulfilled the prediction, they come under one of two alternatives, which equally prove them unworthy of popular trust. They either had not the intelligence to see the necessary consequence of their acts, though so obvious to all other men, or, seeing those consequences, they desired them or were regardless of them, while "urged on by an inordinate greed of official power and plunder."

4. For the great calamity of the war these men owe the nation a signal atonement; but, instead of making any atonement, or even manifesting a decent contrition, they impudently deny their responsibility, and impiously attempt to shift it from themselves over upon Providence. Instead of doing anything to soothe that fear of Abolition hate and misrule which they were so instrumental in arousing, and which was the main cause of the rebellion, they have done all they could to intensify that fear, and to prove that it had been from the first well founded. Instead of doing anything to alleviate or abridge the great national calamity of their inflicting, they have done all they could toward its increase and prolongation, by precluding all chance of amicable restoration.

5. By adopting and propagating the false dogma of the "irrepressible conflict," invented by a secessionist for disunion purposes, these men hoped to disguise their real aim in pursuit of political power; as, by its incessant reiteration now, they hope to disguise their real present object, the gratification of their unappeasable hate in the infliction of a demoniac vengeance upon the whole people of the South, one-half of whom are the mere victims of their own great crime in instigating the war. The preaching of a dogma which carried such persuasive argument in favor and even justification of disunion—though meeting nothing but derision from disinterested intelligence—and their close affiliation with those Abolitionists who for long years had been publicly seeking disunion, and who avowed their hate for the Union and the Constitution as "covenants with death and leagues with hell," brought these men under the just suspicion of being influenced by similar want of loyalty to Union and Constitution. They have done nothing to remove but everything to increase this suspicion.

Since the war has reached a stage where it was deemed impracticable for the non-abolitionized part of the Northern people to withdraw their support, or injuriously to manifest their opposition to its prosecution for abolition purposes, they have ceased all attempts at hypocritical concealment, and shown that Union restoration was a secondary, subordinate object.

6. The counterparts of these men at the South—the original secessionists—skillfully availing themselves of their acts to propagate disunion feeling among Southern people, and having adroitly obtained control of their legislatures, were enabled to precipitate the civil war contrary to the desire of even a majority of the Southern people, according to the very probable showing of President Lincoln. Their attempts at disunion they wish to justify under the assumed right of secession; a right having no basis whatever in the letter or spirit of the Constitution, and wholly repugnant to permanent national prosperity. So far as the attempt rested on any idea of sectional benefit it was wholly a delusion, there being no clearer demonstrable truth than that the South was full as much interested in the preservation of the Union as the North. So far as it rested on the fear of abolitionism it was an ill-advised, unmanly fear, resting mainly upon the accidental election of President Lincoln by a minority of the nation, and the want of proper confidence in the loyalty to the Constitution of a large majority of their Northern countrymen. So far as it depended upon the trick of precipitation, frustrating a fair, deliberate expression of the will of the Southern people, it required the perpetration of one of the greatest crimes ever committed. For this those desperadoes must be condemned as among the worst conspirators and traitors of all time; and their consciences, if they have any, must be agonized by the contemplation of the irremediable ruin they have already brought upon the South. This censure should be increased from the very probable fact that irritation at the loss and despair of regaining political party power had full as much, if not more, to do with the action of those desperadoes than any serious belief in benefit to the South from disunion. Great as the crime of treason always is, its aggravation is enhanced by imputable selfish motives in the perpetrators, especially when directed against a country like ours, enjoying the inestimable blessing of popular self-government,

under a constitution-guarded liberty, and more especially when sundering those cherished ties of every patriot heart which keep us in undivided connection with and boastful remembrance of the pure, unselfish, ever-glorious patriotism of the revolutionary sires.

That genuine patriotism, the life-giving principle of all true national renown, of all permanent national prosperity, has been too successfully assailed in their respective sections, by abolitionists and secessionists, and hence this accursed civil war against the Union.

7. That other treasonable war, of equal importance and still greater peril to the nation—the war against liberty and the Constitution—is being waged by perjured officials. That Constitution, equally glorious and still more precious than the Union, in which is garnered most of our national pride, with all of our national hope, which organized if it did not create our nationality, which is the very political life of our nationality, but, above all, in which American liberty must forever live or know no life, in which is contained the only true *salus populi*, and whose preservation is the highest of all national necessities.

Popular Self-Government.

The right of self-government in a people necessarily implies their right, when framing a government for themselves, to define and limit the powers of their official servants. The novel modern idea that a people cannot rightfully deny to those servants necessary or "indispensable" powers, is a pernicious absurdity, which would effectually destroy the very basis of all right of self-government, and relapse us back more than two centuries to the exploded doctrine of the absolutists of England.

Absolutism can obtain no foothold in this country till the nation proves recreant to the principles of civil liberty as taught by the great founders of the Government. According to that teaching, "absolute despotic power over the lives, the liberties, or the property of freemen, exists nowhere in a Republic, not even in the largest majority of the people." This great principle having been inconsiderately questioned in more modern times, the people of at least two States have thought proper to consecrate it by express adoption into their Constitutions. Of course the usurpation of despotic power cannot obtain even a moral sanction from any supposed or implied approval by such majority of the people. Indeed the most eminent of enlightened philosophic English statesmen went still further, declaring that such power could not rightfully exist under any form of government. All governmental power depending for its moral basis, as he contended, upon the presumed assent of the Supreme Being, such power could rightfully exist nowhere, not even with the assent of the governed, as it would be impious to imply the assent of a beneficent God to its existence.

The Constitution.

After accomplishing independence and testing the inadequacy of the old articles of confederation, when the nation resolved to risk a national government with all powers necessary to a federative nationality, the main object was "to secure the *blessings of liberty* to themselves and their posterity." This object is not merely proclaimed in the preamble, but is legible in the whole scope of the Constitution. All things were subordinated to that main idea, that chief desire.

Hence the great care to prevent consolidation as the death-doom of liberty. In the language of the platform upon which President Lincoln was elected, and which he repeated in his inaugural speech, "the maintenance inviolate of the rights of the States, and especially of the right of each State to order and control its own domestic institutions, according to its own judgment exclusively, is essential to that balance of power on which the perfection and endurance of our political fabric depend."

Hence the reservation, "to the States or the people of all power not delegated;" and the refusal to delegate any not deemed indispensable for national purposes, leaving much the larger amount of all governmental powers with the separate States, including its control of all domestic relations, the control of their elections, and the control of their militia through the appointment of militia officers.

Hence the subdivision of the power granted among three separate bodies of magistracy, neither of which was to exercise any power given to the others—one to make, another to adjudicate, and the third to execute the law.

Hence the guarantee that "the trial of all crimes, except in cases of impeachment, shall be by jury;" also the guarantee of the sacred privilege of the writ of habeas corpus, of the right to bear arms, of the right of petition, of the right of free conscience, free speech, free press, and free ballot, with the right of exemption from "unreasonable searches or seizures," and from any other arrest or seizure but by "warrant issued upon probable cause, supported by oath particularly describing the place to be searched, and the persons or things to be seized;" and, also, the guarantee to each State of a "Republican form of government."

Hence, also, the guarantee of exemption to every citizen against trial or punishment by any military tribunal, "except in cases arising in the land or naval forces, or in the militia, when in actual service, in time of war or public danger; also the guarantee that he should not be "deprived of life, liberty, or property, without due process of law," and that his "private property shall not be taken for public use without just compensation."

Hence, also, were prohibited all titles of nobility, all bills of attainder, all *ex post facto* laws, all excessive bail, and all cruel punishment.

Hence, also, the Constitution proclaims itself to be the "supreme law of the land." This declared supremacy is without exception or limitation. It was intended for all time and under all circumstances. The calumny of its having been intended for time of peace and not for war is a modern weak invention of the enemies of civil liberty, to excuse usurpation or abuse of power. By its own plain showing, it was made for observance more especially in time of war and public danger. In time of peace civil liberty is generally in little danger. It is in time of public danger, in time of civil war, that men's passions are aroused, and under their influences they are most prone to tyrannical persecution. It was to restrain those passions, to prevent such persecutions in such junctures, that the guarantees of the Constitution were made.

Much reliance was placed upon the then comparatively new device of a written constitution for securing liberty. To that end it must be inviolable. To secure its inviolability an oath for its support was required from Federal and State officers. The President, from his great power and peculiar liability to sinister influences, being an object of special distrust, was required to be very emphatic in his official oath. He was required to swear that he would, "to the best of his ability, preserve, protect, and defend the Constitution."

These oaths admit no evasion, no mental reservation or equivocation, but require implicit obedience. A man cannot honestly "take the oath to obtain power and then break the oath in using the power." A President is allowed no mental reservation of intention to break the oath whenever he should deem it "indispensable" to usurp non-granted power, substituting his own opinion for that of the nation as to what is or is not indispensable; nor can he honestly, for any purpose, substitute his arbitrary will for law or constitution, or substitute military despotism for our free Republic.

The excuse of violating the Constitution for the purpose of preserving it has no possible basis of fact or morality. There is but the one only mode for its preservation—that is, by obedience. All other modes, whatever the simulated pretext, are mere treachery. No officer is trusted with discretion to disobey the Constitution. Whenever he usurps such discretion, he perpetrates the basest moral treason an officer can commit. When he does it by suppressing civil authority with military force, he is guilty of actual treason, within both the letter and spirit of the definition of treason, as given in the Constitution. If he escape hanging, it will be only because the laws of his country are not administered upon him. Officers cannot be allowed a discretion to commit treason any more than citizens are allowed discretion to commit murder.

As said by Webster: "The spirit of liberty will not permit power to overstep its prescribed limits, though good intent, patriotic intent, come along with it. *This is the nature of constitutional liberty.* THIS IS OUR LIBERTY."

The Constitution being the creator of our national life,—the only true preserver of free national life,—its defense and protection constitute the very highest duty of American patriotism.

All supersedure of the Constitution by an alleged higher law, law of necessity or of war, are mere pretexts for unnecessary usurpation by would-be tyrants. It gives ample power to meet all the exigencies of any war. So thought the great men by whom it was made; so thought the wise nation by whom it was adopted; and so the nation continued to think with near entire unanimity, till the Government fell into the hands of incompetents, who endeavor to cloak their imbecility under alleged demerits of the Constitution. So also profess to think some of the most respectable and talented of the dominant party. One of them has said in the Senate: "*Necessity is the plea of tyrants*, and if our Constitution ceases to operate the moment a person charged with its observance thinks there is necessity for its violation, it is of little value. I want no other power for putting down even this gigantic rebellion than such as may properly be derived from the Constitution. The more we study its provisions, the more it is tried in troublous times, the greater will be our admiration and veneration for the wisdom of its authors."

Even if it were true that any power necessary to proper efficiency in the government had been withheld, that would afford no justification for usurpation. For, as said by Washington: "Let there be no change by usurpation; for though this in one instance may be the instrument of good, it is the customary instrument by which free governments are destroyed. The precedent must always greatly overbalance in permanent evil any partial or transient benefit which the use can yield."

Martial Law.

1. That which goes by the name of martial law is *no law*. So say the most eminent jurists of England and America, while no respectable jurist has ever said to the contrary. The power misnamed martial law is that which necessarily comes unsought to a military commander in the presence of actual active military operations, because of the silence of the civil law or the paralyzing of its proper functionaries by the operations of the war. Arising solely from the necessity of the occasion, the power is produced by no proclamation, lasts only for the occasion, and needs no revocation. The power is undefined and undefinable, because resting in the discretion of the commander to the extent that its exercise is permissible. As it comes only from necessity, it is limited by that necessity. It exists only because of and in the absence of the civil authority. It is a power to prevent aid to the enemy or obstruction to our own force. So far as it gives control over non-combatants or citizens not attached to the mili-

tary service, it is a preventing not a punishing power. If the commander, or any subordinate by his order, transcends this narrow limit of the power, or abuses his discretion, he is responsible to the law, both civil and criminal.

2. While conducting the nation during war, neither Washington nor Madison ever supposed he could enlarge his power by his own proclamation, or suspend the civil law. Neither of them ever attempted the exercise of a right, under any supposed necessity, to usurp the prerogative of court and jury in the trial and punishment of citizens not attached to the military service.

3. Martial law is not only denounced in the Declaration of Independence, but national abhorrence for that mode of tyranny is amply developed in the State Constitutions. Nearly all of them contain a clause which, if not identical in language, is of equivalent import with the following, taken from one of the oldest among them, and made, like some of the others, in the very midst of the revolutionary war, for the government of a then independent State. "*In all cases and at all times* the military ought to be under strict subordination to and governed by the civil power." "No person can, in any case, be subjected to law martial, or to any pains or penalties by virtue of that law, except those employed in the army or navy, and except the militia in active service, but by authority of the Legislature." "The power of suspending law ought never to be exercised but by the Legislature."

The Act of Indemnity.

1. Congress, not being omnipotent like the English Parliament, has no power to give absolution to Federal officers for either civil or criminal liability for past acts violating the rights of a citizen or the law of a State. In its criminal aspect the power could be deduced only from the pardoning power, which belongs exclusively to the President, and applies only to offenses against Federal law, with no bearing whatever upon offenses against, or penalties incurred under State law. In its civil aspect it is an attempt to deprive a citizen of his vested right to remuneration for the illegal act of an officer. Its violation of justice, on sound principle, is equivalent to an attempt to take one man's property and give it to another. It is arbitrary legislative confiscation, a species of

bill of attainder, without even pretense of fault in the party to be injured.

2. Could the President and higher officials be absolved on the score of motive in the court of conscience, yet it could not be pretended that all their subordinates can be so absolved for their multitudinous illegal arrests and extortions. With the very many known instances of outrages perpetrated by them, to give them all indiscriminately the absolution of the proposed indemnity, would be one of the foulest wrongs with which a party majority ever attempted to disgrace a nation in an enlightened era. The act is a stain on our national character.

Abolition Diplomacy.

The Trent affair proves either gross ignorance in the assertion of absurd pretensions not warranted by the law of nations, or a dastardly betrayal of national honor by the sudden surrender of those pretensions at the first growl of the British lion.

The kidnapping extradition of Arguelles was a usurpation of power to inflict another stain on the nation's honor, by violating the cherished right of asylum, so universally recognized among civilized nations, and heretofore so earnestly asserted by our own. It was a foul thing, done in an illegal, disgraceful manner.

It is the undoubted prerogative of either House of Congress to keep careful watch over our foreign relations, and give expression to such opinions concerning them as the national interest may seem to require. The House of Representatives was acting legitimately within this prerogative when reannouncing and reaffirming the "Monroe doctrine," for the purpose of influencing the action of France in Mexico.

The conduct of the President and his Cabinet, in their attempted effort to soothe the apprehended resentment of the French Emperor at that action, was a disgraceful betrayal to a foreign court of the want of harmony in our own councils—a treacherous, not to say treasonable, promise of aid in counteracting a policy unanimously proclaimed by the representatives of the nation—a ridiculous assumption of exclusive control over our foreign relations—a pusillanimous truckling to the apprehended displeasure of a foreign potentate—a national degradation in the opinion of all Europe—an attempt or treasonable promise to thwart the well-known national will on a great question of policy affecting the whole American continent now and in the long future—a full proof, if any such were needed, of the want of intelligence on the part of the Administration, and of its want of needful moral stamina for the proper discharge of the duties of the Executive Department of the Government.

Currency and Legal Tender.

"Ours was intended to be a hard-money government." So said an eminent expounder of the Constitution, and history confirms what he said. The original draft of the Constitution, like the Articles of Confederation, gave Congress power "to emit bills of credit," which, as interpreted by history and the Supreme Court, was power to create a paper-money currency based on the credit of the Government. After mature deliberation and elaborate discussion, the Convention struck out the power by a vote of nine to two. The only analogous power granted was that to coin money and regulate the value of foreign coin. This far inferior power was not left to be inferred as a necessary incident to the great comprehensive power to regulate commerce, and of course the so much larger, more important power to make paper-money currency cannot be inferred as an incident to that or any other granted power, even if the action of the Convention did not disprove any such intention.

When Congress has regulated the value of coin, the law of the contract gives an all-sufficient tender law, and there is little or no need for any other to secure or regulate the right of tender. The power in no form is given to Congress, not even to make coin a legal tender. It is inferable, from the prohibition upon the States "to make anything but gold and silver coin a tender in payment of debts," that part of the power, all that could possibly be needed for any proper purpose, was intentionally left with the States, where nearly the whole subject of contracts was left, and where this, like all else pertaining to contracts, appropriately belonged. To infer a concurrent power in Congress on such a subject would mar the symmetry of the Constitution, the special purpose of its framers having been to eliminate everything like collision or conflict of power between the Federal and State Governments.

If the power to make paper money were conceded, and the making of it a legal tender were *necessary* to its better circulation, still it would have to be shown that the making of it such was a "*proper*" incident to the power. This cannot be done. The power to rob citizens or dishonor the nation can never be a proper incident to any power.

No honest man will say that a power to raise forced loans is a proper incident to the power to borrow money. Yet, worse is done when the creditor is forced to take a third or a half in discharge of his whole demand, because the forced loan is accompanied by a government promise, express or implied, to refund, whereas no such promise is given to the robbed creditor. Reduced to its pure elements, it is plain robbery of the private citizen for the fancied benefit of the paper-money experiment, to the injury of the national honor and credit.

Besides, the power to make paper money being itself a mere inferred incident to some granted power, to allow this as an incident to that would be to permit a piling of incident upon incident to the utter destruction of the limitation of power intended by a careful specification of all powers intended to be granted.

According to the inexorable law of trade, the doubling or trebling of a full currency always doubles or trebles prices. This has been the experience of all countries, and to none has it been a more costly experience than our own. It has therefore been a long-settled policy of European governments to meet the pecuniary emergency during war by sale of government bonds at any reasonable discount rather than by an inflation of the currency. That discount is only one loss, whereas trebling the cost of government supplies causes much larger loss in the first instance, and it is a loss which is repeated from year to year for every year the war lasts. The inflation policy more than doubles or trebles the needful cost of the war.

Borrowing being the only means for carrying on the war, the necessity for keeping up the value of government bonds should have occurred to every one presuming to control the national finances. To that end a market for them in Europe should have been sought. Instead of this or any other rational effort to keep up the value of the bonds, the most efficacious means were used for putting it down by resort to an inflated, depreciated currency. The excuse for this, according to newspaper discussion, was that an excess of depreciated currency was necessary, as they express it, "to float the loan." It is very strange that there should not have been at the head of our finances that modicum of sagacity necessary to knowing that a thing which is itself constantly *sinking* should not be relied on to *float* anything else.

The sinking of the currency has so sunk the bonds and the national credit that it is much to be feared that a loan in Europe is no longer practicable. Instead of doing anything to extricate us from this unfortunate condition by a reduction of the currency, the empirics are seeking to increase the mischief by a further inflation, through a swarm of new banks of issue. This is done in disregard of the abundant experience of this country and France during their respective revolutions, and of the present experience of the Southern States, that, after a certain point of depreciation in the currency, its holders will cease to fund in Government bonds, preferring the chance of shifting off the currency to that of profitably using the bonds after Government credit as to both is destroyed.

It seems to be conceded now by even the Administration press, or at least by the more intelligent and respectable part, that the enormous extra prices which the people have to pay for all the necessaries and comforts of life, over the necessary result of depreciation in the currency, is a part, and vastly the largest part, of the tax they have to pay toward supporting the war. This too though the Government gets no benefit whatever from that tax. It is a penalty the people are made to pay for a financial blunder. To those who depend on fixed incomes or wages the inflation of the currency causes an indirect tax to the full amount of the depreciation, which is much heavier than would be an income tax of thirty per cent.

This specimen of abolition skill in financiering may be compared to that notable financial discovery made by President Lincoln, and with which he enlightened the world in a message to Congress, when he said: "Certainly it is not so easy to pay *something* as it is to pay *nothing;* but it is easier to pay a *large* sum than it is to pay a *larger* one. And it is easier to pay any sum when we are able, than it is before we are able." This brilliant financial discovery, if it does not enlarge our national renown for wisdom, ought at least to warn the nation against ever again installing *a bad joke* in the Presidency. In all ways Mr. Lincoln assuredly has proved himself to be a very costly as well as a very bad joke.

The Negro Question.

1. Our Government was founded by white men for white people. It was in the contemplation of no one that we should ever be debased into a mulatto nation. Nothing was done by legislation or otherwise to remove the strong natural repugnance of race between whites and blacks, but everything to increase the prejudice and maintain the white supremacy. Intermarriage between the races was prohibited; the blacks were refused all political or social equality, all right of suffrage, or to hold office, even the privilege of testifying against the whites; most of the States prohibited free blacks from emigrating to or settling in them.

2. The black population is a moral, social, and political evil to the States in which it is located; but the evil is confined to those States. Slaveholding may be a sin, though it is countenanced by the example of all nations, ancient or modern, civilized or uncivilized, Christian or pagan; but it is a sin for which they who practice it are alone responsible, none of it attaching to the free States, who have no rightful control over the subject.

For the evil and the sin we have to thank the cupidity of England and that of those among our own countrymen, who carried on the African slave-trade prior to the adoption of the Federal Constitution; and for the twenty years that the trade was kept open thereafter, we are indebted to the cupidity of certain New England and extreme Southern States, who trafficked their votes with each other, and combined to keep open the trade despite the earnest remonstrance of Maryland and Virginia. As said by President Lincoln, "the people of the South are not more responsible for the original introduction of this property than are the people of the North."

While the evils from negro slavery have been felt exclusively by the States in which it is located, the large commercial benefits from slave labor have been diffused all over the nation. Slave labor furnishing, as it has, two hundred millions of annual exports from the South, has been the principal nutriment of our immense national commerce. To the North it has been an unmixed benefit, giving her at the South the most commodious and bountiful market of the world for the products of Northern capital and industry.

3. The true policy in reference to our negro population is to be found in the *separation*, not the *amalgamation* of the two races.

So have thought all our more eminent statesmen who have carefully considered the subject, including such names as Washington, Jefferson, Madison, Clay, and Webster. Jefferson said: "Nothing is more clearly written in the book of destiny than the emancipation of the blacks; and it is equally certain that the two races will never live in a state of equal freedom under the same government, so insurmountable are the barriers which nature, habit, and opinions have established between them."

No public man has ever more fully or frequently than President Lincoln committed himself in favor of the policy of separation. He earnestly recommended to Congress a scheme for gradual compensated emancipation and colonization. He never seemingly abandoned the policy until, from want of manhood, he truckled to the threatened dictation of the traitor cabal of fanatic governors. He tried to escape the disgrace of his submission by anticipating them, and hence his disastrous abolition proclamation, which either unmasked his previous hypocrisy or proved him to be the weak, if unwilling, tool of ruthless fanaticism. Since then vengeance against the South has been his main object, reckless of the interests of both races, using the blacks only as a means for vengeance, regardless of what they may suffer in its accomplishment; this vengeance, too, being for supposed hate of himself, induced by his own acts.

4. The incitement contained in that proclamation to a servile war of knife and torch is denounced as contrary to the usages of civilized warfare by our Declaration of Independence, and also by the diplomatic correspondence of John Quincy Adams under the Presidency of Monroe. In the latter, it is said, in reference to the pretended right to emancipate the slaves of an enemy by proclamation: "The right of putting to death all prisoners in cold blood and without special cause, might as well be pretended

to be a law of war, or the right to use poisoned weapons or to assassinate."

President Lincoln, by his resort to such means against his own countrymen, has done what he can to degrade the nation even below the level of those who murder prisoners, use poisoned weapons, or assassinate in war with a foreign enemy.

5. With the aid of time, the policy of separation can be carried out beneficially for both races, by obtaining in Southern Mexico or Central America sites for colonies so accessible that the negroes could work their own way there, without expense to the Government. This they would willingly do so soon as the colonies began to prosper. Voluntary emancipation would progress rapidly, and public sentiment would justify the free States in even coercing emigration to relieve them from the negro nuisance.

6. The system of Mexican peonage, into which it is now attempted to convert negro slavery, has nothing to recommend it. While it has been reducing a semi-civilized people to barbarism, negro slavery, as practiced in this country, especially in the northwardly slave States, has elevated a race from the extreme of ignorant barbarism to a comparative condition of intelligent civilization. The contrast between the imported African and the civilized negro of our border States, with his physical, intellectual, and moral improvement, is inadequately expressed by the difference between a donkey and a thorough-bred racer. This improvement, too, has been accomplished with as large physical comfort on the part of the negro, as belongs to the condition of much of the laboring peasantry in Europe. Our own experience as to leased plantation negro labor has thus far proved the scheme successful only in enriching the vilest Shoddies at the expense of the cheated, maltreated negro.

7. The scheme of miscegenation and amalgamation is one of equal folly. The law of nature against the propagation of hybrids vindicates its supremacy by a visible deterioration from both races, before reaching the octoroon, when propagation entirely ceases. Besides, the scheme is so disgustingly revolting to the strong natural instincts of our people, as to render its proposal a gross insult to the nation. If our abolition men and women will insist on having it tried with their personal aid, it is to be hoped that our country will not be disgraced by the experiment, but

that it may be made in some foreign land. This natural revulsion is not to be conquered by its fierce denunciation in the halls of Congress as "a base prejudice."

8. We need no further experiments to prove the empiricism of charlatan negro philanthropy. Of all the faults and crimes of the nation from its connection with the negro race, there is none so prominent as that which has occurred during the present war and which is altogether of abolition procurement. Their proclamations, though failing in their main purpose of inciting the use of the knife and the torch in negro insurrections, yet succeeded in seducing them from their comfortable homes to our camps and military stations by the tens of thousands, where, massed together in loathsome squalor, they died off like rotten sheep, by all the pitiable modes of death incident to starvation and unprotected exposure to the inclemencies of the weather.

Such is abolition wisdom and philanthropy; such is the stain upon our national character for humanity, inflicted by an abolition administration.

President Lincoln must have suffered some severe twinges of conscience for this, or he would not have made public acknowledgment of his blunder, by authorizing the people of rebel States to re-enslave those he claimed to have irrevocably emancipated. This he did by *authorizing* the rebel States to subject those he had emancipated unconditionally to a preparatory pupilage before receiving the full rights of freemen.

9. The objections to abolitionizing the Constitution are—

First. It would preclude reconciliation—all chance of amicable reconstruction—leaving everything to the uncertain issue of long war.

Second. Such amendment of the Constitution can be obtained only by the fraudulent manufacture of new States out of Territories not having one-third the population entitling them to admission into the Union, and the fraudulent manipulation of rebel States.

Third. It would be an act of base, ungrateful perfidy toward the border slave States, who aided the suppression of the rebellion under the most solemn, oft-repeated assurances from Congress and President that nothing of the sort should be attempted, yet the amendment requires the destruction, not to say the robbery, of more than two hundred millions worth of property in those States, owned by loyal citizens guiltless of all fault toward the Government, without whose aid the Union could not have been preserved; indeed, it is more than doubtful whether, without that aid, the President and Cabinet would have made even a serious effort at its preservation by force.

Fourth. It would induce a supposed necessity for another amendment giving Congress exclusive separate power to govern what are now four million, in twenty-two years will be eight million, and in forty-four years will be sixteen million of negroes, scattered throughout the nation, as prefigured by the bill of last session creating the Freedmen's Department; or for an amendment that shall at once raise the negroes to all the rights of full citizenship, including that of emigrating and settling where they please, in despite the will of the white inhabitants of the several States.

War Policy, Past, Present, and Prospective.

1. "That this war is not waged for any purpose of conquest or subjugation, or purpose of overthrowing the institutions of those States, but to defend and maintain the supremacy of the Constitution, with all the rights of the several States unimpaired; and *that as soon as these objects are accomplished the war ought to cease.*"

Such was the policy of the war, as enunciated at its commencement with so much unanimity by Congress and ratified with equal unanimity by the nation, silencing all party feeling and volunteering more men than the Administration had use for or would accept.

2. The cardinal principle of this policy was and should continue to be coercion, accompanied by conciliation, for Union restoration and Constitution preservation.

3. The whole war power belonging to Congress, the policy thus announced should have guided and governed every other department; and, after the nation became committed to the war on that policy, it should have served as a guide to Congress also; for it was on faith in that pledge and belief in that policy that the people of the loyal States entered with such hearty unanimity into the war.

4. President Lincoln inaugurated a new and altogether different policy by his illegal abolition proclamation.

Since then the war has been waged for party vengeance and abolition purposes, restoration being subordinated to those objects. This was for some time denied by his supporters, who pretended that restoration was the principal, while abolition was the mere incident. But he himself has placed it beyond further denial by his proclamation "to whom it may concern." He there casts off all dissimulation or attempted disguise, and frankly tells the nation he will permit no peace or restoration unless accompanied by abolition, thus unequivocally making abolition, if not the principal, the equal with restoration, and rendering it as important as if it were the sole object of the war.

5. That abolition proclamation, with its accompanying proclamation of martial law over the whole Union, and attempted suspension of the *habeas corpus* without congressional sanction, are of treasonable aspect, tendency, and purpose.

Supposing President Lincoln and his Cabinet moderately qualified for their stations, each of them well knew—*first*, that those proclamations were gross usurpations; *secondly*, that they would divide the North while uniting the South; *thirdly*, that such division would greatly impair the physical strength of the North, while diminishing the moral force of the Government at home and abroad; *fourthly*, that the task of suppressing the rebellion was one of sufficient difficulty for even the whole undivided strength of the North; *fifthly*, that a moiety, if not a majority of the loyal people of the North held abolitionism in abhorrence, and would not willingly aid in prosecuting the war for its continuance; *sixthly*, that they held martial law, with all other modes of tyrannical usurpation, in equal abhorrence, and would not patiently submit to the suppression of civil authority by military force; *seventhly*, that the military efficiency of a republic always depends upon a hearty approval of the war by a largely preponderant majority of the people.

With this full knowledge on the part of those men, it will be difficult for Charity herself to absolve them from all treasonable purpose, when thus precipitating the nation into an abolition crusade.

To change the policy of the war, as prescribed by Congress and sanctioned by the nation; willfully to weaken the North for any purpose; willfully to hinder restoration; or willfully to prolong the war for the sake of vengeance, or any other mere abolition party purpose, is plain moral treason. It is treason of so dark a tint that it can be absolved only by those who place the gratification of party or fanatic vengeance above the obligations of patriotism. The annals of all bad men furnish no instance of a baser, more disastrous betrayal of public trust.

The very few honest fanatics who really believe that any amount of national peril or disaster can be properly incurred for the sake of their emancipation experiment, may be absolved on the plea of irresponsible insanity. Not so as to these ambitious, power-loving, power-usurping, power-abusing politicians. They are to be judged with all the responsibilities of cold-blooded sane men upon them. They are now on trial before their masters. The nation's verdict will be guilty—*treasonably guilty.*

6. What kind is the vengeance part of the new policy may be judged by the avowals of their party leaders in Congress.

One of them said that the rebels should not be treated like erring countrymen, but "as devils." "Not only their personal goods and their lives, but the fee simple of their lands must be taken from them." Another said, neither South Carolina, Georgia, or Florida "should reappear in the Union. Let these States be set apart as the home of the negro." Another, a Senator, said, "I am for desolation, I am for subjugation, and I am for the exercise of all the power that will crush these infernal, damnable fiends under our feet." Still another, who is one of the most respectable and temperate of their Senators, demanded *unconditional submission*, even if it require "*a pathway of desolation* from the Potomac to the Gulf of Mexico."

7. Unconditional submission is what has never been required or obtained in civil wars among civilized nations, except by the iron despotism of Russia. Unconditional submission to the tender mercies of unrestrained abolition hate is what we can never obtain. *God forbid that we should.* That would prove the Southern people unfit to be our countrymen, unworthy of readoption into the nation.

Not being endued with the radical hate of these men, the nation will teach them at the ballot-box that they are not to be indulged with the luxury of their demoniac vengeance, their anticipated joy over "a pathway of desolation," or the treatment of Americans "as devils" or as "infernal, damnable fiends." Nor will the nation allow the descendants of such men as Washington, Jefferson, Madison, Patrick Henry, Marion, Sumpter, Rutledge, Laurens, and the Pinckneys to be destroyed to make room for the negroes; no, not even for that promised improved race of amalgamated negroes and abolitionists.

The nation will propose an amnesty such as suits its own high honor, magnanimity, and permanent welfare to offer, such as the demands of justice will permit, and such as will not utterly degrade descendants of our revolutionary sires to accept. It will cause coercion to progress as it began and should have continued, hand in hand with conciliation—the only policy for early peace, the only policy for beneficial peace. It will expel the Destructives, drive Constitution-destroying conspirators from power, and thereby give our Southern countrymen the only reliable guarantee for their being restored to equal and protected rights under a government of inviolable Constitution-guarded liberty.

When this is done, all information, public and private, leads to the belief that the Southern people will banish their desperadoes, their last-ditch men, cease rebellion, and restore the Union.

8. Another developed part of the new war policy is the expiatory punishment of the alleged sin of negro slavery.

According to President Lincoln, to punish all participants in that sin, the whole nation must be punished. This, however, being punishment upon too large a scale, substitute victims are to be selected. A party leader, who is the leading representative of Massachusetts, and selected South Carolina and Georgia for that purpose, did so, as he said, because "they are the two States that are responsible for the continuance of the slavery institution. It was condemned in Maryland and Virginia. South Carolina and Georgia breathed into it the breath of life."

The only way in which the responsibility of those two States at all differs from that of Maryland and Virginia was, that the latter earnestly insisted in the Convention on immediate prohibition of the African slave-trade; while the other two insisted on keeping it open, as was done for twenty years. Whatever of fault there was in this, Massachusetts participated in the fault even more largely than those States, by voting herself and influencing other Northern States to vote for keeping the trade open. She so voted for the sake of the large profit she was then making, expected further to make, and did actually make thereafter from the trade.

While her representatives are going back more than seventy years to find this fault for which to punish South Carolina and Georgia so severely, what is to exempt her from punishment, or what is her atonement for the larger share of the sin? They can allege, in extenuation, their disinterested, patriotic aid to the nation in the second war with England, the war for "free trade and sailors' rights," in which they had no peculiar local interest, having neither ships nor sailors. She can allege nothing of the sort. She gave the war no aid, because it interfered with her commercial gains, but hung upon the nation like a palsied limb, and influenced some of her adjoining States to do the same. She even resolved, through her Legislature, that it was "unbecoming a moral and religious people" to rejoice over our national victories.

She denounced the acquisition of Louisiana, and, through her representatives, threatened secession if Louisiana were admitted into the Union. During the war with England she availed herself of its gloomiest period to fulfill her threat, by her notorious attempt to obtain the secession of all New England, despite what would have been its attendant consequences of civil war and the prostration of the then young, feeble nation at the feet of its haughty enemy.

Now, again, she is proving herself a tricky, selfish trafficker in national affairs. She has somehow obtained from the War Department a credit upon her army quota for all the recruits to the navy obtained in her ports by government officers at government expense, without either expense or trouble to herself; while two-thirds, if not more, of those recruits were unnaturalized foreigners or citizens of other States, not even domiciled with her. This credit the Administration had no right or legal authority to give. If she were equitably entitled to any abatement of her quota on account of men furnished the navy, it should have been first authorized by Congress upon some just principle that would have embraced the many thousands furnished by Western States to government boats, and for which they have received no credit.

It is well for Massachusetts that the Administration is above suspicion, *if such be the fact*, otherwise the nation would suspect that she bought the credit with her money. The conduct of her representatives at the last session, on a kindred subject, would increase that suspicion. They first spoke and voted against the repeal of commutation from the conscription law, and then sold their votes for its repeal on the condition of being allowed to fill her quota with rebel State negroes.

After having done more than any other State, except South Carolina, to bring on this war, from which she has suffered comparatively little, but is luxuriating in the enjoyment of her Shoddy beatitude, and in the evasion of patriotic duty by offsetting the volunteered lives of citizens of other States with the roughest of untutored negroes, it is unreasonable in Massachusetts to expect the nation to permit the war to be prolonged upon a policy which promises nothing but the glutting of her vengeance and very possible national bankruptcy.

9. Still another part of the developed policy of the dominant party was frankly disclosed in a speech made recently in the Senate, which was neither contradicted nor rebuked by any of the other party leaders, and from which the following extract is taken:—

"I should like to see every white man in the army returned to his family and his home, and his place filled by a negro. * * * I should be glad to vote for a proposition that would call out a million of negro troops, that the whole white troops may be relieved from the dangers and fatigues of the army; and I hope this Government will increase its energy, and that the time will soon come when we shall be grappling this rebellion with an army of negroes sufficient to close it out."

While we ought to be thankful that there are not negroes enough to furnish this desired army of a million, yet we must remember that there are enough to furnish half a million, which was the number recommended by the war committee of the House. That number can be raised by the fourth of next March, if our armies succeed in penetrating the more thickly negro populated regions of the South. With our white soldiers disbanded, leaving an army of five hundred thousand negroes under the control of an unscrupulous party, with an unscrupulous President, what is to be the result? Will they surrender power if ordered to do so by the ballot-box? Mr. Secretary Seward was kind enough to admonish us, in one of his public speeches, that it would be unreasonable to expect the peaceable surrender of their power until they had held it for another term of four years, its enjoyment having been so much disturbed by the rebellion during the present term. If they will not surrender power, how is the unarmed nation to make them? If they succeed at the ballot-box, what will the liberty of the nation be worth? With their developed purpose to establish a consolidated government of imperial power, and a standing army of five hundred thousand negroes, how are they to be hindered? These are topics for the anxious consideration of every voter. They are topics specially worthy the careful thinking of our white soldiers.

Where the usurpations and unconstitutional abuses of power by a President and ruling party in Congress are so manifold as to leave no room to surmise praiseworthy motives, the nation is justified in its aroused suspicion that the perpetuation of their power is one of these motives. The organization of an enormous army of negroes, while increasing that suspicion, adds to the danger of the fulfillment of that infamous public threat of certain generals and other officers that, after suppressing the rebellion, they would return North, and, with the aid of their soldiers, crush their political opponents. None but a President sympathizing with such a threat, pointed directly at the legislative representatives of the people, would have failed to punish, or at least to rebuke such an infamy. So far from doing this, one of the execrable, traitorous threateners was allowed to retain his position at the very head of all our armies, despite his proved incompetency thereto, and notorious worthlessness as a general in the field.

10. If peace be not, as it has been said to be, "the only proper object of all just wars," it surely must be so in a war against rebellion.

As to the great necessity for an early peace, in reference exclusively to the interests of the loyal States, in view of other suggestions, it is preferable to give the following extract from a speech delivered in the Senate by one of the most intelligent leaders of the Abolition party, while advocating the abolitionizing of the Constitution:—

"Should the war go on until the public debt equals the entire wealth of the country? Should it go on until misery broods over the whole land; until the civil authorities become impotent, and all rights of person and property stand at the mercy of military power? Should it go on until corruption and fraud, the necessary concomitants of civil war, shall have crept into high places, put on the garb of patriotism, and give themselves the means of perpetuating their own power? Should it continue until the nation, exhausted, will welcome the coming of a Cromwell or a Bonaparte; until Provost-Marshals shall be stationed with a military police at every village in the Northern States, displacing the civil authority, governing the people, prescribing new and strange offenses, and punishing them by courts-martial?

"A few more years of civil war, and this picture will be seen. It cannot be otherwise. It is the necessary result of a long civil strife.

"Such is history. We are not exempt from the passions and frailties that wove this web of history for others. Party pride, blinded vanity, may think so. These have driven many nations from the enjoyment of liberty to the profoundest depths of tyranny. Party revenge may be gratified when political enemies come to grief; but that is no compensation for a ruined country. When anarchy comes, we are overwhelmed alike. The Girondist and the Jacobin followed each other in rapid succession to the guillotine."

Status of Rebel States.

Nothing short of success in the rebellion can get the rebel States out of the Union. They have, therefore, to be treated, while the rebellion lasts, and after it is subdued, as States in the Union, except that their rebellion, while it lasts, deprives them of all right or power to co-operate in the management of the Federal Government.

Nothing can be more irrational than to suppose a power in Congress either to expel the rebel States or permanently to exercise despotic rule over them, while the Constitution prohibits even the nation from depriving them by constitutional amendment from their "equal suffrage in the Senate."

If there is anything equally irrational, it is the absurd attempt to deduce, from the clause guaranteeing "to every State a republican form of government," a power in Congress to impose upon a State a government that is not republican.

This would be a plain breach of the guarantee under pretext of its fulfillment. Whatever difference of opinion there may be as to what was precisely meant by "republican government," there can be none that self-government by the people of the State was indisputably a part at least of what was meant. A permanent form of government, dictated by Congress or any extraneous power, was certainly not intended, as it certainly would not be republican or self-government.

So, also, as to the antirepublican idea of giving to one-tenth the government of the other nine-tenths of the people of a State.

The rule of the majority is a fundamental requisite, according to all American ideas of a republic.

After the rebellion is subdued, the nation will not tolerate any protracted arbitrary government of the rebel States, even if Congress has the right so to govern during the rebellion.

It would be the accumulation of vastly too much power in the Federal Government, leading to rapid consolidation and the overthrow of the most necessary safeguard of the nation's liberty.

Suppression of Free Ballot.

President Lincoln has caused or permitted the suppression, by military force, of free ballot in four loyal States. In despite the clearest proof of this, his party in the House of Representatives have given him the distinct sanction of their approval by voting in solid body, with a few honorable exceptions, to retain the representatives of the bayonet and exclude the representatives of the people. There can be no greater outrage than this upon the rights of freemen. If military violence or intimidation is allowed to control our elections, there is an end to even the semblance of liberty among us. As there is not a more traitorously pernicious *crime* against the nation than the military suppression of free ballot by a President, by a general, or by a subordinate under or without the orders of a superior officer, so there can be no baser betrayal of popular trust than the perjured sanction of such *crime* by members of Congress.

Whether this crime be that of actual, plain treason, when perpetrated by a President or a subordinate, as believed by some, or only felony, as thought by others—whether its legally assigned punishment be the gallows, or only the penitentiary, every intelligent patriot must concur in its denunciation as one of the gravest, most pernicious crimes that can possibly be perpetrated against the liberty of the people or against the permanent welfare of the nation. There is no throb of a true American heart in any man's bosom who does not feel for the crime an unstinted abhorrence. If there is any crime by officials better calculated than any other to incite insurrection, it is this. It is better calculated than any other to remind the people of their plain legal right to prevent, by force, the perpetration of treason or felony, to exhaust their patience and induce an armed resistance.

While the nation has carefully tied its own hands, as to any enlargement of the powers of the Government, by requiring a two-third vote from both houses of Congress and a three-fourth vote of the States, this man of yesterday, the mere foundling of a party convention, elected to the Presidency by far less than even a majority of the popular vote—this man, who has never done anything to signalize his claim to confidence in either his capacity or his integrity, has the transcendant modesty to "avow" that he has enlarged and means to enlarge his official power at his own will and pleasure, or, which is the same, to usurp such power as he may choose to say is, in his opinion, "indispensable." With such an unscrupulous avower of unscrupulous principles wielding such tremendous power for mischief, there is no need to wonder at the patriotic fear now thrilling every patriot mind, that he may be insane enough to attempt to secure his re-election by further efforts at the suppression of free ballot. This apprehension has been increased by his very recent interference with the election in Kentucky—the proclamation of martial law over the whole State, under a false, fabricated pretext, and then ordering the judges of the election not to receive votes in favor of the Chief Justice of the State, who was a candidate for re-election. This military order was not published until three or four days before the election, not giving the Conservatives time, as they hoped, to combine on any one candidate, so as to defeat the election of their tool. The Chief Justice has been compelled to seek in exile an asylum from arbitrary arrest and incarceration in a loathsome prison, and perhaps from banishment, for no offense whatever but that of holding political opinions in accordance with those of the members of this Convention, and of the million and a half of loyal men who will vote against President Lincoln. Is the *forbearance* of such a man our only trust against the direful catastrophe of another civil war; and that, too, in the midst of the loyal States? There was a time when the undebauched tone of popular sentiment would have afforded a much surer trust—*his fear* of the loyal hearts and strong arms of his liberty-loving countrymen. The time is *now*, when the people, not trusting to his forbearance, will take care, with proper preparation, for repelling force by force, to prevent him from receiving his re-election by the aid of the bayonet. Should civil war ensue, the fault will be his, not theirs. They will but exercise their plain legal right to protect themselves against armed treason by armed resistance.

Besides the object of controlling the election in Kentucky and aiding forcible emancipation, the recent proclamation of martial law over that State was probably induced with the hope of persecuting her citizens into open rebellion, when an apology would be furnished for the military chastisement of their contempt for and aversion to President Lincoln. To this end they have been robbed of their slaves and horses; they have been arrested and banished for their political opinions, without any form of trial or even of investigation, except what belongs to information obtained from hireling detectives or equally base secret informers. The whole trade of the State has been wantonly placed under the most unnecessary regulations, serving only to enrich their officials by bribes. Her traders are required to obtain a military permit to import from the North and sell within the State. Before obtaining that permit they are required to take an oath, framed expressly to prevent its being taken by Democratic or Conservative men.

Not content with kidnapping her citizens for their political opinions, and incarcerating them at the Dry Tortugas in the dog-days, they kidnapped and banished women and children to Canada for the opinions of their husbands and their fathers, making, at the same time, arbitrary seizure of their property, under pretext of intended confiscation. Under a former martial law in Kentucky they permitted their Provost-Marshals, all through the State, to wantonly harass her citizens, and enrich themselves by notorious bribes and extortions.

Still better to judge what these men are capable of doing for the purpose of retaining power, it will not do to omit all notice of what they have done in Missouri, omitting, for brevity, what they have done in Maryland, Delaware, and the subdued portions of the rebel States. They permitted with impunity the inauguration of the terrible domestic civil war which has raged in Missouri, by three massacres perpetrated in the streets of St. Louis, by their soldiers wantonly firing into crowds of unoffending men, women, and children. When grand juries attempted to have these murders investigated, they would not permit their officers to be summoned as witnesses. They permitted citizens of Missouri to be kidnapped, incarcerated, or banished at the arbitrary caprice of their officers, and arbitrarily suppressed freedom of speech, of the press, and of the ballot. They required military license for men to carry on their business, and, before granting it, required a test-oath, authorized by no law but of their own prescribing. They arbitrarily confiscated the property of some for the pretended indemnity of others, and raised large sums by forced contributions. They desolated three or four entire counties, burning every house, and carrying off for their own use or destroying all the movable property. This was done in the midwinter of that rigorous climate, leaving the aged, the infirm, the women, and the children shelterless wanderers, without sustenance. This fiendish atrocity, so disgraceful to our country, so dishonoring to human nature, if not perpetrated by the order of President Lincoln, he has made himself responsible for, as an accessory to the crime, by his equally guilty connivance.

Such is the detestable tyranny under which we live—such the men who inflict that tyranny on the nation. Are they to be trusted not to try to retain power by any and every means, however infamous? They cannot be watched with too much care; the nation cannot be too careful in its efforts to prevent them. If such be their conduct now, what will it be if President Lincoln be re-elected, when they will no longer have the fear of popular censure to restrain them? The people must arouse themselves to the necessities of the great emergency, or they will suffer themselves and their posterity to be yoked under a despotism.

Conscription.

The Constitution says, "a well-regulated militia is necessary to the security of a free State," meaning it is necessary against domestic usurpation as well as against foreign enemies. It gives Congress power to "call forth the militia, to execute the laws, suppress insurrections, and repel invasions," but expressly reserves "to the States respectively the appointment of the officers."

The conscription act puts the whole militia of all the States under the control of the President, enabling him to call them out at will for the suppression of the rebellion, and to *appoint their officers.* This is in conflict with the obvious intention of the Constitution to keep the militia under the control of "the States respectively," and makes the constitutionality of the act more than doubtful.

Its policy is equally so. If the war had not been turned into an abolition crusade, there would have been no need for conscription. Volunteering, so consonant to the true theory and spirit of a republic, would have supplied ample number of willing soldiers; or, if not, they could have been legally obtained, as in the last war with England, by *drafts* from the militia, with its regularly appointed officers.

Our Armies

have added, by their gallantry, largely to our martial renown, elevated the character and repute of the nation, and secured the admiring gratitude of our country. Their deeds will be exultant themes for proud national song and story during long future generations. It will be a cherished debt of national honor fully to comply with all promises to our maimed soldiers, and in behalf of the widows and children of such as have met or may meet glorious deaths in the service of our country. In behalf of the nation, the survivors are tendered most cordial thanks, and exhorted to a continuance in their gallant well-doing.

Our Civilians.

They have also a patriotic duty, though not so perilous, yet of equal importance with that of our brave soldiers. The efforts of those gallant men in defense of the Constitution against rebel traitors in arms will have availed but little if, after all their hard-earned victories, they returned to find the Constitution desecrated and destroyed by civilian traitors in official stations—to find free speech, free press, free ballot, jury trial, and legal supremacy all gone, with liberty in its last agony, under a ruthless despotism.

But, rest assured, gallant countrymen, your brethren at home, whom you have left in charge of the ballot, will by no supineness, no unpatriotic apathy, permit such disastrous calamity to you and themselves. They are resolved to chase the traitor Destructives, the Constitution-breakers, from the political sanctuary; reinstate the revered, the matchless, the all-glorious Constitution our wise fathers gave us in its rightful supremacy; vindicate man's competency to self-government; silence the malignant sneers of the European absolutists at the imputed failure of the "Model Republic;" and launch the good ship *Republican Liberty* once again on a prosperous career of enduring glory and renown.

CHAPTER II.

THE IRREPRESSIBLE CONFLICT.

Published July, 1864.

This false dogma has no basis of fact, nor is it sustained by any rational teaching of political science. The "irrepressible conflict" phrase, with its sequent dogma, was the invention of a fire-eater, to promote disunion. This tendency was so obvious, that when Messrs. Lincoln and Seward borrowed the phrase and publicly propagated the dogma, for the purpose of sectionalizing the North into a political party to gratify their ambition, they brought their loyalty to the Union into doubt or suspicion. When first promulgated by them, the dogma received the sanction of no disinterested, intelligent men. By all such it was viewed as a mere hypocritical pretext of inordinate ambition, as a very thin, attempted disguise to their personal aims. Its disunion tendency was so obvious, that their advocacy justly brought them under the suspicion of pursuing their aim, reckless of disunion. Their close affiliation with those abolitionists who had the atrocious frankness to avow their hate for the Union and Constitution, as "covenants with death and leagues with hell," increased this suspicion. Regardless of the warning of wiser and better men, that they would infallibly cause civil war if not disunion, they pursued their selfish aim to the accomplishment of the prediction; and, in excuse for their crime, they have incessantly dinned the dogma into the public ear. Since they have openly abolitionized themselves by avowing abolition, and not restoration of the Union, as the main object of the war; since they with their whole party have shown vengeance, not reconciliation, to be the main object, the dogma has been reiterated with new industry, with increased dogmatism. It is their main justification for the obviously disunion tendency of their measures and their blood-thirsty pursuit of diabolic vengeance.

If the dogma were based on any sound theory or actual experience, it ought to have had its exemplification where free and slave labor have their longest line of contact. It is there the very crush of the conflict would have ensued. The Ohio River is that line of contact. Yet no other border between States can show on both sides a more harmonious, rapid, prosperous growth, or a better mingling of the feelings of good neighborship. The inhabitants of the southern border of Ohio, Indiana, and Illinois have never yet manifested any serious general dissatisfaction with negro slavery as prejudicial to them. Abolitionism has been mainly confined to the northern parts of those States, where the inhabitants have no opportunity by observation to obtain information on the subject, and where by no possibility could they feel any evil effect from slave labor south of the Ohio.

The most unanswerable disproof of the dogma is to be found in the unprecedentedly rapid growth of our whole country in wealth and population. This growth has been progressing with even accelerated rapidity during the last twenty or thirty years, while abolitionists and secessionists were giving the slave question every possible agitation. This incontestably proves that all the country needed for an unabated continuance of national prosperity, was to save it from fanatic empiricism and the charlatan experiments of raw or selfish politicians. All the country needed was to be let alone in its well-doing. But this did not suit the personal aspirations of Lincoln, Seward, etc. Hence the preaching of the new evangel of "the irrepressible conflict between free and slave labor," "the house divided against itself must fall," "the country must become all free or all slaveholding," etc. Hence, also, the civil war. Their sinister aid to secessionists and abolitionists in exciting sectional jealousy has caused that widespread sectional alienation and defection from Union love, whose result is the war.

Though there is no truth in the alleged conflict between free and slave labor while kept apart in separate States, yet it must be admitted that there is such conflict between *white* and *black* labor. This is shown too plainly for denial by the legislation of free States prohibiting the immigration of free negroes, and by those mob violences driving back the attempted influx of "contrabands," despite that legislation. This, however, is not a consequence of the slave institution, for it only occurs after the slaves have been set free. It is the sole consequence of the repugnance of the whites to the blacks—the strong, natural repugnance of race. Nature, for wise purposes, while dividing the human family into different races of differing color, language, and physique, has implanted a strong repugnance of race to race. This repugnance breaks forth whenever the white laborer finds the negro interloping and competing with him for employment, and affords the only instance, in our country, of conflict between two classes of labor.

If the dogma were true, then it is strange that they who preach it do not perceive what a strong justification it would afford the South for attempting disunion, and what a persuasive argument it would offer to the slaveholding border States to aid in the attempt. All the present and future interests of the South are so inextricably interwoven with the slave institution, that its defense against immediate abolition is in some measure a necessity. This would be comparatively true even if the blacks were exported; but their presence after emancipation would intensify the injury of impoverishment from robbery, causing a never-ceasing conflict between white and black labor, intensified by all the abhorrence of race to race. As said by Jefferson, "the South has the wolf by the ears, and can't let go her hold." This she cannot do, however uncomfortable her position, while holding on. Such a community of whites and blacks would enjoy such comfort as might be supposed to ensue between a coupled wolf and bear. But the dogma is not true. The Union can be restored, with a renewed lease of life, under the Constitution as it is, leaving the slave question where it was found, under the exclusive control of the several States.

Whatever of sin there was in keeping up negro slavery was confined to the Southern States, those of the North having no legitimate right to interfere with or control the subject. Whatever of "moral, social, or political evil" it caused was inflicted exclusively upon the States where it was allowed. So far as its operation extended to the North, it was an unmixed benefit, giving to the products of Northern free labor a most commodious, bountiful market, without any taste of the "moral, social, or political evil." As a cause for political jealousy, it could not be raised to the dignity of even a plausible pretext while there were eighteen free States, with only fifteen slaveholding, and a corresponding preponderance of free State population. All the antagonism, mutual hate, and mutual abuse of abolitionists and fire-eaters could never have aroused a sectional alienation at all perilous to the Union, if in an evil hour ambitious Northern aspirants, "urged on by an inordinate greed of official power and plunder," had not organized the Free-soil or Republican party on the basis of avowed hostility to an institution closely connected with the peace, happiness, and prosperity of the fifteen slave States. This they did, despite the earnest, reiterated warnings of President Fillmore and other eminent statesmen, that their success in sectionalizing the North, for their benefit, into a preponderant sectional Northern party, by playing upon the universal prejudice against or repugnance to slavery, must inevitably result in the organization of an opposing sectional party at the South; the conflicts between the two leading unavoidably to civil war and disunion. They were further told that it was irrational to suppose that fifteen States would submit to being debarred from all participation in the administration of the Government by the success of a party upon such an inimical, narrow basis. Furthermore, they were told, amid the concurring applause of Northern audiences, that if things were reversed, the people of the North would not submit to the dominating proscription of such a Southern party.

Knowing, as these men did, that, taking the nation as a whole, full two-thirds of it were unalterably opposed to abolitionism; that a million and a half if not a majority of the loyal voters of the North were so opposed, their precipitation of the nation into the abolitionizing of the war, and so closing the door to reconciliation, was a moral crime only a degree less than that of the Southern leaders in precipitating the attempt at disunion through civil war.

The illustrative disproof of the "irrepressible conflict" dogma may be greatly strengthened by a comparison of the relative situations and experience of Pennsylvania and Massachusetts in reference to negro slavery. The former is separated for some hundreds of miles from three slave States by nothing but a mere geographical line, causing the closest contact with negro slavery, subject to all the deleterious effects of the institution, if such there be to any but the whites among whom it is actually located; yet there has been comparatively little complaint among the Pennsylvanians on that border against the institution as prejudicial to them. Their sole complaint has rather been against runaway or emancipated negroes as a nuisance. Abolitionism has found lodgment and active encouragement to much extent only in the remote parts of the State, where the practical working of negro slavery was unfelt and unknown. Pennsylvania has never given active aid to the abolition movement with the ascertained, unequivocal consent of a majority of her people.

Massachusetts, far away from all contact from negro slavery, feeling no effects from it but those of commercial benefit, acting under the irritation of prolonged exclusion from Federal power, and having the expulsion of her two sons from the Presidency to avenge, lent herself heartily to the Free-soil party movement, so soon as it ceased to be under the auspices and for the seeming benefit of antitariff Democrats. Being so deeply tainted with the sin of negro slavery by her extensive participation in its very worst crime, the African slave-trade, and by having sold her vote in the convention for keeping open that trade, she felt that she could not with decency place her co-operation in the movement upon humanitarian grounds, upon any philanthropic pretext. She therefore adopted the dogma with avidity, and has industriously propagated it as a cloak to her real purpose—the pursuit of political power. Nor is it surprising that she was not deterred from this selfish pursuit by the warnings of the danger of disunion, so earnestly pressed by nearly all our eminent statesmen, her own most distinguished sons included. If the feeling of pure, disinterested patriotism, of loyal love for Union and Constitution, had not been entirely worn out by the exacerbating effects of party conflicts, her conduct, as the originator of secession and attempted disunion, proves that the sentiment was greatly impaired. Pennsylvania stands a disinterested witness against the truth of the dogma, while Massachusetts is a tainted, suspected witness in its favor.

As further evidence of the irrepressible conflict between *white and black labor*, may be cited the many mob violences which free negroes have suffered in cities of the free States, and especially at Detroit, from white laborers, in the midst of those professing the most philanthropic sympathy for the poor negro. The unaffected revulsion or prejudice of race was so much more sincere and energetic, that the moral sentiment, real or feigned, had to succumb. So it must continue to be. It is much the bitterest part of the unfortunate doom of the poor negro, that in this, the land of his nativity, he can never find a happy home, even after emancipation. He can never enjoy in full measure the rights of a freeman, not even the most indispensable of all—the sure protection of the law. The inveterate, ineradicable prejudice of race will always prove stronger than the law. As said by Jefferson: "Nothing is more clearly written in the book of destiny than the emancipation of the blacks; and it is equally certain that the two races will never live in a state of equal freedom under the same government, so insurmountable are the barriers which nature, habit, and opinions have established between them." So also thought all our eminent statesmen of the past generation, unless John Quincy Adams be an exception, and so thought that distinguished foreigner and most enlightened observer of our institutions, De Tocqueville.

The fact being that the only conflict is between *white and black* and not between *free and slave labor*, nothing is done by emancipation toward mitigating, much less toward eradicating the conflict and its cause. On the contrary, emancipation at the South will only serve to open there a new and more extended area for the conflict, while it will send to the North vastly increased numbers of free negroes to feel its merciless influence and bring additional reproach upon the impotency of the law. Experience has proved that prohibitory laws cannot keep free negroes from settling in the North. This evasion of the law will long be promoted by abolition sympathizers, until the accumulation becomes so great that black labor will stand forth an obvious competitor with white labor for inadequate employment. Whenever that day comes the black laborer will have to flee or perish, and your laws cannot protect him. His idleness, his thievingness, and his filthiness will afford palliatives if not seeming justification for the mob violence by which he will be oppressed.

If a thorough remedy for the only labor conflict be sought for, it must be found, as it can only be found, not in the eradication of slavery, but in the eradication of the negro.

This view of the subject will enable every voter better to judge the trustworthiness of the dominant party, who have abolitionized the war, and who are undisguisedly prosecuting it, not for Union restoration, but for abolition. It will enable him to judge the statesmanship and patriotism of President Lincoln, as manifested by his recent pronunciamento, in which he proclaims, as an unalterable *sine qua non* to any terms of pacification or restoration, the unqualified surrender by the Southern States of their right to self-government by their submission to his dictated abolition.

CHAPTER III.

SANCTITY OF THE CONSTITUTION.

FIRST PUBLISHED JULY, 1864.

No. I.

"*Give me liberty or give me death!*" the noble sentiment which inaugurated the American Revolution, was also the controlling principle while inaugurating our nationality under the safeguard of the Federal Constitution.

The main object was "to secure the blessings of *liberty* to themselves and their posterity." This object is not merely proclaimed in the preamble, but is legible in the whole scope of the Constitution. To that end a free republic was ordained—that is, *a government of law*, and liberty-securing government of law, was deemed the only government worth having. All things were subordinated to that main idea, that chief desire. There can be no such government unless the law be supreme. To make it so and keep it so resort was had to the then comparatively new device or experiment of a written constitution, defining the powers of the governors and the rights of the governed. This it was hoped and believed would preserve the law in constant supremacy, at all times and under all circumstances. As the organizer, if not the very creator, of our nationality, the Constitution would have peculiar claims to popular reverence and affection. As the great law of the nation's own making, as our great national compact, as the great national compact of a nation of freemen, defining their rights and duties toward each other and all the duties of patriotism toward a common country, as the great conservator of the nation's liberty, it would be entitled to receive, and, as it was confidently believed, would receive, the nation's unstinted reverence and love. All knew the necessity of this. All knew that where law ceases tyranny begins; that there can be no life for liberty but in the unceasing supremacy of the law. But it was also known, by the practical men who framed the Government, that mere feelings of affection, mere sense of duty, were not always sufficient to keep men in obedience to any written law, however sacred and important. It was not deemed sufficient by precept and example to teach that the Constitution should always be viewed as the American *holy of holies*, as the consecrated depository, the only safeguard of the nation's liberty; it was therefore ordered that its support should be more effectually insured by a solemn oath to be taken by all officials, Federal and State. There being one officer who, from the vast extent of his power, his peculiar liability to be influenced by bad passions and sinister personal inducement, was the object of peculiarly jealous dread, an official oath was required of him of especial emphasis. The President was required solemnly to swear: "I will to the best of my ability *preserve, protect, and defend* the Constitution of the United States."

This comprehensive oath admits no evasion, permits no mental reservation, allows nothing but implicit obedience. In the earlier and better days of the Republic the imputation of a willful violation of this oath would have been deemed as a charge of want of personal honor and veracity, as a recreancy to the highest duty of patriotism. That man's conscience is not a thing to be admired, who will take the oath to obtain power and then use the power to destroy the Constitution; who takes the oath with a mental reservation of the right to break it whenever he should deem it "indispensable" to use non-granted power, substituting his own wisdom and discretion for those of the nation as to what are or are not indispensable; who takes the oath and then substitutes his own arbitrary will in lieu of law and Constitution; or, who takes the oath and then in betrayal of his great trust, substitutes a military despotism for our free Republic.

The excuse of violating the Constitution for the purpose of preserving it, having no possible basis in fact or morality, can only serve to justify the worst suspicion as to the real motive of those resorting to such pretext as even an extenuation, much less a justification of their great crime in the violation of their official oaths. There is but the one only mode of preserving the Constitution—that is, obedience. All other modes, whatever the simulated pretext, are mere treachery. No officer is, or ever should be trusted, in a government of constitutional liberty, with discretion to disobey the Constitution. When he usurps such discretion, he usurps discretion to perpetrate the basest moral treason that an officer can commit. If the perpetration be by suppressing civil authority through the instrumentality of military force, then he is guilty of actual treason, within both the letter and spirit of the definition of treason as given in the Constitution. Officers cannot have a discretion to commit treason, any more than citizens can be allowed a discretion to commit murder. Whatever the motive for either crime, it cannot afford even an extenuating sanction in the eyes of the law. Without regard to the motive, the law must inexorably treat both as a *crime*.

As said by the Supreme Court in an opinion delivered by Chief Justice Marshall: "The Government of the United States has been emphatically termed a government of law and not of men. It will certainly cease to deserve this high appellation, if the laws furnish no remedy for the violation of a legal right. * * Is it to be contended that heads of departments are not answerable to the laws of their country? * * * If one of the heads of department commits an illegal act, under color of his office, it cannot be pretended that his office exempts him from being compelled to obey the judgment of the law." So, also, if any executive officer, even the highest, commits crime under color of his office, under the pretext of assumed patriotic duty, it cannot be pretended that his office exempts him from the legal penalty of his crime. Otherwise our Government "will certainly cease to deserve its high appellation." It can be no government of law when officials are allowed a discretion to violate with impunity that great supreme law which was ordained by the nation expressly for their government. If the supreme law has no inviolable sanctity with even those sworn to its support, the ordinary subordinate laws cannot be expected to receive the needful moral support from the great body of the people.

No. II.

Law supremacy is to a law-governed republic what discipline is to an army. Obedience is the vital principle of both. In the one case obedience to the military commander; in the other, obedience to the Constitution, the great commander of the whole nation, in all its functions, civil or military. Continual vitality in the Constitution is the greatest of all national necessities, it containing the only true *salus populi*—it being the only true conservator of free national life. The watching over that life with vestal vigilance, its defense, its protection, are the highest duties of American patriotism.

No republic has ever survived in freedom the military prostration of its constitution, the military assassination of its political life. Revival from such a death is contrary to all rational belief, not only because it is contrary to all past experience, but also because it is contrary to all fair inference from the known foibles and vices of the human character. The ever-eager clutch with which power is grasped, and the hold-fast tenacity with which it is always retained by the strong minded, ambitious few, and the fatal facility of the many to acquiesce in servility, leave little room for belief in such revival. "In crossing a stream it is never safe" to let another get your head under water, when his interest might induce him to keep it under.

All attempts to supersede the Constitution, by an alleged higher law of necessity or of war, are merely the pretexts for usurpations. It gives the Federal Government ample power to meet all the exigencies of any war. So thought the great men by whom it was made, so thought the wise nation by whom it was adopted, and so the nation continued to think with near entire unanimity, till the Government fell into the hands of incompetents, who are endeavoring to cloak their own imbecility under alleged imperfections or demerits of the Constitution. More eager in the pursuit of party vengeance than of the nation's welfare, they chafe restlessly against constitutional restraint upon party persecution; denounce the whole instrument as unsuited to and therefore not made for time of war; claim the right to supersede it by a higher law of their inventing and their administering; and assume the right to use any non-granted or prohibited power, which they may choose to think "indispensable" to the objects they have in view.

Even if it were true that, from an undue care for liberty, the Constitution did withhold any power essential to the proper efficiency of the Government, yet that would afford no justification of their usurpations; for, as said by Washington: "Let there be no change of the Constitution by usurpation; for though this in one instance may be the instrument of good, it is the customary instrument by which free governments are destroyed. The precedent must always greatly overbalance in permanent evil any partial or transient benefit which the use can at any time yield." What is willful false construction but usurpation? Is it not also usurpation to attempt to make an admitted illegal act "lawful" by the simple act of the President in calling it "indispensable?"

Jefferson, in a letter written in 1814, says that Washington "scrupulously obeyed the laws during his whole career, civil and military." This, too, be it remembered, though during the revolutionary war he had to contend with thousands of armed and unarmed domestic tory traitors. He never assumed the right or exercised the power of proclaiming martial law. He may in some very few instances have exercised in a mild way some of the power incident to such law when necessarily arising in the absence of civil authority, within what might be strictly termed the lines of his immediate, actual military operations. But he never was guilty of attempting to make the law, where circumstances according to the established usages of war had not already brought it into being. He never by his own fiat attempted to clothe himself with a power to persecute his fellow-citizens, which otherwise or without his own proclamation he would not possess. His mind and heart were too deeply imbued with the knowledge and love of the principles of civil liberty for any such attempt at self-aggrandizement. In marching his army to quell the whisky rebellion, he took care by general order to remind his soldiers that he and they were merely acting "in aid of the civil authority."

This example was strictly followed by Madison while successfully conducting us through the second war for independence, the last war with England, when she was the greatest military power of the world, while our nation was still comparatively young and feeble. Let it be also remembered that Madison thus "scrupulously obeyed the laws," while a powerful political party in and out of Congress, by speeches and through the public press, continuously denounced himself, his administration, and the war, with fierce severity, and while a very powerful faction were notoriously striving to inflict secession and civil war on the country for the purpose of separating New England from the Union. Even in such an emergency he never lost his equanimity; he never forgot that, as chief magistrate in a government of law, it was his highest duty to give an example of exemplary obedience to the law; he never forgot, as commander-in-chief of the army and the navy, to teach all subordinates, by his example, the duty of willing obedience to civil authority; he neither usurped nor attempted to use any of the enginery of tyranny; he used no mode of terrorism, not even bravado, but scorned such expedients of weak timid men as inappropriate in the government of freemen. Strong as must have been his sense of gratitude toward General Jackson for having "closed the war in a blaze of glory," yet he did not refrain from administering to the general a mild rebuke for his martial law, and carefully forbore all attempt at remitting or refunding his fine.

Such was the example of that great and good man as to what should be the demeanor of a President in such a crisis—the careful upholding of law and Constitution in their supremacy. Great was his merit, and great has been his reward. He lives and will ever live in the affection of the nation, second only to Washington.

With these examples of Washington and Madison before him, stinted must be the mind and pitiable the ambition of him who abdicates the exalted station of chief magistrate in a government of law over a great nation of liberty-loving freemen, and debases himself into a mere Lynch-law President. Such an ambition can be compared only to that of the Greek who sought immortality by burning the magnificent temple of Ephesus.

When a President and his party in Congress have repeatedly violated all the guarantees of liberty contained in the Constitution and effectually silenced the law by subordinating civil to military authority, they have done what they can to justify the exultant shouts with which the absolutists of Europe have been hailing the alleged failure of "the model Republic," the failure of our grand experiment to prove men competent to their own self-government. There is one way and but one way to silence those exultant shouts and call out the exultant peans of the friends of liberty throughout the world—that is, by reinstating the Constitution through the ballot-box and at the same time appropriately punishing those who are laboring for its destruction.

It should be cause for agonizing regret to every enlightened patriot, that, in a great crisis like the present, the Constitution has not had fair play by fair experiment to prove its perfect adequacy to the occasion. To have deprived it of that opportunity is a fault or a folly of such towering magnitude as to be classed among high political crimes. It is a crime not only against our country, but also against the cause of civil liberty throughout the world. By its appropriate punishment, human liberty will receive a renewed lease of life, with hopeful promise of perpetuity, its friends a renewed confidence in the ultimate amelioration of all governments, and the model Republic will be launched anew upon its brilliant career as the hope and exemplar of nations. That appropriate punishment of the Constitution-destroyers by the sovereign people will also wipe out the foul stain they have inflicted on our national character, by vindicating our claims to be considered a liberty-appreciating, a liberty-loving nation.

No. III.

"The spirit of liberty will not permit power to overstep its prescribed limits, though good intent, patriotic intent, come along with it. This is the nature of constitutional liberty. THIS IS OUR LIBERTY.

"The contest for ages has been *to rescue liberty from the grasp of executive power*. Whoever has engaged in her cause has struggled for the accomplishment of that object. On the long list of champions of human freedom there is not one name dimmed by the reproach of advocating the extension of executive power. Their uniform steady purpose has been to limit and restrain it. So far from being the object of enlightened popular trust, it has been regarded as the great object of danger, it has been dreaded as a lion that must be caged."—*Daniel Webster.*

As before remarked, until recently it was the concurring opinion of the whole nation that the Constitution gave adequate powers for the emergencies of any war; that with the Government in competent hands there was no need for usurpation. Even many of the most intelligent leaders of the dominant abolition party have within the last three years publicly professed the same opinion. Take for example the following from a speech delivered in the Senate by one of its most talented and prominent leaders.

"I do not place the power on the ground assumed in some quarters, that, in times of war or rebellion, the military is superior to the civil authority; or that, in such times, what persons may choose to call *necessity* is higher or above the Constitution. *Necessity is the plea of tyrants*, and if our Constitution ceases to operate the moment a person charged with its observance thinks there is necessity for its violation, it is of little value. I hold that the military is as much subject to control by civil power in war as in peace.

"I want no other power for putting down this gigantic rebellion than such as may be properly derived from the Constitution. It is equal to even this great emergency. The more we study its provisions, the more it is tried in troublous times, the greater will be our admiration and veneration for the wisdom of its authors.

"I am for suppressing this enormous rebellion according to law and in no other way. *We are fighting to maintain the Constitution, and it especially becomes us not to violate it ourselves. How are we better than the rebels if both alike set at naught the Constitution?* I warn my countrymen, who stand ready to tolerate almost any act done in good faith for the suppression of the rebellion, not to sanction usurpations of power which may hereafter become precedents for the destruction of constitutional liberty. We will have gained but little in suppressing the insurrection if it be at the expense of the Constitution. Let us preserve it perfect, with all its guarantees for the protection of life and liberty unimpaired."

There can be little or no doubt that such also is the vastly preponderating opinion of all the intelligence of the present day, with the full benefit of our own personal observation and dear-bought experience. Furthermore, there is as little doubt that, according to the belief of a large majority of the intelligent men of the nation, none of the usurpations or unconstitutional abuses of power have aided but have all been injurious to the Union cause. But concede this to be a mistake—say that only an equal number of intelligent men so think, the fact will stand as an unanswerable argument against the policy of such usurpations and as irrefutable proof of the folly of those who resort to them. The most ultra will not honestly contend that state necessity can justify resort to unconstitutional means, when the expediency of those means are in doubt, as they must be when condemned by even a half of the intelligence of the country. If there be any sense in the higher law dogma, the necessity must be obvious and the remedy of indisputable benefit. Resort to mere experiments with doubtful remedies can have no justification on the score of either sense or honesty. The wisdom of the Constitution stands fully vindicated by the practical experience and wisdom of the present day.

"Martial law is no law." So say those eminent jurists Hale and Blackstone. So also concur in saying all the other eminent jurists of England and America. The paradox results from a mere misnomer in calling a *power* by the name of a *law*. It would be only an equal misnomer to call the physical power of a man his law. The power which is misnamed martial law is that power which unavoidably and unsought for comes to a military commander in the presence of actual active military operations, because of the absence or silence of the civil law, in consequence of the absence of its appropriate functionaries, or from their being paralyzed by the operations of the war. It is a power arising solely from the necessity of the occasion—that is, from the enforced silence of the civil law or its functionaries, is produced or created by no proclamation, lasts only for the occasion, and needs no revocation. The power is undefined and undefinable. It is, as said by the Duke of Wellington, "the will of the military commander" —the only really good, practical definition ever given of what goes by the name of martial law.

It is a mere solecism, while discoursing on jurisprudence, to speak of the arbitrary will of a man as a law. The power which thus incidentally comes to the military commander by necessity is strictly limited by the necessity. He cannot go one jot beyond that necessity. So far as it gives him control over non-combatants, or persons not belonging to the military service, it is altogether a power of prevention, not at all a power of punition, for the sake of punishment. It is a power to prevent aid to the enemy or obstruction to himself. If he transcend the narrow limit of his power, or abuses his discretion, he is civilly responsible to the law.

If this exposition of "martial law" be correct—if it be resorted to as a means of prevention, not of punition—then a good citizen need feel no embarrassment as to his conduct under it. All he has to do is to abstain from giving aid and comfort to the enemy, and, should he mistake as to what that means, he will only be restrained by personal temporary detention from a repetition of the mistake. But if this be not the true exposition, if the object be punition as well as prevention, then obviously the proclaimer or enforcer of the martial law should, in simple justice and humanity, let it be distinctly known beforehand what will be punished. Without some such elucidation, no lawyer can tell for his own guidance, or that of his clients, what it is necessary for a good citizen to do, or not to do, in an honest desire to avoid all collision with the military power. This is what most of our good citizens anxiously desire, whether they believe or disbelieve in the power to place the State under martial rule. Such praiseworthy desire should be encouraged and promoted by the military authorities. It is against all American notions of liberty, that a freeman should be punished by an *ex post facto* law, with an *ex post facto* prescribed penalty. It is no mitigation, but an aggravation, if the penalty be left in the discretion of an arbitrarily appointed military tribunal. Far better for him, both for the sake of leniency and for that of future redress, that the penalty should rest exclusively in the discretion of him who proclaimed the martial rule, or of the principal general enforcing it, than in any intermediary tribunal of his appointing.

CHAPTER IV.

SEMI-TREASONABLE ORDER OF WAR DEPARTMENT.

PUBLISHED SEPTEMBER, 1863.

WHEN Congress passed and the President approved the act of last session authorizing the latter to suspend the privilege of the writ of habeas corpus, we had from both a distinct concession or recognition of the principle that the power of suspension is exclusively with Congress. For a joint discretionary power of the sort in both Congress and the President would be so incongruous and injuriously conflicting that no one has contended for it; and, therefore, the concession of its possession by Congress is necessarily the equivalent of a direct negation of the power to the President. Such having been, anterior to this rebellion, the uniform unanimous construction of seventy years' duration, from this time forth it should be held to be the *settled* construction. However gratifying this result may be to those of us who for two long years had insisted on that construction against Congressional and Executive influence, yet this is no time for exultation in the triumph of even so great a principle over pernicious error; but rather for conciliation in that, as in all things, so that there shall be no future need for such triumph over even the political errors of our countrymen. It would, therefore, be unprofitable, if not inappropriate, to inquire too nicely into the motive of the President and his party in Congress for this apparent change of opinion. Let us rather continue to treat it, as it was received at first by the nation, as the harbinger of a change of policy which will hereafter keep all our functionaries within the line of their constitutional powers. The clause of the act requiring all arrests to be promptly reported to the courts for their speedy action, greatly encouraged that hope. It has been also strengthened by the recent declaration of the President, in conversation with General Smith, that he would acquiesce in the decision of the courts against what is supposed to be his most cherished power—his assumed power to emancipate slaves.

There has been a recent military action in this connection of such good promise, that it ought not to be passed over in that neglectful silence with which it has been heretofore treated. Our commanding general in Kentucky, who has had larger experience in the matter of military arrests than any other of our generals, has, by his recent order, struck a much-needed blow at the arbitrariness of such arrests. He has ordered that they shall only be made upon written charges sustained by the "affidavits of two or more responsible persons;" and not even then, until the charge has been investigated and the order of arrest issued from his headquarters. The Constitution says, "no warrant shall issue but upon probable cause, supported by oath or affirmation." Though this is not referred to as the cause of the change in military practice, yet the cause assigned is almost equally gratifying. The general says the order is made "to prevent unnecessary trouble, expense, and *oppression*." Whatever the cause for the change, it is gratifying to find our military officers thus conforming to the injunctions of the Constitution. It is especially gratifying, as signalizing the superiority of the wisdom of the Constitution over the wisdom of our men of the present day. It reteaches that salutary, oft-inculcated lesson, never to suppose ourselves wiser than the Constitution. Coming, as the order does, from so experienced and intelligent a general, it may be taken as full proof that such disregard of the Constitution will mainly result in profitless "trouble and expense" to the Government and "unnecessary oppression" to the citizen.

These cheering hopes of restoration to a Government of law have been chilled by the terms of the suspension proclamation, and its accompanying order from the War Department. The suspension is not confined to localities within or near the site of military operations, but extends over the whole Union, and to localities where there is not the semblance of pretext for being required by military necessity. Nor is it limited to any defined class of cases, but embraces every one the President may choose to imprison, with or without cause, or even the suspicion of justifiable cause. Such extreme laxity in dealing with such a delicate subject, and one upon which popular jealousy is so promptly aroused, evinces rather a reckless, defiant disregard of the spirit of the Constitution, with its sympathizing popular sentiment, than a becoming deference to either. The order from the War Department requires all officers, from whom a prisoner shall be attempted to be taken by judicial authority, after return made of his detainer by Presidential authority, to make forcible resistance with all the military aid that can be obtained. This has a strong squinting toward the perpetration of treason.

The Constitution having confided to congressional discretion exclusively the important trust of determining the when, the where, the how far, and for how long the suspension of the privilege of habeas corpus should be made, the act of last session raises the important question whether Congress can abdicate that trust and transfer it to the President. The preponderance of legal intelligence in and out of Congress, as also of argument, has seemed to be against the power to transfer. It is a long, well-established principle among jurists and statesmen, that a discretionary power confided to one of the departments cannot be legally transferred to or exercised by either of the others. The attempted transfer in this case is in direct conflict with that great principle. The Constitution does not say that in time of war or rebellion the privilege *shall* be, nor even that it *may* be suspended, but only when in those cases the public safety may require the suspension. To determine when, where, how far, and how long public safety so requires, belongs exclusively to Congress, and, as many if not most of our best thinkers suppose, cannot be transferred. This great question has to be decided by the judiciary. Should they decide against the transfer, it would be indecorous to suppose the President would not obey the decision, as his duty requires. It would not do for Mr. Lincoln or any aspiring member of his Cabinet explicitly to avow, before the Presidential election, an intention to disobey such decision. Yet this is exactly what the order from the War Department seems to contemplate, and, in that event, orders all military subordinates to resist such decision with military force. *Will not the resistance be plain treason?*

Says the Constitution: "Treason against the United States shall consist only in levying war against them," etc. What "levying war against them" means has been well defined by English and American adjudications. All lawyers will agree that the suppression of the civil authority by military force is among the plainest or most appropriate illustrations of the kind of "levying war" which was meant. So, also, they will agree as to the following illustrations.

Attempted usurpation by armed force; or by armed force attempting the intimidation of Congress to procure the enacting or repealing of a law, or of the President to obtain a change of his Cabinet or policy; or resisting a constitutional act of Congress, or the exercise of any constitutional power by the President; or the resisting of either department in the exercise of its constitutional functions.

If we were to suppose a legally constituted *posse comitatus* raised by the Marshal for a legitimate purpose, diverted into any such assault upon the Presidential power, it would be none the less treasonable, though the Chief Justice and a majority of the members of Congress should voluntarily join the posse.

So, also, armed resistance to judicial mandate being equally treasonable, it will be none the less so, because made by part of the army under the direct personal command of the President.

The principle equally embraces the forcible suppression of the civil authority of a State—for instance, of its legislature, its courts, or its free ballot. As adjudged by the Supreme Court in Bollman's case, an attempt by force to subvert the Government in any locality, such as a city or State, is treason, though unaccompanied with an intent to subvert the whole Government. A making of war against any one of the States, or an attempt by force to subvert its civil authority, is, therefore, a levying of war against all the States within the constitutional definition of treason. Consequently it is mere absurdity to suppose that there can be such a thing as full treason against a State, while it remains in the Union, as contradistinguished from treason against the United States.

As to the idea that the suspension of the privilege of the writ precluded the issuing of the writ of habeas corpus in all cases, or exonerates from obedience to judicial action under the writ, that is a gross error. The act itself evidently contemplates the continued use of the writ, as that is the most if not the only appropriate mode of carrying out some of its requirements. After directing the Secretaries of State and War to make return within twenty days of all arrests to the proper courts, it directs that, if the Secretary neglect or fail to make the return, the court shall then order the release of the person arrested. Now the proper exercise of this power almost indispensably requires the use of the writ, or, which is the same, of some perfectly analogous process. So, also, a conscript may be detained after regularly furnishing a substitute or paying his three hundred dollars commutation, or a volunteer after having served out his three years' term. In none of these cases is there a conceivable reason of policy why the writ should not be used for the relief of the citizen so unjustly treated; and, though the act is bunglingly bad enough, yet a fair interpretation will exempt Congress from the imputed infamy of having intended to deprive the sufferer of such redress.

The most material and comprehensive portion of the proclamation, as it is also of the act of Congress, is that which extends the suspension to all cases of persons held by order of the President, without regard to the reason or occasion for the holding. It is the order of the President which alone legitimates the holding. No imputed authority as incident to a military commission will do. There must be superadded the express order of the President, either special or general. The act expressly contemplates the use of the writ for the very purpose of ascertaining whether the detention is by virtue of such order. It is true the act, to the eternal dishonor of Congress, makes the return of the officer under oath conclusive, precluding the court from inquiring whether he has ignorantly or willfully made a false return; still it evidently contemplates the use of the writ to obtain the return. A literal compliance with the order may therefore lead an ignorant officer into the unwitting perpetration of treason, by wrongfully resisting the order of the court. Besides, the courts might well say that Congress had no right to preclude the requirement of the production of the President's order to sustain the return of the subordinate, as otherwise the latter would be virtually empowered to make the suspension and enforce it by a false or ignorant return. There is nothing more probable than that inferior officers may ignorantly suppose that, in making all arrests, they act by the authority of their chief, the President. The order obviously requires careful reconsideration and amendment, to prevent such misconstruction of their duty by subordinates, and to save them from the danger of ignorantly incurring the penalties of treason.

CHAPTER V.

AMERICAN PATRIOTISM:—WHAT IS IT?

OCTOBER, 1863.

A GRECIAN sage gave *The habit of duty or obedience to duty* as the definition of *virtue.* An eminent English philosopher pronounces it the best comprehensive definition to be found in any system of morals. It may aid our inquiry as to what is American patriotism; for among the social duties none stands higher than that of patriotism. But this highest type, like all others, has its grades or distinctions, dependent upon local or national peculiarity. We must first ascertain our peculiarity, our distinctive characteristic, in seeking the highest, most imperative duty of our citizens, and thereby develop the true American patriotism.

What is the peculiar distinctive feature of our political organization—of our nationality? What is our national palladium—politically speaking, what is our Holy of Holies? It cannot be the simple right of the people to govern themselve, or the simple fact of our being a republic; for neither is peculiar to ourselves, but we hold those privileges in common with many other people of ancient and modern times. *The great characteristic feature, distinguishing us from all others, is the attempt to give us that highest national boon—a government of law.*

We have been carefully taught that without this there can be neither a proper republic, nor proper self-government, nor proper national prosperity, nor proper civil liberty. To secure this *government of law* the fathers instituted the comparatively modern invention of a written Constitution, defining the rights of the governed and the powers of the governors. To secure liberty in permanency was the great desideratum. This was the *summum bonum* of national existence, to which all other things were ever to be subordinate. We were taught it as the highest order of *salus populi,* the most imperative State necessity, the vitality of the nation, the true *suprema lex*. All else must yield to that; it must be preserved, or its preservation at all times attempted, at whatever cost, inconvenience, or danger. As its loss, according to all experience, was irreparable, it was never even to be put in hazard, for the sake of any other supposable benefit. The occasions when and by whom some of its minor safeguards might be temporarily suspended were carefully defined. Absolute arbitrary power anywhere, at any time, or for any purpose, was carefully expunged from our system of government. Even its temporary use was deemed too perilous for liberty. Arbitrary discretion in officials was reduced to its minimum.

As admitted by President Lincoln and Attorney-General Bates in 1861: "The nation has not chosen to delegate all its powers to this Government in any or all its departments." "It has no powers but such as are granted by the Constitution." "The nation preferred taking the risk of leaving some good undone, for lack of power in the agent, rather than arm any Government officer with such powers for evil as are implied in the dictatorial charge to see that no damage comes to the Commonwealth." That is, the Government, at no time, under no circumstances, upon no pretext, was to assume dictatorial power or any form of discretionary absolutism. Ours was to be emphatically a government of law, not of discretion.

Such being the great distinctive characteristic of our nation, it vindicates our boasted prerogative or mission to teach, by example, the beauty and benefit of civil liberty. From this great mission we learn the special duty of American patriotism. It is to love and protect that which secures our civil liberty. Nor are we left to learn this from our own inquiry into the true spirit of our institutions. It is taught by the plain letter of the Constitution. When inculcating duty to country, it requires from its officials no oath of allegiance, as elsewhere, to either government or country or nation, but an oath "to support the Constitution;" that is, in other equivalent words, to *obey the Constitution* as the "supreme law of the land." That obedience is the comprehensive sum total of our allegiance. Though it may not comprehend all other modes of patriotism, yet there is this to mark its supremacy, that there is no mode antagonistic to it which is or can be true patriotism.

The ancient republics, living amid the ever-recurring dangers of war, taught military discipline as among the highest duties of the citizen and the most important interests of the State. Our geographical position and great strength exempting us from foreign conquest, military discipline can never be with us a paramount national interest. If, contrary to all rational probability, it should ever become so, we shall then soon cease to have free government. But civil or political discipline, for as long as we hope to be free, must continue a paramount interest. Obedience to law, in a government of law, being what discipline or military obedience is to an army, civil obedience is with us the greatest interest of the State, as it is also the greatest duty of the citizen. Obedience to the Constitution is for the nation what self-control is for the moral well-being of an individual. It is thus, and thus alone, that is kept under that fanaticism, whether in religion or politics, which hugs, as the virtue of saints or heroes, the barbarity of the bigot or the baseness of the assassin. It is thus, and thus alone, that the intolerant, proscriptive, vindictive passions of parties are to be restrained within the rules of justice or Christian mercy. There is no moral sense, no conscience in excited parties. When most excited by fancied virtuous animosity, or a fancied national danger, it is then precisely that they most need, as they are also most restive under, the restraint of obedience to the law. It is because of the strong countervailing tendency of bad human passions that their subordination to legal obedience becomes so high a virtue in a citizen or a people. To keep up that subordination without relaxation is the indispensable civil discipline of a people wishing to continue free. Every relaxation is but evidence of disease in the body politic, which, if not checked, will sooner or later destroy the vitals of civil liberty.

As habit of duty or obedience to duty is *virtue*, so obedience to the Constitution must be the definition of true American patriotism. All bastard allegiance to a section, to a party, or to a policy must be a pernicious, sinful substitute for true patriotism.

CHAPTER VI.

HUMANITY VERSUS PATRIOTISM.

NOVEMBER, 1862.

That be far from thee, to slay the righteous with the wicked. Shall not the judge of all the earth do right?

And the Lord said, If I find fifty righteous within the city, then I will spare all the place for their sakes.

Peradventure ten shall be found there. And he said, I will not destroy it for ten's sake.

IN an attempted answer to the opinion of Judge Curtis, condemning the emancipation and martial law proclamations, published on the eve of the late elections, Mr. T. P., professor in a Massachusetts law school, says:—

"Then he tells us that the innocent must suffer with the guilty. This is true, and it is sad. But when the mingled fire and hail of God's vengeance run along the ground, they pursue no devious paths, that they may leave the home of the innocent unharmed; for, when national sins bring national calamities, the innocent suffer with the guilty: it is at all events a fact. And what has been will be."

This is the justification, the sole justification, for inciting the horrors of negro insurrection, published by a professing Christian to a Christian, civilized people in this enlightened age! Having had the boldness to make such an utterance for party effect, he should now, when no party influence operates, be made responsible to public censure for such an insult to and outrage upon the moral sentiment of the nation.

If, indeed, "the mingled fire and hail of God's vengeance" ever does purposely "run along the ground," visiting alike with destruction the just and the unjust, the guilty and the innocent; if, indeed, we are bound by the teachings of our religion to believe such visitations as the special interposition of Providence, we are equally taught to acquiesce in the justice of such examples, by a childlike submission to a perfect wisdom and beneficence, whose ways we cannot comprehend. But when man assumes such authority over his fellow-beings, we may well challenge his right to inflict injustice; and he can find no shelter under the supposed example of a superintending Providence, whose justice or power we have no right to question. Till man is endowed with the divine attributes of supreme power, wisdom, and beneficence, he must content himself with obeying the divine precept—*never do evil that good may come of it.* It is exactly because of his incompetency to play the part of Divine Providence on earth, that he is debarred the right to punish the guilty, by such means as will equally and unavoidably punish the innocent.

What insufferable arrogance for a mere mortal to assume the prerogative of Providence, or attempt to justify his acts by a supposed analogy to the presumed intentional acts of Providence! Such arrogance is impious wickedness. It is because of his shortsightedness, his inability to foreknow the certain results of any course of policy of his contriving, that he is held to the precept—never do evil that good may come of it. Such power was never delegated or permitted by the Supreme Being, or by any enlightened people, or by any national code of morality.

It is because of the inability to stay the hand of the savage negro, to confine his destructive appetites to proper persons and objects, that the inciting of negro insurrection is one of the instrumentalities forbidden in civilized warfare. It is denounced by our Declaration of Independence and the most eminent authorities on the law of nations. It was so expressly denounced by our own Government under the administration of Presidents Madison and Monroe. The man must be destitute of every element of human sympathy who does not find within his own bosom a monitor to tell him that it is equally denounced by every precept of justice and humanity.

Our country has obtained an enviable and influential position among the nations of the earth by being a constant advocate for a mitigation of the avoidable evils of war. It has signalized the disinterestedness of its advocacy by a proffer to surrender, on the altar of humanity, so large a portion of its naval strength as the right to use privateers. Is this policy all to be reversed, and the nation made the scorn if not the odium of the world, by the use of negro massacres in aid of a warfare waged with our own countrymen? This, too, when there is no fair pretext of urgent necessity to excuse a resort to such inhuman means; the preponderance of our military strength, all things considered, being in the proportion of eight or ten to one. If with such preponderant strength we cannot put down the rebellion by legitimate, civilized warfare, we cannot put it down at all. General Taylor, during his invasion of Mexico, protected the foreign enemies with whom he was warring against the savage raids of the Camanches. Though we do not know that the aroused black savage ever showed any touch of pity or human sympathy while inflicting his vengeance, yet we do know that pity for infancy, boyhood, and girlhood has often stayed the uplifted tomahawk in the hands of the red savage of our forests. This, too, toward the children of his foreign enemies. Shall we show less sympathy for the women and children of our own countrymen?

Mr. P. says that rebels have no rights that can interfere with a successful prosecution of the war. If this were true, still the infirm, the women and children, and the Unionists of the South, who have done nothing to aid the rebellion but under compulsion, have large rights well deserving Government protection, instead of an indiscriminate destruction. Then, too, there are the poor negroes themselves, whose destruction by hundreds of thousands is the very probable if not certain consequence of this mode of conducting the war, if it were practicable so to conduct it. Have they, too, no rights, no claim on the justice of the Government for protection against such inhuman policy? Have our *soi-disant* negro philanthropists, our abolitionists, no plea for mercy in their behalf? Does it comport with the honor and fair fame of a great nation to use delusive incitement toward such ignorant creatures, to procure from them an aid which must result to them in a tremendous destruction, from which we cannot save them? But if neither the rebels, nor the Southern women and children, nor the negroes have rights, still it cannot be denied that the nation itself has rights, among the most important of which is the protection of its unsullied honor and its fair claim to rank among the civilized Christian nations of the earth. That is a possession we cannot afford to cast away or suffer to be destroyed. In the long run, it is worth more to us than the glory of many victories on well-stricken fields. Without it, we must sink in the estimation of all Christendom to the level of the Mexican and South American Republics. We cannot afford it as the price of even a valuable worthy object; much less can we afford it merely for the unworthy purpose of indulging a fanatical party in the gratification of their inordinate hate against the Southern people.

If, as Mr. P. says, to some extent the innocent unavoidably suffer with the guilty in all civil wars, this with the right-minded should serve only as an additional reason for trying to diminish, instead of purposely increasing the amount of such suffering.

If Mr. P. will not heed the precept of our divinely-inspired text, in his effort to imitate "God's vengeance," he will, if he wishes to preserve his presumed station in the worthy regards of intelligent gentlemen, hearken to the uninspired precept of great nature's true hierophant—"*Earthly power doth then show likest God's, when mercy seasons justice.*"

CHAPTER VII.

DISUNIONISM.

MAY, 1859.

To the Conservative Union-loving Men of Kentucky and Tennessee.

IT has been thought that you desire a fuller exposition than any yet given of the motives for the political movement inaugurated by the Opposition Conventions of Kentucky, Tennessee, and Maryland. The task of making that exposé has been assigned to the writer, as one intimately familiar with the views of those who were actively participant in starting the movement in Kentucky. It will be performed as fully as the brevity necessary to newspaper publications will permit.

The leading idea was *present and future peril to the Union* from the collisions of the two sectional parties, and the necessity of their being broken up or defeated by a large national organization, having the preservation of the Union for its principal object.

Subsidiary to this, but second in importance to this alone, was the desire to rescue the nation from the misrule of those leaders of the modern Democracy, who, according to the indignant avowal of one of the most talented and honest among them, have made ours "*the most corrupt government in the world.*"

The last speech of Mr. Clay was delivered before the Kentucky Legislature, in compliance with a joint, perhaps unanimous request of its two Houses. That request was probably made in consequence of a reliable intimation that it would be acceptable to him. He seemed to desire an occasion for arousing the attention of the representatives of Kentucky, and through them that of the nation, to the grave subject of *disunion.* How well he succeeded with his immediate audience, may be inferred from the fact stated by a member, that, while he spoke of the value and danger of the

Union, tears of warm sympathy started to the eyes of many, and among them some of the most inveterate old Democrats in the assembly. He spoke of disunion as a danger then rapidly approaching. He said it would not be long before it would become necessary to organize a great distinctive "Union party." Whenever that was done, if it should happen during his life, he declared his purpose to join that party, regardless of all party ties. After his speech, old Democrats, who had warred with him politically for twenty years, cordially shook his hand, and assured him that whenever the Union party to which he referred was formed they would go with him.

Since his death, the rapid development of the disunion tendency has proved the sagacity with which he judged the then aspect of affairs. The South has been flooded with speeches, essays, and newspaper discussions to prove the great benefit it would derive from separation on the slave line. Inspired with undue confidence by apparent success in alluring nearly the whole South into the Democratic party, and thus consolidating it in the fierce sectional contest which ensued the repeal of the Missouri Compromise, its leaders threw off all disguise. In the last Presidential campaign some of them went so far as to avow, to applauding audiences, a long-cherished hatred of the Union. Pending that contest, and in anticipation of a then probable defeat, Governors, Senators, Representatives, etc. organized a conspiracy, the avowed object of which was, in that event, to march upon Washington with an adequate military force, seize the Government before the inauguration of the new President, and dictate the terms of separation. The accidental circumstance of Mr. Fillmore being a candidate, with the consequent defeat of Fremont, alone saved the nation from the attempt to carry out that widespread conspiracy.

One of their chiefs, Governor Wise, in publicly developing the scheme and the means of carrying it out, spoke of a national civil war as what they would have to encounter; but that was not what he most deprecated. It was "the neighborhood civil war," as he termed it, which they would have to carry on with the fifty thousand Unionists of Virginia that he deplored. That it was which gave him pain to contemplate. To meet the exigency of this double warfare, to provide an adequate force against their external and internal foes, he said they would "*arm their slaves.*"

Another of their leaders, Senator Clingman, in a published letter, said they meant to put down the opposition of Union men in North Carolina by the "*swift attention of vigilance committees;*" that is, by organized assassination.

These avowals were nowhere rebuked by any portion of the Southern Democracy. It seemed as though nearly the whole Southern wing of the party was deeply tainted with disunionism. If such had not been the fact, those men would never have dared to make these avowals. The Democratic administration organ, published at Washington under the control of the President, admitted within the last few months, as an undisputed fact, that there is still a "widespread and desperate conspiracy at the South for dissolving the Union." This charge met with neither rebuke nor denial from any Democratic quarter. Such acquiescence under the charge is equal to admission or full proof.

Aaron Burr, for a suspected intention of attempting a severance of the Union, had to endure, during a long remnant of his life, the ignominy of an unrelaxed national odium.

The members of the Hartford Convention brought upon themselves a similar odium for a suspected intention of bringing about a peaceable secession of the New England States, with the regularly obtained assent of their people. This suspicion threw all the members of that convention under a proscription of national hate, which thereafter excluded them from all public trust and confidence. Nor was this all. Such was the popular odium which they incurred, that it effectually broke down the once powerful Federal party, to which they belonged. *Hartford Conventionist* became a stigma of reproach, and remained until recently without a compeer for imputed severity.

General Jackson, in his famous nullification proclamation, said, "*disunion by armed force is treason.*" This denunciation received the almost unanimous approval of the whole nation, outside of South Carolina. It is, therefore, altogether proper to characterize this conspiracy as *treasonable*, and the conspirators as would-be traitors. That they were not actual traitors within even the strict letter of the law, and earning the felon's doom, which it awards to the crime of treason, was only because the occasion did not occur which was to call forth the perpetration of any of the intended overt acts of their treasonable plot.

What degree of reprehension is due to men who, by fair, peaceful means, seek to break up our glorious Union, we need not stop to inquire. There may not be much moral delinquency in an endeavor to convince the people of certain States that their interests would be promoted by secession, nor even in playing upon their sectional passions and prejudices to accomplish that object. But, without consulting the people of those States, without any direct sanction from them, for a few men to assume the right to determine the question and attempt to force them into secession, is a very grave crime. It can find no justification or apology with any intelligent, honest man. When such attempt necessarily involves national civil war, it becomes a crime of the gravest magnitude, to be expiated only by a felon's death. When the purposed attempt was to be carried through, by such coolly premeditated appliances as were to signalize this treason, it merits a degree of popular abhorrence which, as it cannot be adequately expressed, each man must weigh for himself by the promptings of his own bosom. That it has not yet met with such abhorrence may be because public opinion, guided by an overscrupulous merciful justice, will not so punish the known few because it cannot reach the equally guilty but unknown many.

Consider those appliances. A neighborhood civil war to be carried on with the aid of armed slaves! The large slaveholders of Virginia to arm their negroes against their poorer fellow-citizens! To arm negro slaves and incite them to a taste of white men and women's blood! Once tasted, when would their thirst have been slaked? What would have been the result of such a neighborhood civil war? Virginia would have been visited by general massacre and desolation. Or take the North Carolinian's plan for putting down opposition. The murder of thousands of their fellow-citizens by organized bands of assassins, because they would not aid in treason against their country. What can be more atrocious? The very magnitude of the atrocity seems to have saved it from proper opprobrium. Like the big wars that make ambition virtue, it sublimates itself into satanic grandeur. The mind shrinks from the realization of such atrocity. It will not believe such wickedness of rational, accountable men, even though they themselves vauntingly avowed the fact.

Why has the execrable faction of Abolition disunionists earned for itself such general abhorrence? It is because of the belief that they seek disunion and consequent war between the North and the South, in the hope of being thus enabled to incite a servile war, with all its horrid accompaniments. Shall these conspirators wholly escape a similar retribution?

If the contemplated occasion for the treason had occurred, and the whole plot been acted out, what would have been the fate of Kentucky and Tennessee? Though there was not probably a man in either State who would have voted for disunion, yet it is probable that both would have been precipitated into full participation in the national and the domestic civil war. At the first flow of blood, it would have been almost impossible to prevent our impetuous young men from mingling in the conflict. Nothing could have prevented them but the earnest, unanimous remonstrance of the leading men of all parties. Could such unanimous remonstrance have been obtained?

If the misdeeds of the Hartford Conventionists justly sank the old Federal party under the weight of popular odium, what ought to be the fate of the party that honors, sustains, trusts, and submits itself to the guidance of such moral traitors as these? Put down that party; and, though justice may not be fully satisfied, yet all the punishment that can be inflicted will reach these conspirators collectively and individually. Whether they shall be placed individually, like the Hartford Conventionists, under the ban of an enduring political proscription, the nation will determine hereafter.

No sooner had the contemplated occasion for the proposed treason failed to occur, than they began scheming as to the use they should make of the victory obtained by their party in the contest for the Presidency. The scheme for disunion was only deferred, not abandoned. One of the most talented and influential among them, in a published address to the Governor of South Carolina, advocating disunion, gave it as his opinion that "all true statesmanship in the South consists in forming combinations and shaping events to bring about a speedy dissolution of the Union and a Southern Confederacy." The talented Senator Hammond, in a speech delivered to his constituents last summer, expressed the opinion that, if the North succeeded in electing the next President, as it probably would, the Southern States generally would not agree to secede for that cause; but if such a President were elected a second time, or if Congress passed another tariff, then he believed that they would. But it seems from more recent revelations that the disunionists are not so patient as he supposed them to be. The two leading Democratic organs of Louisiana and Mississippi have lately warned the people of those States that in "all human probability" the Republicans would elect the next President, and, as disunion was the proper necessary consequence of that event, urged the selection of such men as candidates as would be best qualified to accomplish that object. Last year there was publicly organized in Alabama what is termed the "Southern League," having disunion for its undisguised object. A Democratic paper published in Mobile announces that at a recent conference of leading men of the party, it was resolved that the attempt at disunion should be vigorously pushed on at once. Still more recently we have the action of the Southern Convention held in Mississippi. There all disguise has been thrown aside. In the event of the Republican party electing its candidate at the next Presidential election, the convention recommends measures to prevent the installation of the Republican President by forcibly retaining power in the hands of the present Administration, or failing in that, to sever the slaveholding States into a separate confederacy.

Mr. Boyce, of South Carolina, a leading Democratic representative, in a letter written and published within the last few weeks, says: "It is but too probable that a hostile sectional party North will soon acquire possession of the Government. *In that event the South should not remain a moment longer in the Union. Then I go for Southern independence at all hazards.*"

While these notes of preparation on the part of disunionists are so distinctly audible, will not the people of Kentucky and Tennessee be aroused to a proper sense of their danger? In voting for Governors, legislators, and members of Congress, will they not select men most reliable for counteracting the project and preserving the Union? It is said that some Democratic candidates, while confessing danger to the Union, are urging the people of Kentucky and Tennessee to intrust its preservation to their party, because, as they say, theirs is the only party having the power to preserve it. With more propriety it might be said, theirs is the only party having power coupled with the inclination to destroy the Union. Its members have control of at least six disunion States, and obtained that control because they are disunionists. The proposition of these Democratic candidates is in effect nothing but an insulting threat. As the danger all proceeds from members of that party, it is saying to the people, let our party continue to rule or it will ruin you. Let the party continue to rob and waste your treasure in paying its venal followers, or it will break up your Government. The patriotic freemen of Kentucky and Tennessee will spurn the proposition. They will scorn to owe even the preservation of their loved country to the bought forbearance of a corrupt party. That country must be saved by the love and valor of its patriot sons or it is not worth preserving.

In the opinion of many thousand conservative Union-loving men, the time has arrived for combining the strength of all such toward preserving the Union. Conventions representing seventy thousand of them in Kentucky, a like number in Tennessee, a like number in Virginia, and forty or fifty thousand in Maryland have so declared. They may fairly be considered as representing, when so declaring, the sentiment of the whole nation outside the Republican, Democratic, and Abolition parties. They have invited conservative patriots of every section to follow Mr. Clay's advice—cast away all party ties, and combine into a great national party, having "*preservation of the Union*" for its principal if not sole platform.

From the well-known fact that full three-fourths of the slaveholders of Kentucky are among the Oppositionists who have organized the movement in this State, it may be inferred that they stand in the same relative proportion in Tennessee and Maryland, and that the Oppositionists embrace full one-half of the slaveholders of Virginia. The inference is also fair that they embrace at least a moiety of all the slaveholders in the entire South. In the opinion of many intelligent persons, though this may not be true, if considered as to the number of slaves held, yet it is less than the truth when the slaveholders, large and small, are all counted by the head.

All that this great body of slaveholders want, in reference to this peculiar property, is peace and quiet on the subject. For its protection they neither desire nor ask the aid of any political parties. Their right is well defined and sufficiently guaranteed in the Constitution. With the feeling of calm security belonging to proper manhood, they believe that nobody will ever dare attempt practically to pass that limit. Even should such an unanticipated attempt ever be made, they have an undoubting reliance upon the superabundant efficacy of their rifles and muskets in repelling the assault. The slaveowners of the border States feel that the generating, through party strifes, of inimical feeling in their neighbors immediately across the slave line, has done and will continue to do them more prejudice than any direct action of Congress could possibly inflict. They are therefore sincere, when saying to the conservatives of the North, all we want on the slave question is that it be put to rest and taken entirely out of party politics. As to protection, we ask none, need none, beyond what the Constitution guarantees and our own muskets can secure.

That this proposition will prove acceptable to the great body of the conservative Union men of the North there can be little doubt; nor can we doubt that they will force their politicians into its acceptance. All information, public and private, proves that they are as heartily sick of the pernicious agitation of the slave question as we are. They are essentially a practical people, and view political questions mainly with an eye to practical results. They see that there is no longer a foot of territory remaining upon which the slave controversy can have any practical result. Law, climate, and geographical boundaries, now permanently established, give a final quietus to the whole subject. As to the non-admission of slave States into the Union, that is a position which the Republican party has never assumed; but, on the contrary, by their vote on the Crittenden amendment to the Kansas bill, they solemnly repudiated it as a party dogma. But as that party was organized mainly with a view to the slave question, and to protect the North against alleged Southern aggression on that subject, it has a lack of nationality, a savor of sectionalism and antislavery propensities which precludes any portion of the South from harmonizing or co-operating with it as a party. It can never be brought integrally into any new national combination. It must be disbanded, like the Whig and American parties, and its really conservative Union members must come individually into the composition of a great national Union party, or no part of the South can co-operate with them.

The proposition for such a combination is sufficiently fair and equal, even in reference only to relative strength of numbers. It is true that, while Fremont received 1,300,000 votes, Fillmore received only 800,000. But it must be remembered that Fremont received 200,000 Abolition votes, which, from present indications, will be withheld from the Republican ticket hereafter, and that more than that number of men did not vote for Fillmore only because he had no chance for being elected. The Oppositionists outside of the Republican and Abolition ranks must nearly equal, in point of numbers, the whole Republican party proper. It is true that the distribution as to localities gives the Republican vote vastly the most availability. But that, in the eye of either justice, patriotism, or enlightened policy, should make no difference with Northern men in yielding up party organization for the sake of a great national fusion. When near a million of their fellow-citizens are asking such a fusion for the sake of the Union, and to relieve the nation from the incubus of the corrupt Democracy, the request comes with an imperative force to which the judicious and patriotic men of the North must certainly yield. A mere sectional triumph in a contest for the Presidency is what they ought not, and, upon reflection, cannot desire. Such a triumph cannot result beneficially to the nation. An administration of the Government for four years exclusively by Northern men would be a most perilous experiment. Whether the Union would stand the strain of such an experiment, is what no discreet man would willingly put to the test. The patriotic warnings on that subject of Mr. Fillmore, in his powerful speeches of 1856, the people of the North have not forgotten. Such a sectional triumph in the election of a President must, as he told them, prove worse than a barren victory. It would arm Southern disunionists with great power toward the accomplishment of their aim. It would give them great aid in their unceasing efforts to play upon the sectional feelings and prejudices of the South—for consolidating the South in sectional opposition to the North, and generating such sectional animosity as would enable them to strike successfully for disunion.

If there are any intelligent men at the North who believe that a Southern Whig or American of distinction would accept a nomination on the Presidential ticket of the Republican party, or would accept office under its President when receiving not a single electoral or even popular vote from the South, it is time that they should be undeceived. No Southern gentleman of high standing would seek the Presidency by such means. Any Southern man who might accept office under such circumstances, for the sake of the emoluments, would be of that class whose support would tend rather to alienate than conciliate Southern confidence in a Northern President so elected. Rightfully or wrongfully, there is at the South an almost universal feeling of jealous distrust toward the Republican party, which it would be vain to attempt to mitigate so long as that party keeps up its present organization. The disbanding of that party and the overthrow of the Democracy are two things needful, indispensably needful, to the restoration of national concord and prosperity. This is so obvious that intelligent men of every locality must concur in the opinion; and there can be no reasonable doubt that the conservative masses at the North will compel the politicians to disband the party and fuse with conservatives from every quarter on the simple platform, "Preserve the Union and quiet the slave question."

This result will be greatly facilitated if the Opposition should succeed at the next election in Kentucky and Tennessee. The available Southern aid thus manifested by those States and Maryland toward the formation of a new national party, will afford great inducement for the conservative masses at the North to bring about the fusion.

But should this anticipation not be fulfilled, should the Republican party fail to disband, and thus secure a thorough, enduring defeat of the Democracy, the conservative Union men of the whole nation will still have the opportunity of clinging together and preserving the nucleus of a great conservative party, to meet a national exigency at some future day. By running a third candidate, as was done with Mr. Fillmore, they will be kept together, and saved from absorption into either the Republican or Democratic party. Kentucky, Tennessee, and Maryland will be kept in their true position of neutrality between the North and the South, and that of pacificators between both extremes for the preservation of the Union.

As the Republican and Democratic parties are purely sectional, their collisions can result in no national benefit, but must necessarily endanger the Union, and they may well be pronounced pernicious organizations that ought to be broken up. Should the proposed fusion take place, the nation will have an opportunity, by a large majority, not merely to condemn the corrupt Democracy, but at the same time to render a salutary, needful condemnation of all sectional parties.

It is a common creed that parties are unavoidable in a republic, and with equal unanimity among the wise they are deemed a great evil. Washington warned us against the "*baneful effects of party spirit.*" He warned us, with peculiar emphasis, against *sectional parties* as the great danger of our national career. Whenever they become so distinctly sectional as are the Republican and Democratic parties, they ought to be put down. That is what the peace, prosperity, and safety of every confederate republic requires. That is what is contemplated by the proposed fusion. Should it succeed, we shall have the desirable opportunity of testing, by actual experiment during a whole Presidential term, the value of our Government when administered free from the effects of party collisions. Senators and representatives, speaking the sentiments of their local constituencies untrammeled by party ties, will give a true expression of the national opinion upon all questions of policy. A President so chosen for the occasion, under no pledge but that of preserving the Union, will have no party at his back to sustain his attempted usurpation or abuse of power, and to cloak his malversation. If future parties must necessarily ensue, still the nation will have had a respite, while its great governmental machine is properly overhauled and righted up, and it will have given a salutary warning against the organization of sectional parties hereafter. It would be a death-blow to such organizations for a long time to come. Future parties will have a more salutary and less perilous basis.

Could anything like a full expression be evoked of the sentiment of Kentucky, Tennessee, and Missouri on the subject of disunion, it would go far toward giving a quietus to the question. In defiance of those three States, Louisiana and Mississippi will never attempt a disunion movement. Without the co-operation of Louisiana, Mississippi, Texas, and Arkansas, the attempt will never be made by the Carolinas, Georgia, Alabama, and Florida. The attitude in which Kentucky and Tennessee shall be placed at the next election is, therefore, a matter of great national importance. Their concurrence in the national verdict of condemnation against the corrupt Democracy for abuse of power, wasteful extravagance, fraud, and corruption will prevent the party from claiming its defeat as the effect of mere sectional animosity, and thereby strengthening the disunion tendency at the South. The party will be compelled to endure the full weight of a really national condemnation, without any such palliative for a deserved defeat.

Its doomed defeat in the next Presidential election is so far apparent as to be virtually conceded by the more candid of the party. One of its most intelligent organs has recently had the candor to predict that the Charleston Convention will never meet, or if it does, that it will be only to disagree and separate without a nomination. No compromise that could now be patched up would prevent defeat. This the leaders see, and, therefore, there will be no compromise. With the spoils lost, the only cohesive power will be gone, and they will lack the motive for even a serious effort to prevent the party from crumbling, as it will, into unavailable fragments. All see that the unity of the party can only be preserved by the South yielding to the new Douglas dogma of non-intervention. This the South would be little likely to do for anything short of certain victory; certainly not for the sake of a barren contest and of—according to Mr. Douglas—such a brilliant personal triumph over the Southern leaders. Neither will those leaders so yield for the purpose of according an amnesty to either Mr. Guthrie or Mr. Breckinridge, who, in their overeager aspirations after the nomination, are attempting to force the obnoxious dogma upon the Democracy of Kentucky. They will be suspected of making this attempt for the purpose of forestalling and propitiating Northern support in the convention to the prejudice of their numerous competitors. This those leaders will be disposed to resent rather than reward.

Should such a split in the Democracy occur, the better part of its Northern members will flock to the Union party. Even should this split not occur, its Northern wing, upon common principles of party tactics, will vote the Union ticket in those free States where there is no hope of benefiting their party otherwise than by thus aiding to defeat the Republican candidate. In this way, and in this worst aspect of results, the election may be thrown before the House of Representatives, where the candidate of the most central and conservative party must succeed.

The prospect is bright and cheering for breaking up these two pernicious sectional parties, whose interminable wrangles over mere abstractions about slavery brought us in 1856 to the very verge of civil war, and whose best ultimate result would be a peaceable severance of the Union. Much depends upon the elections in Kentucky and Tennessee. Victory is before us, if the Union-loving men of those States will exert themselves, as patriots should, when their country is in danger.

CHAPTER VIII.

LINCOLN'S OATH.

PUBLISHED APRIL 30, 1864.

"It was in the oath I took, that I would, to the best of my ability, preserve, protect, and defend the Constitution of the United States. I could not take the office without taking the oath. Nor was it in my view that I might take an oath to get power, and break the oath in using the power.

* * * * * * * *

"I did understand, however, that my oath to preserve the Constitution to the best of my ability, imposed upon me the duty of preserving, by every indispensable means, that Government—that nation of which that Constitution was the organic law.

* * * * * * * *

"I felt that measures, otherwise unconstitutional, might become lawful, by becoming *indispensable* to the preservation of the Constitution, through the preservation of the nation."—*A. Lincoln.*

WHENCE this interpolation upon or new construction of the oath? The Constitution limits the President to the use of well-defined means or measures in the performance of his duty in its preservation, protection, and defense. According to any fair and honest interpretation, his oath confined him to the use of such means and such only. With no propriety can he claim that, while willfully, knowingly violating the Constitution, he is either preserving, protecting, or defending it. If the nation had deemed it wise or proper to permit him or any other functionary to use other measures, which he might suppose indispensable from great national necessity, the Constitution would have so said. Not having so said, his conceded actual or purposed willful violations of the Constitution are plain breaches of the oath he had to take in order to get the power. Mr. Lincoln falls completely within the censure of his own precept, that he might not rightfully "take an oath to get power, and break the oath in using the power."

"Indispensable means"—what are they? They are such for which there is no substitute, such as about the efficacy of which there can be no dispute or even difference of opinion—whose efficacy ought to be foreknown, when it is made the pretense for usurping power not granted. None of this can be predicated of Mr. Lincoln's abolition proclamation. He himself distinctly admits, in the very letter under notice, that by this measure he only "hoped for greater gain than loss," and was not "entirely confident" that the hope would be realized. He confessedly did not feel sure that the loss would not be greater than the gain. It was merely an untried experiment, which might result beneficially, as it might also prove injurious. Surely, in no court of conscience can such means be called *indispensable*, or can he obtain absolution for their use in violation of his oath. Oaths would be of little avail if they were so easy to evade, or if those who take them were allowed an unrestrained discretion in determining for themselves when they can be rightfully violated.

It is a matter of awakening and alarming interest to the nation to find a President who is anxiously seeking a re-election, and who has under his control a million of armed men and a billion of dollars, avowing his intention to disregard the official oath, by the taking of which he obtained his power, whenever and however he may choose to think the violation required by the interest of the nation. The million and a half of conservative voters who desire his defeat, even the most anxious among them, will accord him and his friends much more real honesty in their opinion that his re-election is a more imperative national necessity, far more so, than his submission to the dictation under which he abolitionized the war. Whatever in his own opinion or that of his followers may be the confidence due to his integrity that he will not, to promote his election, be seduced into the abuse of such enormous power, yet he and they ought to know that full one-half of the loyal part of the nation do not share that confidence. On the contrary, they cannot suppress the fear that the dominant party will use that power to secure him another term, and, at the end of that, again use it for its perpetuation in his hands or in those of some equally serviceable man.

CHAPTER IX.

ATTEMPT TO EXPEL MR. LONG.

"I BELIEVE that there are but two alternatives: and they are either an acknowledgment of the independence of the South as an independent nation, or their complete subjugation and *extermination as a people;* and of these alternatives I prefer the former."

Principally for the utterance of this sentiment in debate, Representative Long was arraigned and his expulsion attempted.

Calmly considered, it must be admitted by all that the language used implies that in the event of subjugation he advised extermination, or at least conceded it as a national necessity. The utterance of such a sentiment anywhere, for any purpose, cannot be too much blamed. But blameworthy as it is, it was no cause for expulsion. The right of freedom of speech in debate is too important and of too delicate a character to be tampered with by a party majority. It is much better to leave the utterer of obnoxious or vicious sentiments to the punishment of expulsion from the social circle of Christian gentlemen than to make any strain upon the invidious, obnoxious power of a majority over contempts in punishing a political opponent. Public sentiment in this country has always so held, and in modern times it has been so held in England also. In such cases the majority acts as both accuser and judge to punish a supposed injury to their own party feelings. Such is the just and natural repugnance to that mode of administering justice, that its attempt seldom fails to arouse public sympathy in behalf of the accused.

Whatever may have been his real view in the utterance of such a sentiment, whether as a mere warning or as advice, Mr. Long well knew that "complete subjugation" was the fixed purpose of the Abolition party, and that the greater the misery suffered by the South so much the more welcome to them the final triumph; that of all the mixed motives inciting them in the prosecution of the war, vengeance was the chief, and of all the modes of vengeance extermination would be the most acceptable. If, therefore, he does not really believe in the right to exterminate, he should have been very careful not to give them the least semblance of a pretext for quoting him as admitting their right.

But Mr. Long is liable to grave censure on much higher grounds, in conceding, as he does, that necessity may excuse if it do not justify extermination. Nothing short of this can be made out of his language. Now it is a sin against the sacred cause of humanity to allow that any necessity or supposed State policy can ever excuse the cold-blooded massacre of some millions of women and children.

The policy of extermination has long been confined to the barbarian savages of Africa and our American forests. The latest instance of the sort, with the concurrence of a civilized government, was the extirpation of the Albigenses, in France, some six centuries ago. If it were not impious to suppose direct interposition by Providence to punish in this world the crimes of men, and to visit their crimes on their posterity, it might be affirmed and believed that the French were made to expiate the extermination of the Albigenses by their ceaseless civil wars, their massacre of St. Bartholomew, their reign of terror, and their subjugation by foreign invaders. The modern attempt of the Turks to exterminate their Greek subjects aroused such an outburst of indignation among civilized nations as to cause an armed intervention, which speedily frustrated the fiendish effort. Such, no doubt, would also be the result if our Government were to attempt Southern extermination. Or, as it is probable, and for the sake of our national character it is to be hoped, such scheme would be frustrated by our soldiers following the example of the French soldiers during the reign of terror, refusing to obey the orders of their Government to give no quarter to the enemy, saying they were still ready to do their duty to their country by fighting its enemies, but they would not consent to degrading themselves into the character of butchers or wild savages.

The willful cold-blooded butchery of women and children is not an allowable instrumentality in war for any purpose, or under any supposable immediate necessity, much less as a national policy to obviate a distant danger, which could not arise in less than a quarter or half a century. Neither Marat or Robespierre, or the most blood-thirsty of the cowardly tyrants who ruled the reign of terror, ever uttered so diabolical a sentiment as that couched in the second alternative of Mr. Long, which he seems to contemplate as an allowable policy of national necessity. Why its utterance in Congress has not called forth a loud expression of general indignation it is difficult to understand. It must be that his private and public character has induced the belief that he somehow blunderingly said what he did not, what he could not mean. That it was a mere clumsy mode of insinuating the charge against the Abolitionists that extermination is part of their ultimate policy. Or it may be that the extermination of millions of women and children is such a sublimation of atrocity, a wickedness of such vast proportion that it cannot be realized in human belief that such an idea could really have entered the mind of any Christian gentleman. As to his choice between his two alternatives, there is no perfectly sane man or woman who will not concur heartily with him in preferring to permit disunion rather than enforce extermination. Yet it was for the expression of that preference that he was censured by the Abolition majority of the House, and for which they attempted his expulsion, and not at all for the atrocious sentiment seemingly couched in his second alternative.

Treason, though commonly said to be the greatest of all crimes, yet, intrinsically, it is no worse than hopeless, abortive rebellion. We have been taught that "the right of rebellion is sacred and inalienable." Be it so, yet men may perpetrate great crime in the exercise of undoubted right; and of that class is abortive rebellion, where the only result will be calamity to the oppressed themselves. This is the great crime of the leaders of the present rebellion, which must ever weigh heavy on their consciences, and for which history would visit them with severest censure, even if their crime were not plain treason, though perpetrated under the pretext of a preposterous right of secession. Still, having gone so far, having caused the squandering of near a million of American lives in their mad career, it has been well said that it would be base and unmanly for those leaders to make unconditional submission to the tender mercies of unrestrained abolition hate so long as they have reasonable prospect of success. But after that prospect has ceased, the prolongation of the rebellion will be just as crimeful as its initiation, even if it be not more so. Those of us who, though utterly repudiating the right of secession, yet did not think the rebellion entirely without provocation; who, though fully conceding the right of the Government to quell the rebellion by military invasion, yet opposed such invasion as a bad policy, tending, as it is now clearly proved to have done, more to the prolongation than the speedy termination of the struggle; those of us who, from abhorrence of treason, have sustained the Government in the conflict despite its bad policy, its usurpations, and tyrannical abuses of power, yet have never waived or neglected the freeman's right of censure or his equal right to avow a warm sympathy with the non-combatants, the women, the children, and the negroes of the South, for the terrible calamities they would incur from the war even if conducted on the most humane usage of civilized warfare; those of us who have so thought, felt, and said, would, if they could obtain a hearing, tell those leaders that a hopeless prolongation of the struggle, after all reasonable chance is gone for their success, would, as it regards their duty to the South alone, be one of the greatest crimes that men ever perpetrated against their fellow-citizens.

It was not for the abominable sentiment couched in Mr. Long's latter alternative that he was censured and his expulsion attempted. Not one of the many violent speeches made against him contained a word of censure against that sentiment, but all their censure was directed against him for preferring to submit to disunion rather than resort to the other alternative of extermination. Many of the Abolitionists while censuring him avowed sentiments in debate for which they more deserved expulsion than he did. They freely avowed their traitorous purpose to disregard the Constitution, and willfully perjure themselves by its violation whenever they thought the necessities of the country so required. Mr. Cox, in a brilliant speech, administered to this moral treason the following admirable rebuke:—

"We on this side have determined, in order to save the life of the Government, to save the Constitution from destruction. Under no circumstances conceivable by the human mind, would I ever violate that Constitution for any purpose. As Judge Thomas has said, 'I would cling to it as the bond of unity in the past, as the only practical bond of union in the future, the only land lifted above the waters, on which the ark of the Union can be moored.

From that ark alone will go out the dove which shall return bringing the olive branch of peace.'

"If there is any man in this chamber who holds or utters any other sentiment in reference to the Constitution and his oath than this which I have expressed, I say to him that language has no term of reproach, and the mind no idea of detestation, adequate to express the moral leprosy and treason couched in his language and clinging to his soul."

In the face of this terrible denunciation a prominent Abolition leader, a ratting apostate from Maryland, after its utterance brought himself full within its operation, and making unblushing appropriation of it to himself personally, by the following avowal:—

"If it were a constitutional right so to speak, in my judgment this is one of those cases which so far transcends the ordinary rules of law, one of those cases which carries us so near to the original right of self-defense, one of those cases which appeals so directly to the inalienable right of self-protection, *that without law and in spite of law*, the safety of the people requires his expulsion, and *I would be one to do it.*"

Now this ratter is far too intelligent not to know that there can be no baser moral treason than the perjured, willful violation of the Constitution by a functionary intrusted with power from confidence in his oath for its support, that support being at all times and under all circumstances the imperative duty of a representative of the nation. This would be true even where the supposed need for its violation was urgent and indubitable, instead of being as here a mere pretext for the gratification of party malignity against an opponent. The hollowness of the pretext of a national necessity for violating the Constitution is sufficiently proved even if it had needed proof. His non-expulsion has not caused the loss of the smallest skirmish, or prevented the gain of a single recruit, or the subscription of a single dollar to the national service. How absurd, how totally unfounded the hypocritical allegation of a national necessity for the expulsion! It serves to illustrate how untrustworthy is this ratter and his compeers to hold power for superseding the Constitution under the pretext of necessity. It serves also to show how far the greed of office will carry a ratter in subservience to power; that there is no dirty work of party he will not perform with seeming zeal to repel all suspicion of the sincerity of his apostacy. One would have supposed that he might have contented himself with what he had already done to prove his abolitionism, by his vote to rob many of his own constituents and other citizens of his own State of their lawfully acquired property without compensation. It is fair to presume that this man, like other border State apostates, was reared and lived in a wholesome abhorrence of abolitionism, until the allurement of unchastened ambition and the greed for office led to his ratting. The unblushing effrontery with which he and those other bear their load of odium and infamy is in strong contrast with the conduct, under similar circumstances, of a distinguished ratter in England. Charles Yorke, a son of the great Lord Chancellor Hardwicke, possessed of talents fit to rival his father, "of the most varied accomplishments, and of every virtue in public and private life," in the full maturity of his mind, yielded to the seduction of ambition and received the Lord Chancellorship, with a membership of a cabinet inimical to the political party with which he had always acted. Finding how his conduct was viewed by his former friends, mortification and shame drove him to suicide in three days after his reception of the high office which had all along been the very aim of his utmost ambition. Our border State apostates, instead of fleeing from their shame by suicide, industriously increase it in hue and degree by showing themselves in the lead among the most subservient of the tools of power.

That they may not impute to the writer the manufacture of an opinion for the occasion, he will quote what he published in 1856 concerning the ratting of a prominent apostate of that day.

"Born in the South, reared in the South, married in the South, with all his relatives and connections located in the South, it has an unseemly look, the lending himself to Northern extremists to lead a contest against the section of his nativity. A man is excusable for not aiding his mother in an unjust quarrel, but not for taking active part against her. Such a man is not apt to be what Western people call *whole-hearted*. They suspect him for more ambition than patriotism."

"No one can believe that Fremont honestly entertains the opinions of his party. His pretense of doing so can be viewed no otherwise than as a corrupt barter of his principles and his opinions for the nomination."

"Fremont knows and the world knows that he owes his nomination to Abolitionists of the worst stamp." * * * "It is impossible that Fremont can have any real sympathy with these men, and, by suffering himself to be so used, he is subjected to the suspicion that he has sold himself for the nomination."

The Maryland apostate insisted that the refusal by Mr. Long of extirpation as the alternative for disunion, is the avowal of a disloyalty for which he deserved expulsion. The cold-blooded, vindictive extermination of all our Southern countrymen, the ruthless massacre of millions of non-combatant men, women, and children, is the Christian alternative which he prefers. Language fails in the expression of a proper abhorrence for such a sentiment. It could find lodgment only in the foulest, most malignant bosom. It could find utterance only from bought apostate lips, or from those of the most frantic fanaticism.

Grievously has the South erred, most criminally erred in this rebellion, but most grievously is she paying, and will still further have to pay, the penalty of her crime. But what is the blackest feature of that crime on the part of her leaders; what is there peculiar in the crime of those leaders which gives it marked preeminence in the scale of human iniquity? It is that by precipitancy and terrorism they forced into the rebellion a large portion (President Lincoln says one-half) of the Southern population against their wishes, thereby compelling them, though morally innocent, to endure a full share of the calamity which the rebellion has caused to the South. Now the indiscriminate massacre of the adult male part of that population who have not aided the rebellion can be vindicated upon no principle of justice or State necessity. On the contrary, the release of that part of the Southern people from the thraldom of those infamous leaders affords the strongest of all the justificatory reasons for the war of invasion against the South. But to say nothing of the infamy of exterminating the female and infant relatives of active rebels, what conceivable justification can there be for exterminating the female and infant relatives of those Southern Union men who, from mere impotency to resist, have been compelled unwillingly to acquiesce in the overmastering rebel usurpation? There is none. No principle of justice, no conceivable necessity, can rescue such a massacre from the condemnation which the whole civilized world will pronounce as equal in atrocity to the foulest national or individual crime ever yet perpetrated.

We leave the apostate ratter to wear with what comfort he may the cap of denunciation so admirably fitted for him by Mr. Cox.

CHAPTER X.

EMANCIPATION—WHITE AND BLACK.

PUBLISHED APRIL, 1864.

No. I.

THE amendments of the Constitution pending in Congress indicate a settled purpose to readjust the great fundamental compromises of the Federal Government. While this is being done with a seemingly exclusive view to alleged justice to our black population, it is thought that justice to our white citizens should not be overlooked in the readjustment of the basis of our Union.

Whether from superior sagacity or from closer attention to her own interests, New England had the original compromises all her own way. For the sake of her then profit in the African slave-trade, and the prospective benefit from the protection of her shipping against foreign competition, she sold to the extreme South a twenty year's continuance of the slave-trade. Her States being small in territory, and with neither soil nor climate suited to a large population, she succeeded in obtaining for every State an equal voice in the most important department of the Government. Availing herself of the anxiety of the larger States to perfect the Union, she compelled them to agree that her smallest State should always have a vote in the Senate equal to that of the largest and most populous. Hence little Rhode Island has a vote or political power equal to great New York or Pennsylvania. Hence citizens residing east of the Hudson have each a political power or influence six times greater than those residing immediately west of that river.

The great ethical principle which, in a representative republic, requires the distribution of political power in proportion to population, was thus made to yield to her peculiar interests under the pretext that such a *quasi* State veto was indispensable to the preservation of the reserved or withheld rights and powers of the separate States, including the control of all local State institutions, the regulation of private property, and the defining for itself of the political status of the population of each separate State.

With admirable forecast and sagacity, New England took the precaution to restrict the nation in even its power of constitutional amendment, by making it a permanent, irrevocable feature of the Constitution, that each State should always have an equal vote in the Senate. To this end, the Constitution says that by no amendment shall a "*State, without its consent, be deprived of its equal suffrage in the Senate.*"

Let it be remembered—1. That by reason of the selfish, mercenary greed of New England in keeping open the slave-trade, we are now suffering fully one-third the infliction caused by our negro population. 2. That by reason of the protection afforded by discriminating duties to her shipping and her manufacturers, she has had the comparative monopoly of the richest, most bountiful market in the world, until she has grown insolently rich, even to repletion. 3. That by her dexterity she obtained and many long years has enjoyed a bounty paid by the Federal Government on her codfish, and still continues to enjoy that bounty, while buying the salt with which she cures her fish in the British Provinces, without paying any duty therefor to our Government. 4. That by her gross disloyalty during the last war with England, and by recklessly driving forward with precipitate greed her selfish policy of a protective tariff, she brought the nation to the verge of civil war during the time of President Jackson, and first caused at the South sectional alienation and unfriendly feeling toward the Union. 5. That by her ceaseless agitation of the slave question, with her persistent efforts at interference with a subject over which she had no constitutional right of control, coupled with her blasphemous denunciations of the Constitution and the Union, she has been mainly instrumental in inflicting upon the nation the terrible disaster under which we are now suffering. 6. That after wantonly provoking the South into hating and despising her, she is now seeking to wield the whole power of the nation to punish that hate and contempt by Southern extermination, or by preventing a restoration of the Union, under the pretext of fanatical zeal in behalf of human freedom; while all indulgence of such fanatic zeal, hate, and vengeance is in direct violation of her duties under the Constitution. 7. That, conscious of her inability legally to inflict upon the South, in any other way, the ruin of immediate, uncompensated emancipation, she now seeks its accomplishment by an amendment of the Constitution.

To accomplish this purpose, New England has to uproot the great fundamental compromise, which is the very basis of the whole Federal structure; that exemption of State institutions from Federal control, whose inviolable sanctity was the very object of that equal vote in the Senate, which the Constitution irrepealably guaranteed to her small States. For reforming the Constitution justice is her pretext—justice to her "black fellow-citizens." Let her be put to the test; let her be made to show that justice, not malice or vengeance, is her real motive; let her be made to yield a part of that unjust advantage in the distribution of political power which she selfishly, so unconscionably extorted from her sister States in the original adjustment. While in the frantic pursuit of her vengeance, let her be so far checked as to be told that she cannot be indulged in such an amendment of the Constitution, unless her small States shall at the same time "consent" to being deprived of their "equal suffrage in the Senate." That equal suffrage is such a gross violation of every principle of justice, and of the plain, indisputable, natural right of her white fellow-citizens in the rest of the Union, that she cannot refuse, if justice be her real object. Then let the two propositions go hand in hand—*inseparably welded together*—the abolition of negro slavery and the abolition of the equal suffrage in the Senate.

But that she may have no seeming just cause of complaint, and by way of contrast with her own conduct, let the Constitution be so amended that if she prefers she may be permitted to secede from the Union. What she will concede being nothing more than what pure right and justice require, she cannot refuse that price for the indulgence of her hate and vengeance.

No. II.

New England is just now characteristically employed. Knowing that she cannot effect the abolitionizing of the Constitution by straightforward, fair dealing, she is seeking to accomplish her object by a *swindle*. She has procured acts of Congress for the conversion of three Territories into new States. Neither of these Territories has half enough population to entitle it, in justice, to be admitted as a State, or any local interest requiring a premature admission. The only assignable reason or motive for the trick is to obtain State votes enough to accomplish the proposed constitutional amendment. When the great, and what should be the sacred trust for admitting new States, with an exclusive view to justice to the people of Territories, is thus perverted for a sinister party purpose in obtaining power, it must be pronounced a political swindle by every one having proper moral organization. But even these three States not being enough, the deficiency in making up the three-fourths of the States is to be supplied by the "rotten-borough" rebel States, who are to be placed under the control of one-tenth of their voters; or, rather, of that refuse of their population who, with Shoddyite camp-followers, will equal in number one-tenth of their voters.

Kentucky owns about a hundred millions worth of slave property. Missouri and Maryland together own about as much more. This two hundred millions of property was acquired with the full sanction of law and Constitution. Its protection, like that of all other property, was a leading motive for forming the Union and adopting the Constitution. To pervert any of the national power from the protection to the destruction of such a vast amount of property, in the hands of loyal, unoffending owners, is a shameful swindle, equal in turpitude to an open, plain robbery. It is both a robbery and a swindle.

When England determined to abolish her negro slavery, it was agreed on all hands, even by her ultra fanatics, that justice required the compensation of the slaveowners. So also it was decided by Congress when abolitionizing the District of Columbia. So also it was decided and held by President Lincoln up to the time when he recommended his scheme of "compensated emancipation" to the border State delegations. It being suggested by some one during the conference that Congress would not make the compensation, he made his memorable response: "If so, then that knocks the bottom out of the tub;" that is, out of his scheme. On that occasion he also emphatically declared that a man who invested a thousand dollars in slave property had as indefeasible a right thereto as he would have had to land bought with the same money. Having reiterated his pledge to protect slave property while he remained President, and a gentleman present saying something which he understood as implying that he might forget his pledge, he indignantly responded with the question: "Do you see any of the snake in me?" So right-minded men must view everywhere and always view such a depriving owners of their property; it can only be viewed as gross robbery or shameful swindling. As said by the Supreme Court: "The fundamental maxims of a free government seem to require that *the rights of personal liberty and private property should be held sacred.*"

What has Kentucky done that she should be made the victim of such a robbery? What is her fault that she should be so enormously punished? What has New England to allege against her? It is an old grudge of fifty years' standing. Kentucky, with her ever-living patriotism, went heartily into the last war with England for the violation of "free trade and sailors' rights," though she had not a sailor or a plank on the ocean, and earned, by her patriotic gallantry, a distinguished national applause. Not so New England, though the war was waged for the protection of her peculiar rights and interests; yet, not seeing any immediate pecuniary advantage to her from its prosecution, she hung back with a treasonable apathy, giving it no aid whatever, the nation being still young and feeble and needing the active support of every citizen in the perilous contest. On the contrary, when the peace in Europe enabled England to direct the whole of her immense military strength against our country, and its affairs wore the gloomiest possible aspect, New England availed herself of the occasion to concoct her notorious scheme of secession, which she certainly would have carried out had not peace intervened in the midst of her treasonable machination. Her people earned for themselves that stigma of enduring infamy, the cognomen of *blue-light Yankees.* They did not even forbear from public exultation over that great national dishonor, the vandal sacking and burning of Washington. In the expression of a proper contempt, if not detestation for this conduct, Kentucky took the lead among her sisters of the West. For this contempt, New England will never forgive her. Kentucky long strove to hide those misdeeds in the oblivion of a willing forgetfulness. While New England kept herself under the guidance of her real statesmen, her truly national men, Kentucky extended to her the hand of a cordial brotherhood, encouraging her in her supposed effort to live down her past errors by a regenerated life, and standing by her in her contest about the tariff. Not so with her. She is furnishing new proof of the truth of the old apothegm, that contempt is the unforgivable human offense. The attempted infliction of this swindling robbery upon Kentucky is but a taste of her undiluted venom. Believing, as she does, that slavery is dead in Dixie, under Presidential proclamations and Congressional legislation, and will be crushed past restoration by the operations of the war, and while she vaunts its immediate abolition by the people of Missouri and Maryland, by reason of the military manipulation of the elections of those States, why, under the circumstances, does she, in the absence of all rational motive, press an amendment of the Constitution which will have no practical bearing anywhere but in Kentucky? There is no mistaking her aim. It is a special arrow, barbed by Yankee hate, for Yankee vengeance, and pointed by Yankee cunning, with "Kentucky" for its label. It is a gage of political battle, *a l'ontrance*, thrown at Kentucky. Such a challenge Kentucky never yet and never will decline. Her every loyal son will back her with the loud acclaim—*let God defend the right.* It is true her wrath against Kentucky does not assume so direful a hue as that which she exhibits against the rebel States, seeking, as she does, the extirpation of their property and white population. But, then, their offense has been more recent and aggravating. Over and beyond the Kentucky manifestation of contempt, those States have retaliated her officious intermeddling with slavery by gibing her with an imputed world-renowned reputation for being the most illustrious among nations as a breeder of sharpers and swindlers. With such greater cause for hate against those States, she appropriately places herself under the guidance of her dastard Senator, who had not the manhood to avenge his own personal wrongs, but is now seeking to wield the power of the nation to obtain for her and for himself a satanic vengeance. Nothing short of the extermination of the rebel States will appease them.

In a private conversation with the lamented Crittenden, not ten days before his death, he was asked whether the Abolition party had not been false and treacherous toward Kentucky. His reply was: "Yes; most ungrateful, also. If it could have been known beforehand—the policy upon which the war has been conducted—nothing could have prevented Kentucky from uniting early in secession. If so, she would have carried Missouri, Maryland, and Western Virginia with her; and, in that event, the Administration would not have made even an effort to subjugate the South, nor would the people of the Northwest have volunteered to subjugate Kentucky. The Union would have been gone, and gone forever." To prove the correctness of his opinion, and that he made no overestimate of the value of the service rendered by Kentucky toward preserving the Union, it needs only to cite the following extract from the letter of Secretary Seward to Minister Adams, dated April 10, 1861: "For these reasons the President would not be disposed to reject a cardinal dogma of theirs, namely, that the Federal Government could not reduce the seceding States to obedience by conquest, even though he were disposed to question that proposition. But, in fact, the President willingly accepts it as true. Only an imperial government could subjugate thoroughly disaffected and insurrectionary members of the State. This Federal republican system of ours is, of all forms of government, the very one which is most unfitted for such a labor." "Keeping that remedy (a national convention) steadily in view, the President, on the one hand, will not suffer the Federal authority to fall into abeyance; nor will he, on the other, aggravate existing evils by attempts at coercion which must assume the form of direct war against any of the revolutionary States." After reading this, let any man suppose Kentucky to have joined the South, and then decide what would have been the probable fate of the Union.

If New England refuses, as she probably will, her consent to do justice and right toward her white fellow-citizens of other sections, by yielding a fair representation in the Senate in some proper proportion to population, then the balance of the nation must look to righting themselves without that consent. The way to this is plain, open, and easy. Two-thirds of the States can call a national convention. When so assembled that number of

States can (with the popular ratification of a majority of the nation) rightfully remodel the Union or Constitution to suit the demands of equal justice; provided the non-concurring States are permitted to remain out of the new Union if they so elect. There need be no apprehension that New England will make any such election. She has feathered her nest too well, ever willingly to quit the Union. If she patiently, pusillanimously suffered the robbing, kicking, and cuffing of England for long years, because she could make more money by submission than she could by resistance, she may be relied upon to make the most piteous supplications to remain in the Union, at the price of even much greater sacrifice of political power. To obtain the righting of this wrong, this gross inequality of representation in the Senate, there is needed, on the part of a majority of the nation, only a small portion of that perseverance which has enabled New England to inflict this dreadful civil war on our country.

The inexcusable folly, not to say wickedness, of the amendment of the Constitution, which the Shoddyite Destructives are trying to effect, is apparent from the fact that it will effectually preclude voluntary peaceable restoration, and risk everything on the chances of battle. Every patriot is longing for the fulfillment of President Lincoln's prophecy, when both sides would get tired of fighting and mutually seek reconciliation. The adoption of this amendment will prevent the advent of any such day, because it will take from the Government all power to offer terms of adjustment which the rebels can accept. Nothing will be left to the instructive and conciliating influences of time and disaster, but everything will be referred to the impulse of despair and the uncertain arbitrament of the sword.

No. III.

Since sending to the press the previous numbers, the writer has read the speech of a New England Senator, urging the adoption of this scheme for swindling Kentucky by an amendment of the Constitution, in which he avows that the principal practical effect of the swindle will be in its operation upon Kentucky, thus verifying the imputation herein, that such was its main object. In justification of the scheme, he uses the following language in reference to Kentucky:—

"Halting in her patriotism, limping in her support of the Government, divided betwixt her love for the Union and her love for slavery, preferring to sacrifice her white sons to subdue rebellion rather than put her slaves in the army, she is a most melancholy spectacle, showing to the world how this accursed weight (slavery) could drag down the gallant old State, how it could benumb its energies, paralyze its efforts, divide and arm its citizens against themselves." * * * "How cravenly and unpatriotically did the gallant Kentuckians mount the platform of neutrality and leave the old flag to be borne and upheld by other hands!"

Kentuckians will ponder this reviling of their loved mother, of whom they are so proud. The writer will not be censured while lifting in her behalf the gage of battle hurled by New England for the strong retaliatory terms in which he has portrayed the unworthiness of the challenger. Those who know how Kentucky won her proud reputation for gallantry and for chivalric, unselfish patriotism, need not be told the contemptuous scorn with which her sons will receive this insolent denunciation of her in the Senate chamber. A blue-light Yankee to denounce Kentucky for want of courage and patriotism! Does this miserable Shoddyite hope it is forgotten that during the last war with England, when Kentucky had a white population of only some three hundred and fifty thousand, she lost more volunteers in battle than all New England sent into the field during the whole war? While Kentucky volunteers were repelling British invasion, and protecting New Englanders, settled on the frontiers of Ohio and Indiana, from the tomahawk and scalping-knife, their Yankee kindred were skulking from the conflict, remaining at home in ignominious safety, hatching foul treason against their country, scheming to accomplish the secession of New England, when the then feeble nation was in the midst of a perilous war with the greatest military power of the world, and earning for themselves that enduring stigma of national infliction, their *soubriquet* of blue-light Yankees. It is not yet forgotten that during the terrible conflict New England lent the nation no helping hand, did not give even the cheering of a friendly voice, but, under the bidding of her legislative halls and her pulpits, refused to rejoice over the nation's victories under the hypocritical pretense that such exultation was "unbecoming a moral and religious people," and, under the penalty of social ostracism, she rigorously interdicted all aid to the Government from even the idle capital of her citizens. Now, again, when the nation is encountering another great peril, when the question of its civil liberty is trembling in the balance, she shows her destitution of all moral obligation of obedience to the great national compact; she acknowledges allegiance to nothing but her own "higher law"—that is, the law that suits her present purpose; she is treacherously and traitorously lending her aid toward the destruction of the Constitution and the erection of a despotism on the ruins of American liberty; she sends her sanctimonious sons to the capital to make a solemn oath to support the Constitution, and encourages them in immediately turning round and spitting upon it and trampling it under foot. One of her sons, the other day, had the infamizing frankness to make the following avowal in the Senate: "So far as I am concerned, I shall not stop to inquire whether the employment of slaves as soldiers is constitutional or unconstitutional —whether it be legal or illegal."

Though New England has proved herself a recreant in war, a commercial trickster in peace, and a faithless party to the great national compact, she has the impudent assurance to attempt to assume over her sisters the pharisaical character of a moral censor. Has she no fear of being reminded of her blue laws, her burning of witches, her whipping, branding, and perhaps hanging Quaker men and women, with her persecution and banishment of Baptists? Even in regard to the present great moral touchstone, the question of negro slavery, has she no fear of her antecedents, of being reminded of the poor Indians she reduced to slavery and sold in the West Indies in exchange for negro slaves; of the numerous negro slaves she held in bondage so long as their labor was deemed profitable to her, and most of whom she sold to the South, in preparation for the cessation of slavery as one of her cherished institutions? This precious Senator of hers, in further justification of the attempted robbery of Kentucky, says: "The dire calamities now befalling us are retributions of Providence upon a stupendous crime," that is, the crime of negro slavery. Now there are grades of this crime wide apart. They rise from the simple holding of slaves by purchase or inheritance, under the sanction of law and the approving example of every nation, Christian or heathen, ancient or modern, up to that crime of crimes, the African slave-trade, which stands condemned by the consent of all Christendom, as among the greatest of human atrocities. The Declaration of Independence denounced it as an infamous traffic, and so soon as the nation could exercise its will, untrammeled by the restraint which New England aided in putting into the Constitution, it was with great unanimity denounced as piracy by Congress, and its participants condemned to felon deaths under the gallows. Now this very traffic New England followed extensively, and made more profit from, many times over, than all the balance of the nation. The direful horrors of the middle passage did not touch her conscience so long as she could make money by the traffic. Many of her citizens still kept it up between Africa and the West Indies long after its interdiction by Congress. One of those citizens, who was notorious for having amassed a large fortune in the trade, was sent by her to the United States Senate, where he remained for years, though the reception he met with from Southern and Western Senators sufficiently indicated that they considered his presence as a pollution. What and when have been the "retributions of Providence" upon New England for her larger share of the worst part of this "most stupendous crime?" Has it been shown in the drying up of her courage and of all those generous, self-denying, self-sacrificing feelings which are necessary to patriotism, and reducing her to that unenviable, unlovable thing—all brain and no heart? No other retribution is now being inflicted on her. In the calm security of her local position, removed from all perils of the war, so far from feeling that she is suffering any sort of flagellation, she is hugging herself, with exulting self-gratulation, in the enjoyment of her Shoddy beatitude. While the South is suffering even to the extent of utter ruin, is she to suffer no retribution for her equal share in the crime of bringing on this civil war? This, her responsibility for a full share of the crime, she wishes with blasphemous hypocrisy to shift from herself over upon Providence. This, too, though repeatedly warned and rewarned during the last thirty years by patriot statesmen, her own Webster included, that her officious exasperating intermeddling with the subject of slavery would inevitably cause civil war. And this, too, despite the boastful avowals of her leaders, that they had been diligently seeking disunion for more than twenty years, and habitually denouncing the Constitution as a covenant with death and a league with hell. To leave her unpunished cannot be the award of a just Providence.

An amendment of the Constitution, by which to rob Kentucky of a hundred million worth of property, is the New England prescription which this her precious Senator insists will regenerate Kentucky, and restore her to her former gallantry and patriotism. Why not first try the prescription upon New England herself? She was once brave and patriotic. That was when she was poor. Has her accumulation of wealth been the cause of her present pitiable condition of moral degradation? Then try her remedy—rob her by a constitutional amendment to the sum of three or four hundred million. Her whole history, for more than half a century, proves that the only nerves which reach her moral sensorium are those which pass through her pocket. If the remedy can be efficacious anywhere, it will be with her pre-eminently money-loving people.

This her precious Senator accuses Kentucky of "halting between her love for the Union and her love for slavery"—that is, for her property. Now New England never made any such halt in her patriotism; she never paused between her love of country and her love of pelf. After England had lawlessly pillaged her commerce and impressed her seamen for years, and the rest of the nation could stand it no longer but went to war to redress the national honor, she said no; this war is a thing that will not pay; we can make more money by submission than by resistance; New England will not help—and she did not help. She has borne the penalty of ever since standing, in national estimation, as a section more concerned for the pockets of its own people than for the national honor, and as a selfish, unloving, unlovable, treacherous, traitorous sister in the confederacy of States. This has been the earthly retribution—the Providential she has yet to receive. If that retribution were in the hands of an avenging Nemesis, her radical destructives would be aided in accomplishing their avowed purpose of converting our National Government into a "Consolidated Democracy." In that event it would be within the chapter of probabilities that she would be robbed of some three or four hundred million of her redundant wealth. In that, her hour of agonized wail and distress, the remembrance of her merciful forbearance in this, the day of her power, will cause good men to rush to her rescue just as her *promised* volunteers have "swarmed the highways" to aid the war in all the ebullient exuberance of genuine Yankee patriotism.

The writer has no distinct recollection of ever having read a letter said to have been written by President Lincoln in the summer or fall of 1861, and since published, which he is assured by two intelligent gentlemen contained in substance the expression of the following opinion: We cannot afford to run the risk of losing Kentucky; for if we lose her, we might as well give up the war. Whether he so wrote or not, there is abundant evidence to prove that he so thought. This is strong corroboration of the estimate placed by Mr. Crittenden upon the great value of the adhesion of Kentucky to the Union toward its preservation. But now, though she repudiated the bad example of New England by attending more to the calls of patriotism than those of sectional sympathy and seeming local interests, thereby rendering a most inestimable service to the nation, she is reviled by this Shoddyite Senator, because she will not patiently submit to being robbed for the alleged purpose of improving her patriotism—that is, improving her love for those who rob her. That it would be plain robbery, no just man can deny. That it will inflict a foul stigma on the national character, the enlightened men of every civilized country will agree. They will class it with those unconscionable acts of tyranny, known as repudiations, arbitrary confiscations for no crime, the seizure of private property for public use or the purpose of a public policy without compensation, bills of attainder, *ex post facto* laws, and the rest of all the machinery with which legislative tyrants have wreaked vengeance upon their party opposers, and for which they have brought upon themselves the infamizing condemnation of history.

New England, with three million population, has twelve votes in the Senate, which on principles of fairness would require that New York, with her four million, should have sixteen votes, whereas she has only two. This shows that New Englanders have eight times as much of this political power as is allowed to

New Yorkers. The inequality as to the rest of the Union is in the same proportion. This gross injustice should cease. While New England, for fanatic purposes and for the sake of vengeance, is so pertinaciously insisting upon the emancipation of the negroes, the nation should insist upon its own emancipation from this political thraldom. Justice, whether abstract or practical, demands the emancipation of the *whites* full as much as it does that of the blacks. *White emancipation* should at least accompany black emancipation.

No. IV.

The other day a Senator, who is among the ablest of those who seek the abolitionizing of the Constitution, said in debate: "There are but two sides to the question. The one is Union without slavery; the other the immediate unconditional acknowledgment of the Southern Confederacy." After having shown, to his own satisfaction, the necessity for abolishing slavery in avoidance of future civil war, he proceeds to prove, if that could not be done, the necessity for his other alternative, as follows:—

"Shall this war go on forever? Should the war go on until the public debt equals the entire wealth of the country? Should the whole capital of the people be forced into Federal securities, and these securities made the basis of an irredeemable paper circulation? Should it go on until misery broods over the whole land; until the civil authorities become impotent, and all rights of person and property stand at the mercy of military power? Should it go on until the members of the Senate and House of Representatives shall owe their places here to the bayonet instead of the ballot-box? Should it go on until corruption and fraud, the necessary concomitants of civil war, shall have crept into high places, put on the garb of patriotism, and give themselves the means of perpetuating their own power? Should it continue until the nation, exhausted, will welcome the coming of a Cromwell or a Bonaparte; until Provost-Marshals shall be stationed with a military police at every village in the Northern States, displacing the civil authority, governing the people heretofore supposed capable of governing themselves; teaching how God shall be worshiped, prescribing new and strange offenses, and punishing them by courts-martial? Should it continue until financial ruin brings misery, and misery rushes into anarchy, when no hope but despotism is left?

"A few more years of civil war and this picture will be seen. It cannot be otherwise. It is the necessary result of a long civil strife. Peace parties will spring up; the war party will denounce them as traitors; the publication of newspapers will be suppressed and freedom of speech denied; mobs will retaliate; the blindness as well as the corruption of the war party will strengthen the convictions of the peace party; each party will appeal to violence, the one to hold, the other to obtain power; the ballot-box will become a mockery, a cheat; instead of proclaiming the voice of a free people, it will speak the language of base subserviency or the bold tones of military despotism.

"Such is history. We are not exempt from the passions and frailties that wove this web of history for others. Party pride, blinded vanity, may think so. These have driven many nations from the enjoyment of liberty to the profoundest depths of tyranny. Party revenge may be gratified when political enemies come to grief, but that is no compensation for a ruined country. When anarchy comes, we are overwhelmed alike. The Girondist and the Jacobin followed each other in rapid succession to the guillotine."

This is a gloomy picture which the Senator paints of the inevitable condition of our country if the war last only a few years longer. The painting, if verified in results, is only what was pictured for our warning by the fathers of the Republic. But, thinking as he does, having so clear a prevision of the calamities to ensue from the continuance of the war, it is incomprehensible why he does not devote all his energies toward its speedy termination—to removing instead of creating difficulties in the way of amicable adjustment. A mere perpetuation of slavery in the Union could not possibly produce any greater calamity than that. The uncertain evils of merely apprehended conjectured civil war in the future can be no justification for incurring such horrid immediate ruin, or one which is only to be postponed for two or three years. There would be no statesmanship, no patriotism in that. Why not then leave all other policy for that which promises the speediest termination of the war without disunion? He is a man of far too much intelligence to suppose that abolitionizing the Constitution will have any such tendency. He may think it will tend to perpetuate peace when it is once conquered, but it can give no aid toward such conquest. Its every tendency is the other way. It can only serve to intensify despairing resistance at the South. It not merely will rob her of full two-thirds in value of all her chattel property, but will thereby also destroy nine-tenths of the value of all her real estate. Nor is this all. It will leave in her midst the canker-worm of a hostile race, with which her own people will be at perpetual feud, and causing, according to the inevitable principles of a natural, veritable "irrepressible conflict," the perpetual recurrence of intestine civil wars between the two races, until one or the other is exterminated. It is therefore the merest folly, as no one knows better than this intelligent Senator, to expect that anything short of utter subjugation, the direst necessity, will make the South submit to an abolitionized Constitution. Where, then, is the justification for this Senator, in pursuing a policy so obviously in conflict with his opinion as to the near and great danger to the country from a prolongation of the war? There is nothing even in disunion at all comparable in amount of national disaster to what he says we are bound to suffer after "a few years more of civil war." Why deprive ourselves of the chance that, before the lapse of those few years, though we may fail wholly to subdue her, yet the South may become so tired of suffering and disaster as to seek conciliation on reasonable terms? Why close that door by this amendment of the Constitution? Why trust everything to the uncertain issue of battles? Why deprive ourselves of any chance toward the avoidance of such a tremendous peril?

To remove all future danger from the irrepressible conflict is the pretext. But, by inflicting such tremendous loss of property upon the South, we shall cause a much more dangerous conflict. That wrong would be one which the South would neither forget nor forgive in the lapse of centuries. Her people would be to us what the Irish have been to England for two centuries—a powerful internal enemy, ever ready to join any foreign enemy in the pursuit of vengeance. We should generate a greater in the avoidance of a lesser national danger.

In addition to all this, what is to compensate the loss of national honor in the perfidious, ungrateful robbery of Kentucky? To rob her of her slave property, for the purpose of a great national policy, without compensating for what she holds under the sanction of law and Constitution, will be condemned by the on-looking world and by history the same as robbery by *ex post facto* laws, bill of attainder, or any other mode of arbitrary confiscation. The condemnation will be none the less, because the wrong will be one of national infliction. A nation can commit crime as well as a legislature, and enjoys no exemption from the retribution to be found in the disparaging rebuke of civilized nations. But, above all, what a short-sighted policy must that be which shall persecute near a million of Kentuckians into despising and hating their Government!

The editor of the *Democrat*, in his paper of Tuesday, has given abundant proof of the conduct of New England during the last war with England; but if more is desired, it can be found in Matthew Carey's *Olive Branch*, and in the recent speech of Senator Davis.

No. V.

The "irrepressible conflict" on negro slavery is assumed to be the cause of this disastrous, wicked rebellion, and of all the sectional alienation of national feeling by which it was preceded. This dogma has become a stereotyped phrase of the abolition press. The changes have been rung upon it so long and so continuously, for sinister purposes, that there is some danger of public opinion settling down into an acquiescence in its truth, false as it is. The Legislature of Tennessee, in 1859, when unanimous in its Unionism, gave, in the following resolution, a sound and truthful solution of that sectional alienation, with the consequent rebellion:—

"*Resolved*, That in the opinion of this General Assembly all the evils growing out of the present intense slavery agitation—all the discord, alienation, and bitter hatred now growing up and extending between the North and the South—are the legitimate fruit, not of any necessary and 'irrepressible conflict' between free and slave labor, but of a conflict between rival aspirants in the race of ambition, North and South, urged on by an inordinate greed of official power and plunder—a conflict which can only be repressed by a powerful effort by the friends of the Union, to rouse the people to a conviction of the reality and magnitude of the impending dangers to its existence."

This is the true doctrine. It is sustained alike by the truth of history and the teaching of sound political science. For a century prior to the adoption of the Federal Constitution, and for more than forty years thereafter, no such conflict was either felt or surmised. For fifty years of national existence the two systems of labor were carried on harmoniously together, with a development of national prosperity whose rapidity and promising permanence were wholly unprecedented in the history of the world—a prosperity which was receiving continually increasing development during the thirty years preceding the rebellion, notwithstanding the unceasing efforts of politicians, North and South, for sinister party purposes, to cause such a conflict by the incessant agitation of the subject. It was an untruthful, unsound dogma when first uttered by its fire-eater inventor, and which could not, as it did not, receive acceptance among intelligent men, for long after it had obtained recognition and adoption from Messrs. Lincoln and Seward. Rational men of every section—true lovers of the Union—repudiated the dogma as *visibly* unsound and untrue, and for the obvious reason that, whatever of more than mere semblance of truth there might be in it, yet, in its despite, the national prosperity had progressed with an all-sufficient rapidity, *disproving* any need of change, and proving that to be let alone was all that was needed for the fruition of a geometrically increasing national prosperity and an enduring national happiness.

After thus disproving the dogma, it will be proper to prove the soundness of the theory announced by the Tennessee Legislature: that is, that our present national calamity is due mainly, if not exclusively, to those conflicts of politicians in pursuit of office and power, which have raged almost unintermittingly since Washington's administration. While the dogma is being made the pretext for unsettling the great foundation of the Federal Constitution and the adoption of an abolitionizing amendment, which will effectually destroy all hope of an amicable, an enduring, a beneficial restoration or reconstruction of the Union, the public mind should not merely be disabused as to the imputed necessity for such change, but pointed to the true source of the evil while in pursuit of a corrective.

That distinguished English writer, John Stuart Mill, who stands pre-eminent as the political philosopher of the age, in descanting, some few years ago, upon the structure of the executive department of the Federal Government, expressed the following opinion: "Another important consideration is the great mischief of unintermitted electioneering. When the highest dignity in the State is to be conferred by popular election once in every few years, the whole intervening time is spent in what is virtually a canvass, and every public question is discussed and decided with less reference to its merits than to its expected bearing on the Presidential election. If a system had been devised to make party spirit the ruling principle of action in all public affairs, and create an inducement not only to make every question a party question, but to *raise questions*, for the purpose of founding parties upon them, it would have been difficult to contrive any means better adapted to the purpose." His philosophical theorizing on our scheme of an elective Presidency is fully sustained by the practical observation and opinion of the Tennessee Legislature. To the pernicious excess of partyism, generated by contests for the Presidency, is mainly attributable "all the discord, alienation, and bitter hatred between the North and the South" which have caused this calamitous rebellion. To that, therefore, and not to the irrepressible conflict dogma, should the national attention be directed, in any attempt to eradicate the cause, for the purpose of preventing the recurrence of such rebellions in the future. The dogma is a thing of comparatively modern invention for party purposes; whereas the seeds of sectional alienation and hatred had been sown and diligently cultivated, for the sake of party success, for more than fifty years. Party action caused the hatred, and the hatred was then played upon to infuse prejudice against negro slavery. The latter was not the motive, but only used as a means to gratify the former. New England, which figures so prominently and unanimously in favor of abolitionism, never bethought of the crime of negro slavery until long after the Missouri Compromise controversy. Then her politicians said little or nothing about the alleged crime of slavery. Then the gravamen relied upon by her was the inequality and proven injustice of the original compact, giving the South representation for what ought to be considered as property, and not as part of its population. So recently as the organization of the first Free-soil party by Van Buren, she lent the movement no aid, its leaders being antitariff Democrats, and she not seeing how its triumph would inure especially to her benefit, though gratifying her sectional animosity. It was not until the organization of the Republican party promised the gratification of this feeling, while at the same time enhancing her political power, that she cordially co-operated in a political movement having hostility to negro slavery for its avowed object. Her antecedents in reference to the African slave-trade, and the sale of her own slaves to the South, were so notorious as to preclude her from undertaking single-handed, or as the prominent leader, any crusade against negro slavery, on exclusively overrighteous or moral grounds. She merely fomented and used Northern prejudice to obtain the power by which to "feed fat the ancient grudge" she bore the South, from hatred generated in contests for the Presidency.

What rational, practical observer of the influence of partyism upon poor, erring human nature, now and in the past, can doubt that the defeat of Jefferson, in the first contest for the Presidency, had very much to do with the extreme to which the State-rights doctrine was carried by the Virginia and Kentucky resolutions of '98 and '99? Who doubts that the exacerbation of political defeats made the whole Federal party of the North unanimous against the Missouri Compromise? Who doubts that the resentments of a common defeat combined the friends of Jackson, Crawford, and Calhoun, otherwise so discordant, into a cordial opposition to the administration of J. Q. Adams? Who doubts that the defeat of the latter gentleman, operating upon an irascible, unforgiving temper, had much to do with his aid to the antislavery movement? Who doubts that political vengeance was the exclusive motive with the Van Burens for the organization of the first Free-soil party of any importance? Who doubts that the revenging of Democratic triumphs was the main cause for casting aside the old Whig party and seeking a party consolidation of the free States, under the Free-soil antislavery banner? But, above all, who doubts that avenging the defeat of the elder Adams, and his party followers, was the main cause of New England opposition to the acquisition of Louisiana, to the last war with England, and to all measures in support of that war, driving her people, in the midst of that war, to the very verge of the foul treason of secession?

The only answer to these queries point to the indisputable historic facts, which prove that the contests for the Presidency have been the principal cause of the sectional alienation and hatred which has ultimately brought to its aid sectional prejudice on the slave question. There never was any semblance of the irrepressible conflict, until parties, for party purposes, aroused and used that prejudice. The great fundamental fault in our governmental structure is, therefore, not where the dogma points, but is to be found in the mode of obtaining our Presidents through an untrammeled popular election. It is there the corrective must be applied, in seeking, by constitutional amendment, to eradicate the cause of the present national calamity and preventing its recurrence in the future.

In addition to other superabundant proof, we have the testimony of John Quincy Adams and Governor Plumer, of New Hampshire, as to the prevalence of the disunion sentiment among the leading politicians of New England for years before the last war with England. Mr. Adams, after saying that the New England projects for disunion culminated in and found their final catastrophe in the Hartford Convention, tells us: "The postulates of disunion were nearly consummated. The interposition of a kind Providence, restoring peace to our country and the world, averted the most deplorable catastrophe, and turning over to the receptacle of things lost on earth, the adjourned Convention from Hartford to Boston extinguished *the projected New England Confederacy.*"

Josiah Quincy was probably the ablest representative that New England ever had in Congress, excepting Webster. He more distinctly and much more nearly represented New England sentiment than Webster ever did. During his speech made in 1811, opposing the admission of Louisiana as a State, he was called to order for the utterance of disloyal sentiments, when he reduced the following to writing, as what he had said, and what he meant to abide by:—

"I am compelled to declare it as my deliberate opinion that, if this bill passes, the bonds of Union are virtually dissolved; that the States which compose it are free from moral obligations; and that, as it will be the right of all, so it will be the duty of some, to prepare definitely for a separation—peaceably if they can, forcibly if they must."

It appears from a recent debate in the Senate that the twelve New England Senators have the chairmanship of *fourteen* committees, four of them being the most important, and wielding more power and influence than all the other committees combined. Of at least two of the other committees next in importance to those four, New Englanders are chairmen as Senators from Western States. Nothing could well exemplify better the necessity for curtailing the undue share of power held by New England in the Senate, the flagrant injustice of which can receive no alleviation, but only aggravation, by the increase of the whole population of the nation. The grievance can be redressed no otherwise than by an amendment of the Constitution.

If further proof be desired of disunionism in New England prior to the last war with England, or of her misconduct during that war, it may be found in Ingersoll's History of the War, and in Randall's Life of Jefferson, vol. iii.

CHAPTER XI.

MILITARY RULE OVER ELECTIONS.

THE memorial presented in this chapter was sent, with the subjoined letter, to an eminent citizen of New York, for the reason therein given. Why he did not procure its publication in a New York paper has not been explained, and cannot be conjectured. Its publication there in April, 1864, was obtained through a Democratic Senator.

"DEAR SIR:—

"For more than a month I have been intending to write you concerning matters of grave import to our country. The recent suppression of free ballot in Kentucky has ended my hesitancy. That you may understand the nature and extent of that suppression I send you a copy of my memorial to the President on that subject. It was written and intended as a private communication, to be sent by mail. Various reasons have changed that purpose. It is now sent to you, with permission, if you deem it proper, to turn it over to the New York press, where it can still be published without danger to the paper making the publication. The danger to myself personally is wittingly incurred. The times allow no flinching from patriotic duty.

"What I have been wishing to urge upon your consideration is, that our national liberty is in a crisis of imminent danger, demanding the instant and active effort of every patriot to ward off that danger. If further proof had been needed it is furnished by the suppression of free ballot in Kentucky. I know not how it may be with you, but thinking men with us, unaffected by patronage or party bias, generally believe that the dominant party have no intention of permitting the Federal power to be taken from them by the ballot-box, if fraud, money, and military violence can prevent it. Hence the urging forward of the obnoxious conscription when we have already more armed men than we have any need for in suppressing the rebellion; the urging on of the raising of the standing army of three hundred thousand negroes, forty thousand of whom, we are semi-officially informed, have already been organized; the threats of abolition officers to return after peace and regulate the politics of the North by 'crushing the heads' of Democrats under the iron heels of their soldiers; the unscrupulous character of the leaders of the dominant party, showing by acts, and even avowing in words, a total disregard of all constitutional obligations; and hence, also, the suppression of free ballot in Kentucky.

"The apparent apathetic acquiscence under the martial law and abolition Presidential proclamations of last September sank me deep into the 'vale of despond.' Such was my despondency that, if unencumbered by a large family, I would have sought a freeman's asylum in Switzerland for the small remnant of my life. But then came those glorious October and November elections, showing the still true loyalty of the masses, and proving how unwise and unpatriotic I had been in despairing of the Republic. They pointed the way to a resuscitation of the Constitution and the reconstruction of constitutional liberty. My heart again glowed with hopeful, fervid zeal for the liberties of the nation. Popular condemnation at the next Presidential election of all tyrannical usurpation and abuse of power was to inaugurate a new and enduring reign for constitutional liberty. Such was the fond patriotic hope. We have no other. Without that, the days of constitutional liberty are numbered. Without it, our whole future is gloomed over with the portending shadow of anarchical despotism.

"For more than six years I have been vainly endeavoring to arouse our political men from the exclusive consideration of their ephemeral party contests and make them heed the coming national perils. Notwithstanding such mortifying want of success, at the bidding of the people despair is cast behind, and the effort is now being renewed, in thus calling your attention to the threatened danger, and invoking, by every incitement of patriotism, your active aid toward whatever you may deem necessary for securing to the people a free Presidential election, unawed by military power.

"To that end permit me most respectfully to suggest that you immediately urge forward with unflagging zeal the arming, organizing, and disciplining the militia of your State; your example will incite the authorities of other large States to do the same. Therein, and therein alone, lies our only hope of safety. If by a corrupt squandering of national treasure, aided by the intimidation of Federal bayonets, the Destructives can so manipulate the next Presidential election as to retain their power, we had as well prepare the funeral obsequies of American liberty—a funeral that will even bury all hope of resurrection. By the theory of our Government the people are themselves the conservators, the sole trustworthy guardians of their liberty. To enable them to prove so they must be armed and disciplined. To accomplish that not an hour is to be lost. Every patriot must push forward the needful work with unflagging zeal, as if each man was working for very life. In the mean time shall down-trodden Kentucky look in vain for sympathy from her sisters of the North? Will they utter no words of popular denunciation against the tyrannical suppression of her right to free ballot—that cherished right, so indispensable to all, without which there can be no liberty, no free Republic?

"Very respectfully,

"S. S. NICHOLAS.

"LOUISVILLE, August 10, 1863."

The hopeful augury of this letter, based on the fall elections of 1862, was entirely dispelled by those of 1863. The writer immediately relapsed back to his old belief, the only creed of common sense, that an unscrupulous party, controlling the patronage of a billion of money and the services of near a million armed men, cannot be beaten at an election so long as it adhere together, the only chance for extrication from their thraldom depending upon splits and division among themselves. To this effect he wrote, in the winter of 1864, to leaders of the Democracy in Congress predicting just such a result of the election as actually occurred, if the Democracy kept up a party opposition and started a party candidate of its own for the Presidency, whereas if they would at once commence disavowing all purpose of further party opposition, have no convention, or if any, then only to declare it inexpedient to nominate a candidate, the desired split in the dominant party would necessarily and inevitably follow. The soundness of this surmise was amply verified by the irrepressible manifestations of desire to split in favor of Chase and Fremont. Whatever nomination the seceders made under those circumstances would have been mainly induced with a view to the Democratic support, which, if obtained, would have insured the election of their nominee. When so elected he would have been compelled to lean upon conservative support for political strength to carry on the Government, which would have compelled a willing or simulated conversion of himself to conservatism, with an overhauling, denunciation, and redress of the bad acts of President Lincoln's administration. This probably would have led to the resuscitation and continued life of the Constitution; whereas the reelection of Lincoln having given a seeming popular ratification to those bad acts, the Constitution, with the liberty it guarded, are irretrievably gone. As has been said, after the Constitution has been so mauled to pieces with popular assent, you had as well attempt to restore an addled egg. The whole science of chemistry cannot restore the one, neither can political science restore the other. Instead of our former constitutional liberty, the nation will, in the long future, have no government but that of an unrestrained, irresponsible party majority. The celebrated Chatham, in comparing "the arbitrary power of a king with the arbitrary power of a House of Commons," said: "Tyranny is detestable in every shape, but *in none is it so formidable* as where it is assumed and exercised by such a number of tyrants." It was in the same speech he said: "Power without right is the most odious and detestable object that can be offered to the human imagination." These utterances of the great Chatham are in the genuine spirit of that memorable declaration of the distinguished Lord Halifax, one of the founders of English liberty, made near a century before: "Life would not be worth having in a country where liberty and property were at the mercy of despotic power." Yet sad to say, such, to all appearance, is our inevitable doom if nothing can be devised better than that with which we have been experimenting, only to prove a disastrous failure. There is no hope unless the nation can be rescued from the thraldom of party majorities.

To the Honorable Abraham Lincoln, President of the United States of America.

This memorial of your fellow-citizen, Samuel Smith Nicholas, of Louisville, Kentucky, showeth:

That foul wrong and dishonor has recently been inflicted by some of your subordinates upon his and your native State.

It may be proper, by way of self-introduction, to premise that for more than thirty years he has abstained from all affiliation with political parties; consequently has seldom voted during that time, and did not vote at the late election, pursuant to a resolve announced weeks before; that for more than that time he has advocated something like the Henry Clay plan of gradual prospective emancipation; that he claims to be, as he has always been, imbued with that heart-devoted love for Constitution and Union once so universal among Kentuckians; that though the maltreatment received by Kentucky from both sections has absolved her from any supposable obligation of special partiality for either, yet, in case of disunion, his advice will be for her to remain with the North; that for more than six years he has been publicly predicting this rebellion, as the result of the mutually aiding machinations of secessionists and abolitionists; that he has done as much as any other man to disprove, to decry, and denounce the pretended right of secession, and predicting all the calamities that have overtaken the South in the attempted assertion of that right; and that at an early day since the commencement of the war, foreseeing the present destroyed condition of the Constitution, he urged the necessity, and has continued, in a series of publications, to urge the great necessity of vigorous remonstrance against Congressional and Executive usurpations, and for arousing the nation to a proper sense of the near danger to its liberty.

To enable you to judge the significance of the military orders about to be quoted, it is also proper to premise that for more than a year military officers in Kentucky have freely indulged in the "pressing" of horses, slaves, and other property, giving the owners such certificates, or no certificate, as they thought proper.

Kentucky has never been proclaimed as in rebellion, nor could it have been truthfully done as to any part of the State. She has suffered much from rebel invasions and raids, from which the Government failed to protect her; but no part of the State has ever been in organized rebellion.

The canvass for the late election was conducted by tickets, one of which was headed by Judge Bramlette, the gubernatorial nominee of the so-called Union party, while the other ticket was headed by Governor Wickliffe as the nominee of the so-called Democratic party. As said by Judge Bramlette in his speeches, there was no difference of opinion as to the unconstitutionality and inexpediency of the radical measures of Congress and the President. "We are all agreed," said he, "in opposition to them." The canvass seemed to turn upon the comparatively immaterial issue of a further grant of supplies, Congress having already granted all that could possibly be needed until the 1st of July next. The one party contending that it was wrong to place Kentucky in political antagonism to the administration by voting against supplies—a policy, as they said, equivalent to stopping the war and succumbing to the rebellion; the other party contending that it was every way wrong to vote supplies to enable the administration to carry out its imputed policy of inciting slave insurrections, abolitionizing the South, desolating all its private property, raising a standing army of three hundred thousand negroes, and subjecting the loyal States to martial law, in destruction of their right to free speech, free press, free ballot, and jury trial. They said the refusing supplies, except on prescribed conditions, did not necessarily stop the war, but would only reduce the President to the necessity of either resigning or changing his policy. Under this sort of dispute the opposition party had fastened upon it the designation of the "no more men and no more money party." As early as July 16, the military officers gave public manifestation of their purpose to take the management of the election into their hands. On that day Colonel Johnson published his order at Smithland, directing the judges and clerks of the election in adjacent counties "not to place the name of any person on the poll books to be voted for at the election, who is not a Union man, or who is opposed to furnishing men and money for a vigorous prosecution of the war against the rebellion. Any person violating this order will be regarded as an enemy to the United States Government, and will be arrested and punished accordingly."

On the 24th July General Hartsuff published his order that "in impressing property" it should be taken exclusively from rebels and "rebel sympathizers." "Among rebel sympathizers will be classed those nominally Union men, but opposed to the Government and the prosecution of the war."

On the 25th July General Boyle published an order of similar import, saying, in addition, the negroes of loyal citizens should not be impressed, but only the negroes "of citizens who are for no more men and no more money to suppress the rebellion, their supporters, aiders, and abettors."

On the 28th July Colonel Foster published an order: "None but loyal citizens will act as officers of the election; no one will be allowed to offer himself as a candidate or voted for who is not in all things loyal to the State and Federal Governments and in favor of a vigorous prosecution of the war. No disloyal man will offer himself as a candidate or *attempt to vote*, and all such efforts will be summarily suppressed by the military authority."

On the 30th July General Shackelford published the same or a very similar order, indicating that both came from some superior.

On the 29th July General Asboth ordered that the name of no candidate should be placed on the poll books who is not "unconditionally for the Union, or who may be opposed to furnishing men and money for suppressing the rebellion"—"any voter, judge of election, or other person who may evade, or refuse compliance with the order, will be arrested and sent before a military commission."

There were probably other orders by other officers in reference to the election which your memorialist has not seen. Not content with these; not content with the gentle suasion and threats of Generals Hartsuff and Boyle, nor with the stern threats and efforts at intimidation of the other officers, in aid of the Bramlette ticket, General Burnside, to make surety doubly sure, on the 31st July, by his published order, assumed to place all Kentucky under martial law. The following is the pretext which he offers for so doing: "Whereas, the State of Kentucky is invaded by a rebel force, with the *avowed intention* of overawing the judges of election, of intimidating the loyal voters, keeping them from the polls, and forcing the election of disloyal candidates at the election on the 3d of August; and, whereas, the military power of the Government is the only force that can defeat such an attempt, the State of Kentucky is hereby declared under martial law." He further warns the judges of election that they "will be held strictly responsible that no disloyal person be allowed to vote," but without explaining, as the other generals did, who were to be deemed disloyal.

It may be that General Burnside has given the public little reason to impute to him much of either information or judgment in matters pertaining to constitutional law or politics, or much intelligence of any sort. But charity itself cannot suppose any man could attain his commission, with so small a modicum of intelligence as to credit the story, if any such there were afloat, that the small raid of which he speaks was made with the "avowed intention" of overawing the elections of Kentucky. The whole force of the raid was probably not much more than a thousand men — not enough, certainly, to overawe, even if unopposed by our troops, more than three or four, much less an hundred, counties. The enemy must have known his force was wholly inadequate to produce any material effect on the election, and that any raid for any purpose, at such a juncture, would, as his did, aid the Bramlette ticket. But the general states a most material and important fact in this connection; he says the purpose was "avowed." When, where, and how was the avowal made by the guerrilla chief? It is most singular, very surprising indeed, that the general should be the only person who ever heard of such an avowal. The whole of the Southern armies might be searched, and it is improbable that any officer as high in rank as a colonel could be found fool enough to make a raid for such a purpose; much less, to be guilty of the extreme folly of avowing his intentions.

Every motive of prudence or propriety, even if he believed what he states, required General Burnside to have forborne all interference with the election till his aid was called for by the civil authorities of the State. That he received no such call is presumable from the fact that he makes no reliance upon it in extenuation of his act, but resorts to a bungling fiction. The presumption rests upon firmer ground than even that. None of our civil functionaries were capable of such dastard treachery to the State. All of them knew that to have done so would have infamized the perpetrator for as long as a proud, high-minded people can retain resentment against a wanton trampling on their dearest right, accompanied by the most insulting, degrading dishonor.

Obvious as it was to common sense at the time that there was no necessity for the proclamation of martial law, or military interference with the election, the rapid flight of the raiders, and the result of the election, have proved that there was not the flimsy pretext of necessity for either.

On August 1 Colonel Mundy, commanding at Louisville, issued his proclamation, with generous assurance to the citizens that their election should be protected against the interference of raiders, of whom no man had the slightest fear, but giving no promise against his own soldiers, as to whom at least one-half of the voters stood in the greatest apprehension. On the contrary, he said there would be a military guard at each voting place, accompanied by detectives, who knew "the record of each resident in the several precincts, to point out to the guard any who shall attempt to perpetrate a fraud against the election law;" and that "all who shall present themselves at the polls, and fraudulently attempt to vote, will be immediately arrested by the guard, and confined in the military prison." Accordingly, on the day of election there were ten soldiers with muskets at each voting place, who with crossed bayonets stood in the doors, preventing all access of voters to the polls but by their permission, and who arrested and carried to the military prison all that they were told to arrest. But there were not very many arrested; it is said not more than thirty or forty, all of whom, with one or two exceptions, were released the next day, it becoming early apparent that there was no need for undue intimidation to secure the success of the Bramlette ticket. Out of some eight thousand voters in the city, less than five thousand votes were taken. How many of the missing three thousand were deterred from attempting to vote cannot be ascertained, nor is it necessary, for the intimidation of three thousand voters is no greater outrage than the intimidation of only five hundred. The interpretation generally put by the Opposition party upon the order of Colonel Mundy was that no man was to have the privilege of having his right of voting tested by the judges if pointed out to the guard, as proper to be arrested, by any one of the colonel's detectives. He not having the semblance of legal or rightful power to interfere with the election, the most sinister suspicions were naturally aroused, and very many deterred from going to the polls, for fear they should be victimized to personal or party malice. Indeed it is rather matter of surprise that so large a number of the Opposition party did go to the polls. Similar intimidation was not only practiced in other parts of the State, but, from published proof and reliable information, there is no doubt that in very many counties the judges were so dastardly infamous as to submit to the military order, and not permit the Wickliffe ticket to be voted for. The result is that there was not only direct military interference with the election, but it was conducted in most of the State under the intimidation of Federal bayonets.

Under the degrading corruption of public sentiment produced by our ceaseless party conflicts, it has become a common act of complicity of all parties with election outrages, never to complain of an outrage which worked for the benefit of a man's party. Hence, Mr. President, you will probably hear few or no complaints from the successful party against the military enormities perpetrated at the election; but rest you assured that there is not an enlightened Kentuckian, untainted by patronage or with party hate and prejudice, to whom those enormities have not proved like the iron of despotism, piercing the very core of his moral sensorium. It is needless to enlarge upon the ridiculous character of the flimsy pretext for laying all Kentucky under martial law, even if the pretext had been true. Nor is it necessary to define the legal character or denomination of the crime committed by General Burnside and his subordinates in the perpetration of this great outrage against Kentucky. If your memorialist was right, in a matured opinion published by him more than twenty years ago, and which he still approves, then they were all guilty of plain treason. For, according to the teaching of that eminent lawyer and statesman, Edward Livingston, levying of war against any one State is a levying of war against all the States, and the suppression of civil authority by armed military force being the very plainest exemplification of treason, and, in the holding of an election, the civil authority being in the discharge of its very highest, most important function, it is difficult to escape the conclusion that its military suppression is *plain treason.* But leaving that for the courts, and not expecting you to act in advance of their decision, there is a point which every one of your intelligent countrymen, whether legally learned or not, can decide and will decide, that is, the suppression of free ballot in Kentucky by your military subordinates was an illegal, unnecessary, tyrannical abuse of usurped power.

What shall be your action toward those subordinates, it is for you to determine, not for your memorialist to suggest. That it may be such as is required by your duty as a citizen and a public servant; such as is required by every incentive of true patriotism; and such as is required by proper care for your own fair fame, now or hereafter, toward relieving it from the imputation or suspicion of complicity with such foul wrong, is the earnest hope of

Your fellow-citizen,

S. S. NICHOLAS.

In October, 1864, the regular Committee of the Democratic party of Kentucky, composed of respectable and intelligent gentlemen, published a temperate, well-matured address, in which was collated military orders and other proof showing the interference of the Federal authorities preceding and during the election, from which address the following abstracts are made:—

1. The people were warned that when property was needed for the United States army it would be taken from *rebel sympathizers*, the receipts given therefor to be marked "disloyal," and not to be paid till the end of the war, or on proof that the owner was a loyal man.

2. Rebel sympathizers defined to be, all those not in favor of a vigorous prosecution of the war, and an unconditional supply of men and money for that purpose, and votes given at the election to be a test of *loyalty.*

3. Persons offering to vote whose votes are rejected, to be arrested by the military.

4. Judges of election to be held responsible by the military if they permit any disloyal men to vote.

5. The Democratic ticket ordered to be struck from the poll books in many places.

6. Oaths unknown to Constitution or law required from voters and judges.

7. Under an illegal trade regulation, "boards of trade" were organized in nearly every town, without whose permission no merchandise could be imported into the State or transferred from one part of it to another, and no permit to be given except to those whom such board chose to deem loyal; the commercial prosperity of every trader, manufacturer, and mechanic being thus placed at the mercy of these inquisitorial boards. Speaking of these trade regulations and the operations under them, Governor Bramlette, in his message to the Legislature, said: "It is a most shameful, corrupt system of partisan political corruption and oppression."

8. More than a third of the voters deterred from going to the polls.

9. "We publish statements showing outrages committed at different places in more than twenty counties. Our materials are ample to swell the list almost indefinitely, but these are sufficient to indicate the general character of the whole." "In twelve counties not a single vote was permitted to be cast for the Democratic ticket; in eight others it received less than ten votes in the county; in fifteen others less than fifty; and in sixteen others less than one hundred; these fifty-one counties embracing many of the strongest Democratic counties of the State." "In only twenty-eight counties was Mr. Bramlette voted for by a majority of those entitled to vote."

10. Two Democratic candidates for Congress were imprisoned to prevent them from canvassing; many voters and several judges of election were also imprisoned.

These abstracts are made from the address of the Committee for the purpose of showing that there was no exaggeration in the preceding memorial. Every citizen can judge what free ballot amounts to or is worth in this country under the dominance of an unscrupulous political party.

General Scott on Martial Law.

General Winfield Scott, by long odds the ablest military legist our country has produced, published, in 1843, a review of the author's pamphlet on martial law, to be found in the first volume, from which review the following extracts are made for the purpose of neutralizing, if not annihilating, whatever of respect may be supposed to be due to General Jackson on the subject of the right of a military man to proclaim martial law in this country. It will also serve to dispel the false notion that an officer is bound to obey the unlawful order of his superior. See the review, p. 284, vol. i., Autobiography of General Scott.

"This timely publication, understood to be from the pen of an ex-judge of the Kentucky Court of Appeals, discusses the extraordinary doctrines recently avowed in Congress and elsewhere, attributing to the commander of an army the right to proclaim and enforce *martial law* as against *citizens* (including legislators and judges) wholly unconnected with the military service.

"The monstrous proposition avowed has raised the indignant voice of '*A Kentuckian*,' and it is only necessary to read him to consign the speeches and writings he reviews to the same repository with the *passive obedience* and non-resistance doctrines of the Filmers and Hobbses of a former age.

"In England the land forces are governed by an annual mutiny act and a sub-code called 'articles of war,' made by the king under the express authority of the act. The preamble of that act always recites, among other things: whereas, no man can be forejudged of life or limb, or be subjected to any kind of punishment within this realm, by *martial law*, or in any other manner than by the judgment of his peers and according to the known and established laws of this realm, yet it being requisite for retaining the forces in their duty that *soldiers* be brought to a more exemplary and speedy punishment than the usual forms of law will allow, be it therefore enacted, etc.; followed by a careful enumeration of crimes for which officers and soldiers shall be punished by court-martial.

"It is in view of the high principles of civil liberty consecrated by Parliament as above, that Tytler, for a long time Judge Advocate of Scotland, says, in his essay on Military Law: '*Martial law* was utterly disclaimed as binding the subjects in general.' So also Chief Justice Loughborough said in 1792: 'Martial law, such as it is described by Hale and Blackstone, does not exist in England at all; it is totally inaccurate to state martial law as having any place whatever within the realm of Great Britain as against subjects not in the line of military duty.'

"Notwithstanding those conservative views, long embodied in the laws and public opinion of England, which hold in utter abhorrence the application of martial law to any person not at the time in the military service, one general and several eminent statesmen are found on this side the Atlantic who ignorantly suppose that that law, described by Hale and Blackstone as 'no law,' is a part of the law of these States, which every commander may indulge himself with, at his own discretion, against the free citizens of republican America.

"There is nothing in our military code to give the slightest pretense that any part of it can be applied to citizens not attached to an army. But in a matter so infinitely important to the existence of free government and our civil liberties, the Constitution is not silent. The fifth amendment expressly declares: 'No person shall be held to answer for a capital or otherwise infamous crime, unless on a presentment or indictment of a grand jury, except in cases arising in the land or naval forces, or *in the militia when in actual service*, in time of war or public danger.' The sixth amendment is to the same effect: 'In all criminal prosecutions the accused shall enjoy the right to speedy and *public* trial by an impartial *jury*.'

"If these clauses do not expressly secure the citizen, not belonging to an army, from the possibility of being dragged before a council of war or court-martial for any crime, or on any pretense whatever, then there can be no security for any human right under human institutions. Congress and the President, if they were unanimous, could not proclaim martial law over any part of the United States without throwing those amendments into the fire. And if President Madison (begging pardon of his memory for the violent supposition) had sent an order to General Jackson to establish the odious code over the citizens of New Orleans, it would have been the duty of the general, under his oath to obey the Constitution, to have withheld obedience; for, by the ninth article of war, officers are not required to obey any but '*lawful commands*.'

"General Jackson took the responsibility with as little of necessity, or even of utility, as of law. In this he stands distinguished from every American commander from the Declaration of Independence down to the present day. * * * Whatever may be our astonishment at the fact that a court of American officers should have proceeded under illegal orders to try a citizen under such charges, they saved themselves and the country from that last of degradations—the finding the prisoner guilty *because* accused by the commanding general. Mr. Louallier was acquitted.

"When Pompey played the petty tyrant at Sicily, as the lieutenant of that master despot Sylla, he summoned before him the Mamertines. That people refused to appear, alleging that they stood excused by an ancient privilege granted them by the Romans. 'What!' said Sylla's lieutenant, 'will you never be done with citing laws and privileges to men who wear swords?' Roman liberty had already been lost in the distemperature of the times. *Inter arma silent leges* found its way into our young republic in the thirty-ninth year of its existence. This odious reply of Pompey to the Mamertines shows that the lovers of law and of human liberty would have gained nothing if he had gained the battle of Pharsalia.

"Under the thirty-third of our rules and articles of war, General Jackson's own officers were bound to aid in causing the writ of *habeas corpus* to be executed against him, as also in executing the precept for his appearance before the judge, if he had refused to appear and to submit to the sentence of the court. This article is as old on our statute book as our glorious revolution of 1776, and as old in England, whence we borrowed it, as the glorious revolution which drove out James the Second and his martial law, which has never again appeared there from that day to this.

"It is vulgarly supposed, particularly by those who, dressed in a little brief authority, lust for more, that the suspension of the writ of *habeas corpus* lets in martial law upon the citizen. The suspension by Congress would certainly, for the time, enable power to hold any citizen incarcerated without cause and without trial, but if brought to trial it must still be before one of the ordinary courts of the land. It is a curious fact that this writ has been but twice practically suspended, (by Generals Wilkinson and Jackson, in both instances at New Orleans,) and never once constitutionally anywhere in the United States since the Declaration of Independence."

CHAPTER XII.

THE PRESIDENCY.

AFTER more than thirty years' consideration of the subject, the author thought it best, before finally turning it over to the care of others, to perfect the details of the Hillhouse scheme for electing our Presidents, presented in the first volume. The result will be seen in the subjoined proposed amendment of the Constitution, which was presented for the consideration of the Senate February 9, 1864, through the kindness of Governor Powell, a Senator from Kentucky. This was done from no expectation of immediate action on the subject, but with the view of arresting public attention and preserving the details of the scheme for future use, if there should ever hereafter be a call for it.

Undue pertinacity will not be imputed to this continued effort to thrust upon public consideration some such amendment of the Constitution, when it is remembered with what a cluster of eminent names the scheme has been indorsed. Senator Hillhouse, of Connecticut, the originator of the plan; Chief Justice Marshall, of the Supreme Court; Chief Justice Parsons, of Massachusetts; Chancellor Kent, of New York; Roger M. Sherman, the eminent lawyer, of Connecticut; Wm. H. Crawford, of Georgia, long a distinguished Senator, and afterward Secretary of the Treasury under Monroe; William C. Rives, of Virginia, long a Senator, and then Minister to France; Judge Curtis, of Massachusetts, formerly of the Supreme Court; William A. Graham, of North Carolina, formerly Secretary of War; John Bell, of Tennessee, formerly Speaker of the House of Representatives, and afterward Senator,—are some of the more eminent men who have approved the plan. The list could be much extended by introducing those who have approved qualifiedly. These are enough, and more than enough to satisfy any one, who has not thought on the subject, that the plan must have intrinsic merit worthy his investigation.

That the present calamitous civil war was not caused by the exploded dogma of "the irrepressible conflict," the reader is referred to the chapter on that subject, and to what is briefly said in the fifth number of the chapter herein on emancipation. That it was occasioned by party conflicts for the Presidency, he is referred to the discussions contained in the first volume, and the predictions therein of just such a civil war, as the inevitable result of prolonged party contests for the Presidency, under the present plan for electing our Presidents. He is also referred to the successful effort made by Northern Federalists, from hostility to Democratic rule, to play upon Northern sympathies by an alleged unfairness in the division of political power by the allowance of a quasi three-fifths negro vote, whereby the South was driven to acquiesce in the original Missouri Compromise. He is referred to the recklessly disastrous repeal of that measure, mainly accomplished to promote the strength of a single aspirant to the Presidency; the party support of Kansas frauds and oppressions; the organization of a Northern sectional party with antislavery for its only distinctive feature, which, if successful in attaining power and using it on the then established proscriptive policy of all parties, would have excluded the whole South from any participation in the offices and honors of the Government, a sectional thralldom which applauding Northern audiences, responding to Mr. Fillmore and other speakers, declared they would not submit to from a Southern sectional party, but would resist, if necessary, by rebellion or secession. He is also referred to the death-grip tenacity with which Southern leaders of the Democracy clung to the power of making Presidents; and, so soon as they found, by the election of Lincoln, that such power was irretrievably lost, the alacrity with which they flew to secession and civil war for redress.

So soon as the first purely sectional party contest had succeeded in achieving the Presidency, all considerate men saw that disunion was the inevitable, immediate or remote consequence. All men ought to have seen, at the same time, that making the Presidency the lure and reward for the formation of such parties, was a radical defect in our form of Government, and that there was the root of the evil, which had to be eradicated before we could entertain a rational belief in our national longevity or prosperity.

Costly has been the price of this clear proof. We have had to pay the loss of life or of health to more than a million of our countrymen, the very flower of the nation, besides a loss in national wealth that it would be difficult to enumerate. It remains to be yet tested whether we have not incurred a more precious loss than all that. We have yet to learn whether the destruction of the Constitution, under violent, inconsiderate, vengeful party action, has not inflicted a permanent loss of our liberty; whether the nation, for all time to come, will not have to remain under vassalage to irresponsible party majorities. The resuscitation of the Constitution, and with it the revival of the liberties of the nation, can never come while the present plan of electing our Presidents remains. Permanent security to liberty is incompatible with that plan. The Fathers taught that it was incompatible with any scheme of government which did not afford a better *practical* check to the power of majorities than their supposed virtue and forbearance. The paper guarantees of a written Constitution, ratified by official oaths, are proven to be of no avail, when a dominant party holds both Houses of Congress and the Presidency. The judiciary are impotent. An appeal to the people is equally unavailing. The great body of the people are equally demoralized, equally imbued with unreasoning party spirit and vindictive hate. The re-election of President Lincoln is ample proof of this. Despite the blundering incompetency of his administration; despite its perfidious betrayals of pledges; despite the multifarious usurpations and tyrannical abuses of power; despite enormous taxation, a ruined currency, a dishonest tender law, and impending national bankruptcy,—the nation, by his re-election, has fully ratified the action of himself and his party. All those outrages on the Constitution and the principles of civil liberty have been confirmed as rightful by the high court of last resort. After arraignment before the great national tribunal—the people themselves—they have been approved at the ballot-box, and will stand for the future as authoritative precedents in favor of the untrammeled power of party majorities. Constitution-guarded liberty stands proved to be a mere delusion. "The Model Republic," as now constituted, is proved to be a mortifying failure.

The nation may continue long to present an aspect of seeming strength, wealth, and prosperity, but the great vivifying principle, the spirit of liberty, which made it attain that position among the nations, with unprecedented rapidity has departed from among us. It remains to be seen whether its absence will cause the national decline to be as rapid as its elevation. However that may be, it stands as a demonstrated fact that the substance, the reality of liberty, is irretrievably gone, unless some plan can be devised by which political parties can be prevented from grasping, at one and the same time, by the same party action, both the legislative and executive powers of the Federal Government. When combined in the same hands, they are proved to be uncontrollable. The legislative and executive powers, instead of performing their intended function of mutual checks, only serve as mutual aids, mutual cloaks in the usurpation and tyrannical abuse of power.

It would be worse than idle to attempt the eradication of political parties and party spirit. That is an unavoidable bane, incident to every republic, resulting from a natural and incurable vice of poor human nature. All that can be hoped for by any practical statesman is some palliation of the evil, by promoting its subdivision into many distinct localities, and discouraging its concentration into only two or three great national parties. Our dear-bought experience has taught us that the inevitable result of such great national parties, in an extended country like ours, is their becoming sectionalized, and with their sectionalizing, civil wars and attempts at disunion. What the great final result will be it needs no gift of prophecy to tell. All experience teaches that men will resort to despotism as an asylum from anarchy.

It is time that intelligent Americans should disabuse their minds of our long-cherished confidence in the imputed superior virtue, patriotism, and intelligence of our people, which was to save us from that common doom of all other republics. Our constantly-recurring protracted party contests for the spoils has thoroughly demoralized the whole nation with only lamentably few exceptions; those exceptions being so few as to constitute only a very meager minority of our voters. We long deluded ourselves with the fond belief that this loss of political morality was mainly confined to party hacks and leaders. But it has gone much deeper than that into the body politic. The rank and file are thoroughly infected. The spirit of party has eaten out all spirit of true, disinterested patriotism. Fealty to party has everywhere, and with the vast majority of men, been substituted for true loyalty to country.

By way of exemplar proof, let us test this by putting the vaunted patriotic Democracy to the test of a very brief exposition. Until our present experience, under the pressure of the great treasonable rebellion, fealty to party, passive submission to party dictation was never so fully exemplified as by the rank and file of the Democracy, who have been so earnest and unanimous in their denunciation of the Abolition party. But suppose situations reversed—that there had been a similar rebellion against Democratic rule, and the very same measures for its suppression had been used by their party leaders—does any sane man doubt that the great body of the Democracy, four-fifths at the least, would have seemed to approve and ratify all that was done? Look at its composition. In proportion to numbers, it contains fewer native Americans than the Abolition party. Even educated foreigners, after long residence among us, seem incapable of understanding anything of the principles of civil liberty beyond the rule of the majority. That is their *beau ideal* of good government before leaving home. It is for its enjoyment that they emigrate to this country. They are slow to learn the value of or necessity for a constitution-protected liberty. They are slow to yield their assent to the rule of law, as preferable to their rooted predilection for the rule of a majority. With most of our own uneducated countrymen that is also the limit of political knowledge. A border State ratter, a former leader of the Democracy, now a leader of the ultra Abolitionists, openly advocates in the Senate a change of our Government into a Consolidated Democracy; yet no man of either party rebukes such supersuperlative folly. The Democracy have everywhere proved themselves ultra Destructives, by the overthrow of all the conservative elements of our State Constitutions that have come under their rule. The very many of their prominent leaders who have apostatized to abolitionism have done so as undisguised ratters, thus proving that there is no political honesty among many of even the *elite* of the party. Most of the conservatism of the nation was embodied in the ranks of the Whig party. The former Whigs who have affiliated with Abolitionists are more numerous than those who have affiliated with the Democrats, though the great body of the party has co-operated with the latter, without affiliation, during our present troubles. The inference is, that there is or ought to be much more of genuine conservatism, of loyalty to the Constitution, and the principles upon which it was formed, in the ranks of the Abolition than in those of the Democratic party.

Let us briefly consider the action of the Democracy at its late Chicago Convention. There never was, there never can be an occasion when party interests could be more imperatively required to yield to patriotism. The contest to be inaugurated involved everything dear to Americans. It involved Constitution supremacy, and with it the whole of American liberty. The contest was of most doubtful issue, however wisely shaped. The party had to contend against the influence of a billion of patronage and the army vote, and also a noted prejudice in the minds of many against the party as the not altogether guiltless instigators of the civil war. It was well known that very many believed that they had wittingly or unwittingly instigated the war by the repeal of the Missouri Compromise and the management of Kansas affairs; also by the suspected procurement, or at least by the publicly avowed party approval of the disastrous Dred Scott decision. Under these circumstances, then was the time, if ever a political party could be induced to do so, for laying aside the ingrained selfishness of all parties, and making the nation believe that it was influenced altogether by disinterested patriotism, and not at all by hopes of party aggrandizement. How did they act? They placed two Democrats on their ticket, instead of selecting for one of the positions some Conservative who had never belonged to their party. They gave no promise not to use power for party advantage, not even to cease or mitigate their abominable proscriptive party policy, showing that the country might go to perdition, unless in the process of saving it their party should be restored to power. Fearing that they might censure something that was popular, they made no specification of usurpations and tyrannical abuses of power, but contented themselves with vague, pointless generalities for a platform, showing the want of even that courage for which alone the party had theretofore obtained honorable distinction. The effect of their action was little more than courting a comparison of the trustworthiness of their party with that of the Abolitionists, instead of advice to lay aside, for the occasion, all party ties, in a grand patriotic rally for the salvation of our country.

Nor, in this connection, should there be a total omission of the former Whig party. Its leaders were sufficiently bold and frank in the private avowal of conservatism, but the party was ever timid and time-serving in its action. Never willing to breast and resist what might prove to be a too popular current, they permitted, without even a struggle, those important conservative outposts—the State Constitutions—to be broken down by the Destructives; showing that the most intelligent and least vicious of modern parties was not to be relied on for a manful maintenance of the test of its own principles; showing that political parties are not to be relied on for that mutual check which is the only conceivable benefit they can be supposed to render a republic. In all else they are evils, and nothing but evils. Whatever can serve to mitigate the amount of mischief they necessarily inflict by their contests, deserves the earnest attention of American statesmanship. Partyism is the great root of all our political ills, which, as it cannot be eradicated, must be restrained, or in some way obviated, before we can have a rational belief in the permanent restoration of American liberty and prosperity. To the solution of that great problem all American intelligence should be earnestly devoted. The subjoined plan for electing our Presidents is one man's contribution to the general national stock of many supposable expedients.

The result of the late Presidential election, with its accompaniments, afford the amplest proof that the present plan does not entirely secure to a majority of the nation the election of our Presidents. It stands fully proved that an unscrupulous party, having control over a billion of patronage and a million of voting soldiers, cannot be deprived of power by the ballot-box. So thorough has been the author's long-felt conviction of this, that, in February, 1864, he wrote to leading Democrats in Congress, earnestly recommending an immediate cessation of all party opposition, accompanied with the declaration that there should be no Democratic or Conservative candidate for President. This would have left the dominant party liable to those splits which are the inevitable fatality of all unopposed large parties. Their seceding minority, opposed to the re-election of Mr. Lincoln, would have shaped their nomination and platform to conciliate the support of Democrats and Conservatives, and their candidate, if elected, would have been compelled to lean upon them for support. By this sort of *pis aller* something would have been accomplished for the country much better than the retention of power by the incumbents. The answer given to this solicitation was, that the argument was good, and the scheme plausible, if it were only practicable; but that it was impracticable, for the Democracy could not be induced to cease party action for the brief space of only two years.

It is not probably true that the actual frauds had any very material influence upon the result of the election; but there is scarcely a man of the million and a quarter of Opposition voters who does not believe that gross frauds were used; not one who does not believe that the fraudulently obtained electoral votes of Tennessee, Arkansas, and Louisiana would have been counted if necessary to Mr. Lincoln's election, and that they were obtained with that express object. Such being the unanimous belief of the one side, it is fair to presume that very many of the other side concur in the belief; enough, at least, to make the believers a majority of the nation. From this time forth a majority of the nation can have no trust in the truthfulness or purity of the ballot-box. How long can such a system last? It cannot be very long before it finds its overthrow in some violent popular explosion, to be followed by another civil war, ending in despotism; or by other oft-recurring civil wars, to the utter destruction of all our national happiness and prosperity.

It is a melancholy reflection, based on probable fact, that for the votes given at the last election in protest against Abolition usurpation and misrule we were indebted in very large measure more to party ties than to patriotism or true allegiance to our country. This is undoubtedly true as to most of the foreign and very large part of the more ignorant native voters. This places our national patriotism and intelligence at a very low point, showing how deficient has been our teaching in political morality and political information. This must be all equally true as to a large part of that better class of more intelligent, non-fanatical voters who voted for the continuance, and thereby a seeming approval of Abolition misrule, whose predominant motive was as much disapprobation of the Democracy as approbation of the Abolitionists. Lamentable is the condition of any republic which shall have to depend upon party spirit, instead of patriotic spirit, for its preservation. If, indeed, this substitution of partyism for patriotism be due to our party conflicts for the Presidency, then nothing can be plainer than that something should be done to remove the office from the immediate certain reach of party effort, thereby removing the greatest of all incentives to the formation of national parties and their disastrous collisions.

Much pains have been bestowed upon the details of the following plan, to obviate the only objection, with few exceptions, ever yet stated by candid intelligence against the plan—that is, its supposed liability to be thwarted by fraudulent management of the lot. With this view, all the details will be found, on careful consideration, to be necessary to the prevention of fraud or the success of any sort of party management toward controlling the result. It is confidently believed that those details will stand the test of the severest criticism.

JOINT RESOLUTION PROPOSING CERTAIN AMENDMENTS TO THE CONSTITUTION OF THE UNITED STATES.

Be it resolved by the Senate and House of Representatives of the United States of America in Congress assembled, That the Constitution of said United States be amended as follows:—

Article No. —.

Section 1. Congress shall, at the first session after the adoption of this amendment, and from time to time thereafter, apportion among the several States the electors of President and Vice-President according to the ratio of population, in Federal numbers. One elector to each State having less than a million; two to each having one but less than two million; three to each having two but less than three million; four to each having three but less than four million; five to each having four but less than six million; six to each having six but less than eight million; and seven to each having eight million of population. Each State having but one elector shall be an electoral district, and each of the other States shall be divided by Congress into districts equal to the number of its electors, to be composed of coterminous territory, and, as near as may be, the districts to have equality of population.

SEC. 2. The voters of each district qualified to vote for members of the most numerous branch of the legislature shall elect an elector. The elections for electors shall be held during the month of October next preceding the commencement of every Presidential term. The several State Legislatures shall prescribe the time and manner for holding those elections and making returns thereof; also for deciding them when contested, and making new elections therein; but Congress may discharge this duty, in whole or in part, when deemed necessary.

SEC. 3. The electors shall convene in the Senate chamber, at the seat of government, at noon of the first Monday in February next preceding the commencement of the ensuing Presidential term and form an electoral college. Two-thirds of all the electors shall be a quorum of the college. The Chief Justice of the United States, or in his absence the President of the Senate, or in the absence of both the Speaker of the House of Representatives, shall be the presiding officer of the college. The presiding officer shall cause all the electors elected, whether present or not, to be listed in the alphabetical order of their names, and in that order divide them into six classes of equal numbers; distributing by lot separately among the several classes such electors at the bottom of the list, if any, as are left out in the division. He shall by lot, under the supervision of one from each class, designate the several classes by numbers from one to six. When a quorum is present he shall announce that the college is formed, and note the time at which the enunciation is made; but, when necessary, the enunciation shall be postponed until after the verification, by a majority of the electors present, of the returns and qualification of members.

SEC. 4. After the college is formed, the electors present of each class shall, after the college is formed, choose an elector from the class next succeeding it in number, except class six, which shall choose from class one. In open session of the college, the presiding officer, under the supervision and control of the six so chosen, or a majority of them, shall cause two of those six to be designated by lot. From those two the college shall choose one, who shall be President for the next ensuing term of four years, and the other shall be the Vice-President for that term. The voting by class or college shall be *viva voce*, in open session of the college. In cases of tie, the casting vote shall be given by the presiding officer, who, if he be also an elector, shall not vote except in cases of tie. The college may adopt rules for expediting a decision by the several classes, and to prevent more than two persons from receiving an equality of votes on the final vote of a class. If there be a failure to choose one of the six from any class, within the time prescribed by the college, the members of that class shall themselves make the choice. There shall be no reconsideration of a vote given.

SEC. 5. If the college fail, except from exterior violence or intimidation, to make an election of President and Vice-President, within twenty-four hours from the time when the college was formed, it shall be dissolved, and the offices of its electors vacated. Thereupon the presiding officer shall order a new election of electors on any day not less than thirty from the date of his proclamation, and at least thirty before the next month of June, which election shall be held, and the electors chosen shall convene at the time and place designated by the proclamation, and proceed to the election of a President and Vice-President, as before directed, within twenty-four hours from the time of their formation into a college, and under like penalty for their failure. Should the failure to elect be caused by exterior violence or intimidation, the functions of the college shall not cease, but it shall reconvene when and where a majority of its members shall by proclamation direct, and make or complete an election, as before directed, within the time specified under like penalty.

SEC. 6. Should no election of President and Vice-President be made by an electoral college before the first day of June next ensuing the commencement of a Presidential term, the Senate of the United States shall convene in its chamber at noon of the first Monday in July next thereafter, constitute all its elected members, whether present or not, into an electoral college, as though each Senator had been elected an elector, and proceed in all respects, as before directed, within twenty-four hours, to choose a President and Vice-President to fill the vacancy. Should the Senate fail so to elect, the discharge of the duties of President and Vice-President, for the residue of that term, shall devolve upon such officers of the government as Congress shall have theretofore directed.

SEC. 7. No office shall be incompatible with that of an elector, except the office of Chief Justice of the United States.

SEC. 8. An act or resolution passed by Congress, which shall be returned by the President with his objections, shall be valid without his signature if repassed by each house of Congress, by a vote equal to a majority of all the members elected thereto.

SEC. 9. It shall not be deemed compatible with the duty of President habitually to use the patronage of his office for the special advantage of any particular political party, or to suffer the patronage of any subordinate officer so to be used.

SEC. 10. Should a vacancy occur in both the office of President and in that of Vice-President while there are two years remaining of the then Presidential term, the Chief Justice of the United States, or in his absence the Secretary of State, shall convene the electoral college, after thirty days' notice, by proclamation, who shall fill the vacancies for the remainder of the term in all respects as if it were an original election.

SEC. 11. Every elector, before entering on the duties of his office, shall, by oath or affirmation, promise to support the Constitution of the United States, and declare that he has not, and will not, pledge his vote as an elector in favor of any person or toward aiding any political party.

CHAPTER XIII.

A NEGRO ARMY.

PUBLISHED FEBRUARY, 1863.

THE bill from the House pending before the Senate authorizes the raising of an army of three hundred thousand negroes for five years, with black and white officers. Against that bill we propose to present the Senate and President a respectful but earnest remonstrance, under the influence of as pure a loyalty and as honest and uncompromising an aversion to disunion as actuates any member of the Senate or the Executive Department.

He must be a shallow statesman who does not recognize *public opinion* as the *still* great ruling power in this country. It is the efficacy of this power that makes a republic so formidable in a popular, so inefficient in an unpopular war. It was that power which enabled us to astonish the world by an impromptu levy of a million of armed men. The want of that power is what now places us in imminent peril of national dishonor. While we had the full benefit of all that unstinted power in apparently successful operation, the on-lookers from Europe told us that our effort was hopeless, and many of our best thinkers were almost despondent of any restoration of the Union by means of coercion alone. How perilous must be our situation when full one-half of that power is seemingly paralyzed by our internal dissensions, and our rulers are threatening to aggravate those dissensions by this negro army, while doing nothing, absolutely nothing, to soothe our divisions or conciliate public confidence. He must be a bold man, if not a reckless ignoramus, who cherishes the belief that this war can be successfully prosecuted by any minority party or by any other than a largely predominant party, and that, too, sustained by an equally predominant public opinion.

It is the duty of the press to endeavor to ward off this new peril by informing the Senate and the President as to the true state of popular feeling in reference to this proposed large standing army of negroes. Considering the large proportion of foreigners, and the "reckless, landless resolutes" of our own country composing our present army, it has, with the considerate, been matter of the deepest concern how such a vast body of armed men were to be gotten rid of at the end of the war—how we were to escape that military despotism predicted for us by our fathers as the almost inevitable result of such a struggle. This jealous apprehension was intensified and still further diffused among the people by a departure of the party in power from its reiterated pledges as to the purposes of the war, the ignoring of every semblance of conciliation, and adopting a policy precluding all voluntary submission by any part of the Southern people, and insuring a long, protracted, merciless, exterminating war. The thought obtrudes itself upon every thinking mind, how insecure our liberty when dependent upon the tender mercies of the victorious soldiery of such a war. The seemingly reckless increase of our army intensified this fear. The attempted usurpation of power in the abolition proclamation showed there was no limit to the power that the dominant party would not attempt to usurp, and that there was no sacrifice of personal opinions and official pledges that the President would not make in submission to the dictation of a faction of the worst men of his party. Then came the martial-law proclamation, looking like an effort to frighten the nation into submission to the unbridled sway of that fanatic faction. The proclamation of the usurped power and deliberate intention to punish by a military commission whoever should be guilty of whatever he and his satraps might choose to think "disloyal practices," was at once, to every intent, assuming to himself, or for the fanatic faction that dictated to him, a military dictatorship over the nation. A faction who through their most influential leaders had claimed the power, and announced the intention, when deemed necessary, for Congress to appoint a Dictator, even to the superseding of the President. A faction who through their leaders in and out of Congress have again and again proclaimed their deliberate intent, if deemed necessary by them in the accomplishment of the purpose for which they prosecute the war, ruthlessly to exterminate the whole white population of the South and supply it with a better race of people, meaning probably an amalgamation cross of the abolitionist with the negro. A faction, one of whose leaders has very recently thanked God for all the defeats of our armies, as those defeats had brought us the crowning blessing of the abolition proclamation.

With these reasons for jealous, suspicious distrust of the purpose of the dominant party, the Senate and President should have no difficulty in crediting our assurances that this attempt to create so large a standing army of negroes will everywhere intensify this suspicious distrust, recruit the ranks of the opposition, widen the division at the North, and take from the administration the indispensable support of popular opinion.

Much of that jealous distrust of a large standing army, which the founders of the Republic so sedulously inculcated, has been allayed by the generous confidence in their fellow-citizens, which is common to the people of most republics. This has been carried so far with many as actually to believe that American soldiers could never be induced, contrary to the experience of all other nations, to aid in establishing a military despotism. It is believed by many that our citizen soldiers could never be brought to obey their officers in firing upon their fellow-citizens while resisting usurped tyrannical power. But who can base such a hope upon a large standing army of negroes? An alien foreign race, bound to us by no ties of affection or sympathy as the equal children of a common country, but who have the supposed injuries of long servitude to avenge against the whole white race. Do the Senate and President imagine that the people are not revolving all this? Think they that the people view with apathy these dark portents? If so, we entreat the Senate and President to be warned, for nothing could be further from the truth. The people look upon this measure not only with aversion but with anxiety and distrust. Its enactment, if it should be enacted, would necessarily deepen and widen the perilous dissensions already existing. It is in vain for the dominant party to protest the purity of their intentions. So many of its most solemn pledges have been willfully violated that its protestations no longer command the public trust. The single fact of the black army being enlisted for *five* years, while our white soldiers are enlisted only for three years, is sufficient of itself to arouse the most jealous apprehensions as to the sinister purposes of the Abolition party.

In illustration of the reasons that the people think they have to fear our army when the war is over, we will refer to a recent publication by General Milroy and some other abolition officers from Indiana. After denouncing as traitors the Democratic members of the Indiana Legislature for fulfilling the wishes and pronouncing the opinions of their constituents, these officers assume to declare for themselves and the whole army: "When we have crushed armed treason at the South, we will upon our return, while our hands are in, also exterminate treason at the North, by arms, if need be, and by the blood of traitors wherever found." This infamous threat from his subordinates, it is to be hoped the President has not seen. In other days its authors would have been promptly dismissed in disgrace from the army. If such threats can be made with impunity by army officers against the people, who are taxed to pay, clothe, and feed them, and be held in terrorem over the representatives of the people, the days of freedom are nearly gone. We had as well be preparing the obsequies of American liberty. Take this threat, in connection with the notorious fact that the last elections in Missouri were carried under the terror of the bayonet, and the Senate and President must see that this is no time for increasing but for soothing these fears of the people. If they do not so see and act, they need not be surprised at the daily increasing clamor for peace.

Instead of unnecessarily swelling the vast expenditures of the war, by organizing a negro army that must be powerless for everything but evil, we should endeavor, by the most vigilant and rigorous economy, to retrench the present expenditures. Such retrenchment is both a military and a political necessity of no flexible order. Unless our expenditures are circumscribed within some reasonable limit, our defeat is imminent. We will destroy our national credit. When that is destroyed, we shall have used "the last man and last dollar" of impassioned patriots. There will be nothing left for sacrificial offering on the altar of country. Every effort should be made to ward off that result. Without the credit, we cannot obtain the dollar, and, without the dollar, we cannot obtain the man. These may be unpalatable truths; but they are truths, and they are less unpalatable now than they will become hereafter, if we fail boldly to grapple with them. It behooves us, in this emergency, to act like men, and not like children.

Our revenue from taxation and tariff will not cover more than a fourth, or at most a third of our expenses; for the balance we have to depend upon our credit. Treasury notes are only a temporary, partial expedient. Secretary Chase, together with the finance committees, see and admit that an increase of their amount will only serve proportionally to their depreciation, and a corresponding increase in the amount of our expenses. The Secretary says he has negotiated a permanent loan only to the amount of twenty-five millions; that no more can be obtained, or, if at all, only to a moderate amount, and at a ruinous sacrifice; yet such loans are the only means of carrying on the war. Adequate taxation would be so enormous as not to be thought of. He missed his opportunity for negotiating such loans by letting slip the time when the Administration was sustained by an undivided public sentiment and the aroused patriotism of the North was at fever heat. Much of the loan, if then effected, would have found a market in Europe, furnishing the means at home for taking new loans. The solid, redundant capital seeking permanent investment to such vast amount does not and never did exist in this country. Probably it never will exist here while the great bulk of our real estate remains unimproved.

A year ago the necessary loans would have been effected for an economical prosecution of the war upon a reasonable scale. It could have been effected then, because the North was unanimous and zealous in supporting a vigorous prosecution of the war. Why can it not be done now? There is no other reason, but that the unanimity and zeal of a year ago are now gone. Why are they gone? It is because of a change of policy by the Administration not acceptable to the nation; because the policy of the Administration is no longer to maintain the Constitution as it is and restore the Union as it was. It is because the leaders of the dominant party have thrown off all disguise, showing they will submit to no restraint from the Constitution, that abolition is their object, and avowing their determination to consent to no restoration which shall permit the South to retain its slave institution. What is the remedy? The obvious one of retracing the steps which brought about the change in national sentiment. A retraction of the unconstitutional and abolition action of Congress and the Executive will bring us back where we were. A retraction of the martial-law proclamation should be accompanied by a solemn assurance that there shall be no future attempt to trample on the guaranteed liberties of the people. Unanimity restored, the North will supply the means. Capital in large amounts does not exist for such a permanent loan, but it is distributed through the nation in small sums, which, in the great aggregate, are an enormous amount. In that restored state of things, an appeal to the nation for a patriotic loan would, as it did in France, bring all this out. Every old woman would lend the Government her spare hundred dollars.

If some such policy as the one here indicated is not pursued, the Government must almost certainly sink under the pecuniary load of the war. Our armies cannot be kept in the field without money. Most respectfully, and with all deference to other opinions, it does appear to us that the money can be obtained in no other way. The ultra abolitionists are probably, all told, not two hundred thousand voters, with comparatively little wealth, and even less influence, when deprived of that which they derive from the Administration. It is every way proper that they, and not the rest of the nation, should be made to yield in such an exigency. A large, a very large majority of the nation is unalterably opposed to the destruction of the whole white population and property of the South. It is sheer madness to attempt to carry out any policy against the will of such a majority.

CHAPTER XIV.

AMENDMENT OF THE CONSTITUTION.

Letter to a Member of the Kentucky Legislature.

PUBLISHED FEBRUARY 11, 1865.

DEAR SIR:—There can be no doubt of it, I see no room for intelligent doubt that the constitutional amendment must entirely annul all such legislation as the pending bill to apprentice slaves. Every lawyer knows that such must be its effect, giving right of action to the freed negroes for the full value of their hire, from the time they are so illegally held under such apprenticeship. In this aspect, the bill is a ludicrous specimen of that "practical statesmanship" of which certain gentlemen are arrogating to themselves the exclusive monopoly—a scheme to avoid the mischief of the amendment, which will be nullified the instant the amendment takes effect!

The futile scheme of Governor Bramlette to obtain compensation, by a conditional ratification of the amendment, I should be sorry to consider a fair specimen of his "practical statesmanship." I cannot, in ordinary charity toward him, bring myself to suppose that he really believes it has any practicability whatever. I have too much respect for his "practical statesmanship" to believe that he entertains even a hope that abolitionists will accord bare justice, much less what they would esteem great generosity toward Kentucky. He knows, as every lawyer knows, that the legislature has no power to make a conditional ratification. All it can do is to say yes or no. Such a ratification would only enable the abolition Congress to consider the condition as mere surplusage, and treat the ratification as unconditional, which they would certainly do. Men who have the effrontery to attempt by fraud to engineer a seeming ratification of such an amendment, when it is notorious that vast majorities of the people of more than a fourth of the States are unalterably opposed to it, will have the effrontery to do this also, or even worse, if necessary to their purpose.

They know that the courts would treat the apprenticing as a mere nullity, from being an obvious fraud upon the higher law, in disparagement of the rights which slaves were about to acquire under the amendment. But they will not trust to mere judicial decision. By the second clause of the amendment they have secured to themselves full power to nullify any legislation which goes to restrict the emancipated slave to the *munificent* remuneration of "a new suit of clothes and twenty-five dollars," in full for seven years' labor.

I have always believed that the clause giving Congress the seemingly unnecessary power to enforce an amendment which adequately enforces itself, was introduced for the express purpose of affording Congress the apology of assuming exclusive jurisdiction over our negro population, the exercise of which, as prefigured in the "Freedmen's Department," created at the last session, would give the Federal Government more local patronage than the governments of the slave States now enjoy. In the exercise of this power they will tolerate no apprenticeship other than the natural one of the child to its negro parent, and will make it felony to hold an emancipated negro under such apprenticeship.

All honor to glorious, unterrified Delaware. She promptly refuses to bow down and lick the foot that spurns her. That is not merely acting with proper spirit, but in accordance with the highest order of true "practical statesmanship." If Kentucky follows her example, the assent of the requisite three-fourths of the States cannot be obtained, and the nation will not be improvidently afflicted with that great obstacle to reconstruction and permanent pacification.

It is inconceivable to me how any Kentuckian could fancy any possible benefit to our State, which could induce the giving of her vote toward the *robbery* of her own citizens and the infliction upon her of that dire doom of two hundred and fifty thousand lazzaroni negroes, who would effectually repel the influx of all white labor or capital, and would certainly drive off much of that which we now have. The exercise of the principal labor of the State by lazzaroni free negroes would be much more degrading to labor and much more repulsive to white laborers than a humane, well-ordered slave-labor system.

CHAPTER XV.

PACIFIC RAILROAD.

PUBLISHED JANUARY, 1859.

SENATOR SEWARD has received much commendation for his Pacific Railroad speech. It is treated as the development of an enlarged and enlightened statesmanship. Its true claim to such praise needs investigation. It is certainly entitled to commendation for a fearless sort of candor.

He admits that the road will cost a hundred million, and ten million annually above its earnings to keep it in operation. He admits that it is not a commercial enterprise; that the benefit to commerce will not justify the expense; and that by no calculation can it be proved a money-making or money-saving enterprise for the nation. He says its objects are political. He enumerates its political objects and advantages thus:—

First. A mail conveyance.

Second. A conveyance for soldiers and military stores.

Third. The introduction of society in the recesses of the continent.

Fourth. Maintaining peace and authority over the Indian tribes.

Fifth. The protection of our Pacific coast.

Sixth. The consolidation of the Union between the Pacific and Atlantic States.

As to the first and second of these objects, there is no denying that the road would greatly facilitate the transportation of the mail, of soldiers, and military stores; but the only question in reference to them is that of economy. Taking only five million as the interest of the capital to be expended and ten million as the annual expense for keeping up the road, and we have an annual cost of fifteen million. The interest on this sum is nine hundred thousand dollars, which, it is believed, would on an average greatly overpay the annual cost of mail and army transportation. The timely establishment of arsenals and furnishing them with ample munitions during peace, is all that is required for any contingency, and can be done for less freight by way of the ocean than it could be done by way of the road even if it were made. The mail transportation is too insignificant an item to need separate comment. In an economical point of view, the result is, that we should pay annually fifteen million for what we can do without the road for one million. This disposes of his two first reasons.

His third and fourth objects may also be considered together. What is the particular motive for hastening the introduction of society into the recesses of the continent, he does not explain, and it is not easy to conjecture what his motive may be, unless he wants population there merely because they are *recesses*, and because of the difficulty in governing the population after he has got it there. Those recesses now belong to and are inhabited by the Indian tribes. Every principle of good faith and of national honor requires that we should permit them to retain those remote recesses, so long as their possession is compatible with our national weal, or at least with our national convenience. With such an indefinite amount of unappropriated good land within our own limits and outside their reservations, why seduce our people into invasions of their inferior lands and inferior site? Why but to defeat his other object, the maintaining of peace with those tribes? The way to maintain peace with them is, everywhere that we come in contact, to present to them a comparatively dense population capable of self-defense against their assaults. The true way is to keep away the temptation to hostilities from the apparent facility of success. The true way to promote those hostilities is to thrust among them a sparse, unsustained population, whose feebleness will invite assaults from savage cupidity and vengeance. In close connection with this branch of the subject, is a view of it which brings in doubt the practicability of the whole scheme, and which tends to show that, instead of building the road to seduce population into those remote wild regions, we are compelled to the observance of a more rational policy, that of waiting their settlement, for the necessary protection of the road when built. There is no practical doubt in the proposition that money will build the road, and that an indefinite amount of men and money can protect it when built. There is as little doubt that the whole of our present army would not be more than sufficient for its protection. A military station at intervals of ten miles would be wholly inadequate, if the Indians were resolved on its destruction. With our experience of the insecurity of railroads from the depredations of mere individual love of mischief or thirst for vengeance, in the midst of our densest and most orderly population, how can we trust to the absence of those passions among savages who can indulge them with perfect impunity? A prudent man would rather say that an extermination of the Indians to a distance of one hundred miles on both sides of the road would be the first necessary step toward its security! Is Mr. Seward prepared to pay this also as part of the price of the road? A railroad may be compared to a long chain, the breaking of any one of whose links destroys the usefulness of the whole. Is it prudent to lay such a long and costly chain, when the destruction of many links depends upon savage forbearance? In view of the great difficulty, the scheme may be pronounced *impracticable*, as a thing to be pushed through immediately, without regard to the present location of our white population. The road can progress no faster, comparatively speaking, than that population. On the main trail from the Missouri it might be sent forty or fifty miles into the Indian country, with Indian permission, in advance of population, there wait its coming, and then start again. This is the only mode in which it can be safely and reliably made on any northern route. From Red River through Texas it might be prudently laid to the present outer limit of white population, and after the lapse of a few years take a fresh start. Every mile of road on either route would aid emigration to the Pacific. Two such roads should be immediately commenced, to be prosecuted upon some such gradual plan of completion. Any other is utterly chimerical.

As to his fifth reason, *the protection of our Pacific coast*, it might be sufficient to say that its position gives it better protection than is enjoyed by our Atlantic or Gulf coast. Furnish them with the needful fortifications and munitions of war, and the people on the Pacific are abundantly able to protect themselves against any force that would probably ever be sent against them. In case of war, we could send them aid long before an invading army of any size could reach them from Europe. But there would be the absence of all motive for sending such an army to so remote a point, when our richer Eastern cities are so much nearer of access, and affording equal facility for being sacked. This reason has so little force, that it is obvious the hundred million would be better employed in strengthening the defenses of our Atlantic and Gulf coasts.

Nor is there any greater force in his final and main object, *the consolidation of the Union between the Pacific and the Atlantic States.* Men of as much sagacity as Mr. Seward, and who have bestowed as much well advised thought upon the subject as he has, believe that the Union to which he refers cannot be consolidated. This is another impracticability. Fast as we of the Atlantic coast are, we yet are not fast enough for the adventurous, enterprising spirits who rule and will continue to rule our Pacific coast. At least half the intelligence of the nation agreed with Mr. Clay and Mr. Van Buren when they declared that we already had too much territory even before the annexation of Texas. An equal portion of that intelligence saw no benefit in the acquisition of California, except that, by coming into the possession of our race, it gave a vent to much of our turbulent population, and presented the facile and probable means for ultimately ridding us of all our Pacific possessions. Public rumor and private information are greatly at fault if this anticipation be not in the process of rapid fulfillment. A large portion of the people on the Pacific are already eager for separation. The most prudent and considerate only wait for better preparation. Fortify their harbors, stock their arsenals, and build this road to facilitate the access of emigrants, and they will, with comparative unanimity, call for the separation. The very means he proposes to produce consolidation will promote separation, just in proportion as emigration to the Pacific will be promoted. They will, by filibustering, either drag us into foreign wars, or keep us in such constant dread of being dragged into them, that we on the Atlantic side will be glad to be rid of them, and will give their departure a joyful acquiescence. Whatever benefit we now have from their commerce as distant colonies, we should continue to enjoy without the trouble of governing them. We should enjoy, in an increased degree, the great benefit of being drained by them of our turbulent, filibustering, mob-exciting population, and postponing that great national evil, an excess of population. What Mr. Seward aims at in his better consolidation is, therefore, not attainable—and if it were, is not desirable. It is best for both sections that we should separate and constitute distinct amicable confederacies. Our country is entirely too large to be properly governed by any one government. When reasonably filled up with population, it would be only equally preposterous to attempt to manage all the nations of Europe by a single government. Detach our Pacific possessions, and it is still to be greatly feared that in less than fifty years we shall have a population of a hundred million. The opinion of no man is worth quoting who does not feel a salutary dread of having our republican institutions subjected to the test of even such a moderate amount of population as that. The statesman who will look only half a century ahead; cannot fail to recognize excess of population as the great peril of our national career.

The separation of our Pacific possessions will tend to keep down population, and postpone that peril. Our true national policy is to promote that separation. As a means to facilitate and expedite it, we should promote emigration thither. To that end we should start two railroads in that direction, to be carried so far only as common sense and common prudence show it safe to carry them.

The judicious expenditure of a hundred million in internal improvements would greatly tend to strengthen and consolidate the Union of the States east of the Rocky Mountains. This Union needs such aid, and would justify the expenditure, though there should be no resulting pecuniary benefit. The power to make such improvements may well be conceded by the Democracy since the recent discovery by their President of such an enormous incident to the war-making power. If that gives the power to make a road through California to San Francisco, there can be no disputing the power to make such a road through other States, for the better defense of New Orleans, Savannah, or any other city.

CHAPTER XVI.

TEXAS BEFORE ANNEXATION.

The vast importance of correct views as to the various questions of policy involved in the proposed annexation of Texas supersedes all necessity for apology on the part of any citizen in proffering his opinions to the public, as a contribution to the general stock. Without attempting to embrace the whole subject, it is proposed to take a cursory glance at some of the more leading questions involved.

The present population of Texas may be stated at from one hundred and fifty to two hundred thousand, including from twenty to twenty-five thousand slaves. Of these slaves, the efficient hands employed in agriculture do not exceed twelve or fifteen thousand. These cannot produce annually more than from sixty to one hundred thousand bales of cotton. Her present national importance may be properly estimated by this item, which is too insignificant to excite uneasiness or jealousy in any quarter.

Her ability to increase this amount of production depends entirely upon accessions to her laboring population. This again depends upon poor white immigrants from Europe and slaves from here, her constitution forbidding the importation of slaves except from the United States.

The chance of her obtaining such labor from Europe may be satisfactorily tested by the well-known fact, that cotton has never yet been cultivated by the labor of Europeans, and that no field labor has ever yet been obtained from them in such a climate. Until the healthier and more congenial latitudes of the Union and British America are densely filled, it will be preposterous to anticipate any considerable European emigration to Texas. Even if commercial capital and government influence should, for a time, force the flow of the stream in that direction, no permanent result of importance would be yielded. Such population must sooner or later dwindle and perish in the field labor of that climate.

Nor is her prospect better for any considerable accession of slaves from here. Any amount of unimproved cotton lands of the first quality can still be had within our bounds, nearly as cheap as in Texas—so cheap that the difference in price would not constitute an inducement with the slaveholder for expatriating himself. There is no capital in Texas, nor the means of accumulating any, to enable the present inhabitants to import slaves. The expenditure of the large sums which must have gone to the accumulation of her enormous debt of thirteen million, ought to have brought in a much larger number of slaves. That resource is now gone. The public credit is sunk and gone forever. Her only future dependence for slave labor rests entirely upon the immigration of slaveholders from the United States.

What then are the inducements upon which the hope of any such emigration can be based? They consist exclusively in the *alleged* superiority of her climate and soil for the production of cotton.

To counterbalance these, there are the disinclination of every people, and especially Americans, to expatriation; the disinclination to become citizens of a country that must forever remain an inferior and dependent, if not insignificant power; the disinclination every man of sense and substance must have to adopt as a new home a country already irretrievably insolvent, and incur for himself and property the unavoidable burdens of a population of only two hundred thousand attempting to maintain an independent government.

A recent pamphlet has endeavored to prove that Texas will present superior and attractive advantages to cotton growers, by reason of a treaty with England, admitting Texas cotton into England free of duty, in consideration of similar free admission of English manufactures into Texas. Such an argument may be worth something among our venerated senators, but it would be difficult to find a respectable slaveholder so silly as not to know that it mattered nothing to him whether he paid his taxes for the support of government indirectly at the custom-house or directly to the tax gatherer. No intelligent man could fail to come to the conclusion that the burden on him for the support of government must always be much lighter as a citizen of this Union, than as a citizen of Texas. As to supposed difference in the relative degrees of security, for both life and property in the two countries, nothing need be said.

In the absence of all well-founded hope to obtain the necessary labor to till her soil, it is idle to talk about the extent of her domain and the fertility of her soil. These alone can never constitute a respectable State or a rival in any branch of commerce. Any such supposable rivalry can, therefore, have no bearing of weight upon the question of annexation.

Her doom as an independent nation, if she remain such, is feebleness and dependence. But the more zealous advocates of annexation, though at one moment they preposterously magnify her prospective growth and population, to excite our fears of rivalry in the cotton trade, in the next insist upon this very feebleness, as what must drive her into the arms of England, and through our fears of that dreaded enemy alarm us with the apprehension of having a thorn driven into our vulnerable side.

This simulated fear, so degrading to our national character and which ought to be so offensive to our national pride, is based upon an idea, the direct reverse of a well-established European maxim: that is, that a weak neutral is one of the best frontier barriers a nation can have. But the whole idea is preposterous and unsustained by the slightest probability. Their origin and near neighborhood must ever disincline the Texans to making or fostering a foreign alliance injurious to us. Even in the event of ill blood between the two nations, their good sense would tell them that the momentary gratification of any ill will, by aiding a temporary invasion through their borders, would be dearly paid for by incurring the lasting hostility of this nation, which must lead to their ultimate extermination. Why should England go so far off as Texas to seek a point for invasion, when the whole Gulf coast, from Mobile to the Sabine, presents an unintermitting succession of such points, all so much better than any in Texas, in proportion as they are nearer to the main object of attack, New Orleans?

A recently published letter of General Jackson's intimates the opinion that England might, secretly and unknown to us, land in Texas an army of thirty thousand men, and by an overland march of three hundred miles surprise and capture Orleans. The venerable general does little credit to the sagacity of England, in supposing she would take such a circuitous path to such perfidious violence. No man knows better than he does, that, with less than one-third the force, she can take Orleans any day in the year, by landing within two hours' march of the city. No man knows better, that neither ten, nor thirty, nor twice thirty thousand men could permanently hold Orleans, and that such an army could reasonably expect a permanent lodgment only in their graves. Sickness alone would dispose of at least the half of it in a single season. If with a million of bold and hardy yeomen, now with the aid of steam, almost as it were within bugle-call of Orleans, we cannot repel any force that can be sent against it, from a distance of five thousand miles, we deserve to lose it, and had better set about placing ourselves under the vassalage of some braver and more warlike people, capable of defending us. Is it not time that England should cease to be such a raw-head-and-bloody-bones scarecrow for us? There is no nation from a war with which she has so little to hope and so much to fear as with us. Since she has become satisfied of our ability to defend ourselves and injure her, war between the two countries will never be of her seeking. She would no doubt be glad not to be so dependent upon us for cotton, would therefore like to see Texas grow up to a successful rival as an independent State, in raising cotton, and therefore will encourage her all she can by soft words and honeyed assurances of good-will. But no English ministry will venture directly to encourage the propagation of negro slavery, and without that Texas can never become of sufficient commercial importance to induce England, at any serious expense or inconvenience, to seek a close alliance with her. She has too much sagacity ever to receive it as a colony, to be reared up by her resources, and then snatched from her by us, as soon as we found it worth the taking. If there is even room for doubt as to our ability to defend our southern frontier against her invasions, with what hope could she expect to defend Texas, open as it is at every avenue to our invasion? Indeed, she would have better luck than with any colony she has ever yet planted, if the colony itself did not eagerly jump into our arms the moment we extended them for its reception.

Nevertheless, as not merely General Jackson, but Mr. Adams, Mr. Clay, and Mr. Van Buren have all in their turn sought to obtain Texas, as necessary to the security of the great emporium of western trade, it is in vain for inferior men to argue the reverse. The Western and Southern people have been made to believe that the country is necessary to them. Furthermore, the land is undoubtedly very good, and for all good land they have a most insatiable craving. Sooner or later, have it they will. Rightfully or wrongfully, therefore, any discussion of the subject, for practical uses, requires the concession that the country is needed, and ultimately will be obtained, either for money or at the price of blood. The only open question is as to the time, manner, and conditions in obtaining it.

Annexation will add but little, if anything, to the wealth or commerce of the whole Union. The abstracting of slaves and capital from the States where they are now employed and the concentrating them upon Texas will enhance the value of its lands and may increase the yield from the slaves, but will be attended with a corresponding diminution of the value of the lands and the amount of population of those States from which they are drawn. Supposing this drain to come principally from the Carolinas, Georgia, Mississippi, and Alabama, or that their inferior lands are thrown out of cultivation by the competition, then they will lose slaves, capital, and population, and incur consequent diminution of general State wealth, just in proportion as Texas acquires. There is now within the Union a superabundance of land to grow more cotton than can be sold. The effect, therefore, must be, without adding materially to the aggregate wealth of the whole nation, to impoverish the cotton-growing States and enrich Texas. The difference to our Northern Atlantic brethren will be nothing. They will still have the same amount of slave-drivers working for their benefit; the same extent of monopolized market for the use of their shipping and the sale of their manufactures. On the supposition that Texas would become a considerable cotton-growing country without annexation, as the Northern States, to that extent, would lose their monopoly, their manifest interest is in favor of annexation, as, in any event, that of the Southern States is against it.

Yet, however obvious this is, still it must be taken as an undoubted fact that the Southern States are anxiously in favor, while the Northern States are earnestly opposed to annexation.

The reason for this plain departure from self-interest on both sides must be known, properly to understand the whole subject. This reason is to be found in the fanaticism of the one side and the fear of it on the other, and in the jealousies and graspings after power among the political leaders of both sides. These jealousies and antipathies, when so strong as to make the parties themselves overlook their immediate pecuniary interests, must constitute an important feature in the case, not to be neglected in any attempted adjustment of the subject.

The people of the three slaveholding States of the West,—Kentucky, Tennessee, and Missouri,—who have an identity of local interest, institutions, manners, and customs, and who hold the command of the Mississippi, may be said, like all the other people of the West, to think it would be better to have Texas, and mean to have it some day, but are in no violent hurry about it. Their interest, in common with that of all the other Western States, is that the cotton-growing region should remain where it is, and where they have the monopoly in the supply of various articles of commerce, some of which they would entirely lose if the cotton growing were transferred to Texas. These three States also, though having an immediate interest in the slave question, are but moderately affected with the antipathies growing out of it, do not wish to make it themselves, nor suffer it to be made by others, either the subject or object in a political or sectional scramble for power. They do not favor at present, nor mean to favor at any distant day, either a slaveholding or non-slaveholding alliance among the States. They are for the Union as it is, and mean to keep it as it is, in despite the jealousies and animosities of the extremes. They know that no line of demarkation for separating the States can ever be drawn without their assent, and they never mean to assent to any such line. They view negro slavery as a curse upon their own white population, and are by no means content to look upon it as an irremediable evil, which they are bound to entail upon their posterity. They stand in the same position as Virginia and Maryland, both as to feeling and interest, in regard to prospective emancipation. These five States have a peculiar and identical interest on that subject, which is no little involved in the Texas question.

The slave question, properly considered, is of the utmost importance to the future destiny of the nation. Its proper consideration has already been too long neglected. It is time for every statesman, wherever located, to look it full in the face, notwithstanding its repulsiveness, and to attempt either remedy or palliative against the mischief with which we are threatened. This is his duty, fully as much on the score of patriotism as of philanthropy.

Our slave population, in half a century, will by natural increase amount to twelve or thirteen million. What are we to do with twelve million of slaves, having the physical and mental improvement to be attained in that time? One of two things must ensue. They will either exterminate the whites south of the North Carolina and Tennessee line, or the whites will have to thin them off by cutting their throats. The least revolting and most probable of these alternatives will inflict an indelible stain upon our national annals.

African colonization has ceased to be viewed as even a palliative for this appalling evil. If there be any efficient remedy, there is none other than that of colonization upon our own continent. For that purpose, Texas, or a part of it, affords the only remaining suitable position. The climate, though enfeebling and ultimately destructive to the white man, is admirably suited to the negro. The fertility of the soil affords that easy means of subsistence suited to his indolent nature. The free negroes of the better sort would eagerly flock to it from every quarter of the Union. The means of access are so easy and cheap, that the poorest would work their way there, without charge to the Government or to any colonization society. The work of voluntary emancipation would rapidly progress throughout the States of Maryland, Virginia, Kentucky, and Missouri. The drain from these States, by emigration of owners and sale of slaves, for the use of the slaveholding part of Texas, would leave it a comparatively easy task to bring about a coercive but prospective and gradual emancipation. According to every probability, those four States, and possibly Tennessee also, would adopt systems of gradual emancipation in less than twenty years.

The subdivision of slaves, in those five States, among a multiplicity of owners, which takes the females from field labor, secures their union in marriage, and affords to the sick and infants proper care, is what renders those States the great prolific nurseries of our slave population. When slaves are held in large gangs, and the females worked in the fields, they do not propagate near so fast. Indeed, it is said that among the Creole planters of Louisiana, from working the females, or from inattention to infants, their propagation is not nearly sufficient to keep up their numbers. Break up those great nurseries for slaves, where they duplicate in less than a quarter of a century, concentrate the slaves into the large proprietorships of the South, and they will not duplicate in less than forty or fifty years. Without entering into any conjectural estimate of the probable amount of voluntary emancipations, it is perfectly within the bounds of probability that from these causes alone, our slave population, at the end of half a century, instead of amounting to twelve, will not exceed five or six million. Indeed, if colonization and emancipation should become a sort of fashionable mania, it is within the bounds of probability that our slave population may be kept down to something like their present numbers.

But all this depends upon making a portion of Texas a free negro colony. The enlightened portion of the people of those five States, even those most anxiously desiring emancipation, will never move seriously or zealously in the matter until they can see how emancipation is to place the slave in a better situation than the free negro of the non-slaveholding States, nor until they can know that the emancipated slaves are not to be left as a lazzaroni population on our hands. We have been taught to believe that the free blacks of the non-slaveholding States are the most degraded and miserable portion of our whole population. The agitation of the subject by abolitionists has, for the last ten years, kept down its agitation among ourselves. But present us, through a free negro colony in Texas, with the practical means for a beneficial general emancipation, and there will be no want of zealous, intelligent, and influential men among us to give the subject a thorough and effectual agitation—provided, always, that the abolitionists will be kind enough to let us alone. Our ability to do this will not be doubted when the fact is recollected that in each of these five States, the non-slaveholding voters outnumber the slaveholders in a ratio of four or five to one. But it is only bare justice to the slaveholders themselves, of the writer's own State, to say that a majority of them are ready to co-operate, when they can be satisfied that emancipation will be beneficial to the slaves.

The more intelligent portion of the people of these five States will never acquiesce in the idea that negro slavery is to be entailed upon them and their posterity in perpetuity. If they wish to be rid of the evil,—if they are not blind to the future destiny of their States,—let them attend to the adjustment of this Texas question and the terms of her admission into the Union. They hold the power in their hands to require it to be adjusted in a manner to suit their peculiar interests on this subject.

The bulk of the present population of Texas is concentrated upon its eastern division. Let it be stipulated in the pending treaty that the country shall be divided into two parts, by a line commencing at the mouth of the Brazos River, running up it to the thirty-second degree of latitude, and thence the nearest course to Red River; or at the mouth of the Colorado, running up it to the thirtieth degree of latitude, and thence to Red River. The eastern division, which would be about the size of Missouri or Georgia, to be at once admitted into the Union as *one* slaveholding State. The western division to be guaranteed against slavery, and held for the purpose of promoting free negro colonization from the United States—but never to be admitted as a State into the Union; after the lapse of a century, or sooner, if found to be in a condition to take care of itself, to be emancipated as an independent power. The holders of private land claims in the western division to be permitted to surrender them to Government, at a graduated price of from ten to twenty-five cents per acre, according to the quantity held by a single person. All the good lands in the eastern division are already taken up by private claims, and should be taxed five cents per acre per annum till this, or whatever else may be deemed an adequate remuneration, is made up to the owners in the western division.

If our Government is firm in adhering to some such arrangement as this, as an ultimatum, there is no danger that Texas will not accede. There cannot be a doubt but that the more intelligent and far-sighted among them are very sick of the experiment of carrying on an independent government with so small a population. They must be nearly hopeless of any considerable or valuable accession to their population in their present situation. They cannot but be apprehensive that much of the most valuable part of their present population will sell out and return to this country. The immediate enormous increase in value which would be given to the lands of the eastern division by annexation would induce them to accede upon almost any reasonable terms. Put them to it, and they themselves will devise the mode of compensating and satisfying the holders of land in the western division.

But, where the difficulty of satisfying these holders? If we succeed in sending them free negroes in sufficient quantities, they will prefer retaining all the better locations to surrendering them at any reasonable price; for we shall furnish them with an abundance of the very best and cheapest labor they can expect from any quarter, and enable them, without capital, to till those lands most profitably, and, after making fortunes by so doing, it will be at their own option to leave them and come away, or not.

The ultimate destination of the negro colony being separation, the permanent enlargement of the Union would be only some two hundred miles of Gulf coast, extending back some three hundred miles to Red River. It would be only *one* new slave State to come in with Wisconsin, as Florida did with Iowa—a mere keeping up of the present relative numerical strength in the Senate. It will be fixing a final terminus to the slave boundary in the Southwest. The fixing of such a terminus in the Northwest settled the agitating Missouri question. This must be settled in the same way. The Indians will easily prevent the negroes from encroaching upon them to the north. The natural destination of the latter, when the colony is no longer large enough to hold them, will be across the Rio Grande into Mexico, where by that time the government will be in the hands of the mixed negro and Indian breeds, and it will be easy for the two people to affiliate. Our western Indians will be completely sheltered in from any access to or contact with the injurious influence of any powerful foreign nation. The permanent character of the treaty allotment of homes made to the Indians by our Government will compress the whites within the present limits of the Union, and the roving mania will have to cease or find a vent in Oregon.

This arrangement would also go far toward conciliating, if it did not entirely conciliate Mexico, and thereby secure our national honor from unnecessary imputation. She would be glad to have such a barrier to the encroachment of our migratory population. With that and the Indian settlements on our west, she would deem her whole border sheltered from such unauthorized encroachments. She would be glad to see any such voluntary terminus put to what she deems the grasping ambition of our Government. She must have lost all hope of ever regaining Texas; and favor and liberality extended toward her, in adjusting the northern line of Texas, would entirely conciliate her.

The arrangement, while it fostered and promoted the peculiar views and interests of the five States more particularly interested in prospective emancipation, would allay if not satisfy the political jealousies of the North and the South. The West would be satisfied as to the security of her commercial emporium, and the craving for the good land would be appeased. The South ought to be satisfied with the accession of another slaveholding State; and the North ought to be satisfied that the threatened addition of four new slaveholding States is mitigated down to a single one, with the best sort of a guarantee that the evil to them, such as it is, must there stop, to say nothing of the increased chance of emancipation in some of the present slaveholding States. The considerate and better advised of the Southern people, such as are not mere politicians, must be more than well pleased that the injury to them from a cotton growing rivalry in Texas should be circumscribed within reasonable limits.

A more favorable occasion may never occur for obtaining the country, and at the same time conciliating these various interests and attaining the paramount object of aiding emancipation.

CHAPTER XVII.

CONSERVATIVE ADDRESS AND RESOLUTIONS.

ADOPTED BY THE CONVENTION HELD IN LOUISVILLE, FEBRUARY, 1859.

THIS convention of delegates to organize a State opposition to the further rule of the self-styled Democratic party, and to propose such an opposition by all good men throughout the nation, will state some of their objections to that party:

1. *It is essentially a Disunion Party.*

It hugs to its embrace many avowed disunionists, who, if they do not control, have great influence over the party; who, by constant agitation of the slave question, for sinister purposes, are rapidly driving the whole nation into two great sectional parties, as the precursor of disunion.

The modern Democracy, at the time of its organization, found the nation comparatively free from sectional strife. The feeling of patriotism and loyalty to the Union prevailed throughout the nation. Disunionism existed nowhere, or, if harbored in the breasts of a few, it was carefully concealed. Now, avowed disunionists may be found in every locality. Under the rule of this party all real patriotism has died out in the breasts of large masses of our countrymen. Its later career has been signalized by nothing so much as angry sectional strife, engendering the bitterest sectional animosities. We have factions in the North and in the South openly denouncing the Union in the severest terms that hatred can invent, and avowing its destruction as their principal aim.

On the eve of the last Presidential election, the conduct, public speeches, and published letters of many of the leaders of the party left little room to doubt that there was an organized treasonable conspiracy to seize the Government and break up the Union by armed force, if the election went against their party. One of the governors published his intention, in that event, to march on Washington, seize the Government by force, and to meet the opposition of sixty thousand Union-loving men in Virginia, *by arming her slaves*. Another prominent leader, who is now enjoying a seat in the Senate with the full approval of the party, in a published letter declared that any resistance to the enterprise by the Union men of North Carolina should be crushed by "*the swift attention of vigilance committees;*" in other words, by murder and assassination. "The domestic neighborhood civil war," which the Governor of Virginia said he anticipated, was to be carried on by these Democratic conspirators against their Union-loving fellow-citizens in the one State by the aid of armed slaves, and in the other by organized bands of murderers and assassins. The unrebuked public avowal of such atrocious purposes sufficiently prove the disloyalty, not merely of the leaders themselves, but also of a large portion of their followers. It is not to be believed that these men would have formed such a conspiracy or avowed such purposes unless they felt assured that they would be sustained by their party in the South. Such belief is ample proof of the general diffusion of the disunion sentiment with the great body of the party at the South. The existence of this formidable conspiracy, though frequently charged, it is believed none of these men ever pretended to deny. These facts and the industrious circulation for years past, by leaders of the party, of pamphlets, speeches, and essays, directly advocating disunion as desirable for the South, abundantly sustain the charge that it is a disunion party. But while calling for condemnation on its leaders, it is by no means intended to include the mass of their too confiding followers, and especially in Kentucky, who we fondly, proudly hope and believe are untainted with disunionism, and who will scorn any party domination leading them to that result.

2. *It is a Disorganizing, Destructive Party.*

It has destroyed the conservative elements of nearly all our State Constitutions, and gave evidence, through the utterance of some of its most influential leaders, of an intention to attack the

Federal Constitution in the same way but for the disastrous check which the party recently received.

Through its party chief and other leaders it proclaims its execrable dogma that no majority of the people can give permanent protection to minorities or individuals against the unjust aggressions of party majorities, by means of their great governmental compacts, their written constitutions. In this land of constitutional liberty, to this nation of freemen, who were taught by the great founders of the Government that constitutional liberty was the only liberty worth the having, the party proclaims, through the official message of its President, this new dogma, destructive of the stability and value of all constitutions. It proclaims, through him, the doctrine of *unrestrainable power of temporary party majorities*. To prove that they cannot be restrained to even a fair and reasonable mode prescribed by a constitution for its own alteration, President Buchanan says: "The will of the majority is supreme and irresistible. It can unmake constitutions at pleasure." He argues at length to prove that majorities cannot be confined to any particular mode, however reasonable, in altering, revoking, or remaking constitutions.

Another influential leader, one who might be selected as a specimen incarnation of the principles of modern Democracy, said, in the Senate: "The importance of State Constitutions in this country has been greatly exaggerated. In their declaration of principles they but repeat the common law which our fathers brought with them, and which would be law without such repetition. The limitations in them can be modified by the people at their pleasure. Any provision which pretends to take away that power or delay its exercise, is impotent against a majority of the people." In other words, it is impotent against the power of any temporary party majority. In still other words, the dominant party in a legislature may, within a period of two months, by the vote of a bare majority of the people, obtain power to persecute the minority into exile or even hang them for their political or religious opinions. Though this does not verify the novel discovery of this Senator, that our bills of rights "are mere repetitions of the common law," yet it must be conceded that this new theory would render them as impotent to restrain legislative power as the common law, which here and in England only lives by legislative permission.

Thus the modern progressive Democracy, through its President and other leaders, openly avows this new creed, treasonable to the cause of civil liberty, of which it has long been suspected, denying all sanctity or value to constitutions, and viewing them with disfavor, as unnecessary temporary restraints upon the *divine inalienable rights of majorities.* This party finds no cause for veneration or respect in the fact that our constitutions are the great organic compacts and covenants of the people with each other, when alone they are acting in their real sovereign capacity; that they are the great measure of right between majorities and minorities; that they are the only restraint against despotic government—that is, upon the power of a party majority; and that they afford the only security to individuals or minorities in the enjoyment of private property, freedom of conscience, freedom of speech, freedom of the press, and all other privileges that are the *birth-rights* of American freemen, and which are not the mere *concessions* of majorities. The citizen must be secure against persecution by the majority for his religious or political opinions, and secure in the enjoyment of his private property, or there is no civil liberty. He cannot be so secured but by inviolable written constitutions. This party teaches that our nation ever since its existence has been absurdly engaged in the repetition of futile efforts to secure civil liberty by means of inviolable constitutions, placed beyond the immediate reach of the heated, vindictive passions of temporary majorities. For constitutional liberty we are invited to substitute the unbridled government of the immaculate Democracy. The independence and equality of the States, the compromises of the Federal Constitution, with its protection to local rights and institutions, are to be subjected to the will of a majority of the people or of the States, or of both. The only barrier against the consolidation of all power in the Federal Government is to be yielded up to this new dogma, *the inalienable, irresistible, divine right of the majority!*

3. *It is a Double-faced Party, having one aspect for the North and another for the South.*

Many of its Northern leaders earnestly advocate a strongly protective tariff, while many of its Southern leaders say that the adoption of another protective tariff will justify and cause a dissolution of the Union.

The Northern leaders advocate squatter sovereignty, while its Southern leaders hold it in abhorrence.

Its Northern Representatives, under Southern dictation, vote for a law saying Kansas shall not be admitted into the Union without a population of ninety-three thousand, and then, to secure their re-election, pledge themselves to vote for her admission regardless of the amount of population.

Many of its Northern leaders favor internal improvements and vote for the most costly improvements ever devised, while its Southern leaders deny the power to make improvements, and the policy of such measures.

Its Northern leaders are opposed to the opening of the African slave-trade, while many of those from the South are anxiously in its favor.

Many of its Northern leaders thought the Lecompton Constitution a cheat and a swindle, which it was dishonest and tyrannical to attempt to force upon Kansas, yet some of them, under the influence of peculiar party suasion, voted a bribe to the people to induce its adoption; while all the Southern leaders voted for the force bill and the bribe, yet some of them, at least one of them, and he the most independent and talented of the whole, (Senator Hammond, of S. C.,) has since confessed that, even while so voting, he believed the Constitution to have been an execrable fraud which the South itself ought to have kicked out of Congress.

4. *It is a Party with no common Policy or fixed Principles.*

Its members agree with each other as little in regard to fundamental principles of government as they do in regard to measures of national policy.

Old-fashioned Federalists, with President Buchanan and Chief Justice Taney at their head, combine with Locofoco Democrats.

Nullifiers and strict Constitution State rights men unite with antinullifiers and the loosest latitudinarians.

Distributionists of the proceeds of the public lands mingle with opponents of that measure, and both unite in squandering the public domain for the benefit of unnaturalized foreigners and pet corporations.

Red Republicans, Socialists, and Agrarians fraternize with Southern nabobs, who advocate a property qualification for voters, (and a slaveholding qualification for representatives,) and who proclaim in the Senate the doctrine that "laboring men are everywhere the mudsills of society," and that "every man is a slave who depends upon the wages of his labor for a support."

Such are the discordant materials of the party that the President, with a proper regard to sections, cannot even organize a cabinet that harmonizes either with him or each other on the most important subjects. We find him compelled to the humiliating toleration of a Secretary of the Treasury who denounces and exerts his official influence to thwart a favorite and most important measure which the President recommends to Congress. Others of his cabinet also oppose him upon other measures. One of the chief organs of the party makes bitter complaint that it is broken into fragments, and that even those fragments are subdivided into cliques by different aspirants to the Presidency.

What Mr. Calhoun said of the party before it came under his guidance, its whole career proves to be true—"It has no cohesive principle but the power of public plunder."

5. *It is a Sectional Party.*

It has agitated the slavery question for party purposes, until it has driven nearly the whole North from its ranks. While thus agitating for the purpose of consolidating the whole South under its party rule, it was reckless of that necessary consequence, the sectionalizing of the whole North with its superior strength into an opposing party; reckless of the evil effects of bringing the whole nation to an angry, sectional contest on the slave line, and utterly reckless of the consequent peril to the Union. It was guilty of the blunder of supposing that the consolidation of the South under its rule would more than compensate all that it would lose in party strength at the North. It has not merely succeeded in sectionalizing itself, but also in sectionalizing a great opposing party at the North, which seems to have antislavery for the principal article of its creed.

While there is not a foot of territory left upon which the opposing ideas of these parties on the slavery question can have any practical bearing, yet their abstractions are made the absorbing topic of political discussion, to the infinite injury of great national interests, and the driving of nearly the whole nation into one or the other of two sectional parties, a prolonged strife between which cannot but result in disunion. While most Democrats started and have kept up the agitation of the slave question for a supposed party benefit, the disunion Democrats have co-operated with the Abolitionists in aiding the agitation, from their mutual hate of the Union.

Everything tends to prove that so long as the Democracy retains power, the Disunionists will allow the nation no peace on the slavery question. When Kansas no longer promises to keep it alive, they try to give it new vitality by advocating the opening of the African slave-trade, a scheme which, as it has no chance of success, can be founded on no motive but that of agitating. They stimulate the agitation by encouraging the smuggling of cargoes of Africans. They audaciously insult the whole nation by giving impunity to the piratical felons who effected the smuggling. They incite their grand juries to a practical sort of nullification of the nation's law, and justify them for refusing to indict the persons engaged in this piratical traffic.

With the same view, they are manifesting mock zeal for the acquisition of Cuba, while they know that Spain, through all departments of her Government, has solemnly declared that she will not sell, and when a pertinacious thrusting upon her of the offer to buy, can have no effect but to aggravate her against us, and indefinitely postpone the chance of peaceful acquisition. The scheme, if sincere, would be a gross blunder; as an electioneering trick, to furnish material for the next Presidential campaign, it is a most shallow artifice. Its surroundings have created a popular suspicion that the scheme to obtain thirty millions of secret-service money covers up an undetected plan of public plunder for private or party benefit. Groundless as that suspicion may be, there can be no doubt that the principal motive with most of the party is the reagitation of the slave question, with a view to our national elections. Impracticable as the scheme is, and so obviously calculated to injure the chance for peaceable acquisition, however desirable it may be, it must be urged from a motive paramount to the desire of acquiring Cuba, and reckless of all prejudice to that object. The motive can be found only in its desire to agitate the slave question; and for party advantage to play upon a supposed insatiable national greed for foreign territory.

6. *It is a Corrupt Party.*

It is not only corrupt itself, but has caused much corruption in most other parties. It introduced into the National Government the spoils principle for distributing patronage; and the infectious example has diffused that system throughout the nation. It is unavoidably a corrupting system. Party allegiance is the test for all offices, from the highest to the lowest. All offices and employments, national, State, county, town, or corporation, are the immense spoil for which parties contend through the ballot-box. The necessary natural consequence ensues; the ballot-box has become thoroughly corrupt. Bribery, box-stuffing, illegal voting, forged certificates of naturalization, false returns, and all manner of frauds have become the regular accompaniments of every national election. For this corruption, the Democracy is more responsible than any other party, or all other parties. It has systematized and extended this corruption so far that it is somewhat doubtful whether the incensed nation can wage a successful resistance through the ballot-box against its corrupt office-holders. According to Democratic discipline, all holders of civil office, and all contractors, have to pay a heavy tax on their salaries and earnings toward raising an enormous corruption fund for carrying elections. This fund, wielded by more than a hundred thousand well-drilled officeholders, renders the party truly formidable.

Useless offices are multiplied, and extravagant compensation allowed to increase the power of the party. Witness the many custom-houses where the duties collected are not a fifth, and, in some instances, not a tenth of the expense of collection. The grossest frauds and peculations are winked at from supposed party necessity. There is no vigilant, honest eye anywhere superintending the expenditure of the people's money.

The details of all this corruption cannot now be gone into; but by way of summary proof, take the indignant avowals of two distinguished Democratic leaders, made in the Senate, without contradiction or rebuke from any quarter. One of them, Senator Toombs, said that in his opinion "ours is the most corrupt government in the world." The other, Senator Johnson, of Tennessee, said that if the people only knew the extent of the corruption, "they would come to Washington and pitch the whole concern into the Potomac." Such was not the character of the Government when it came into the hands of this party. All this corruption has grown up since then.

In a published letter, written by President Buchanan in 1852, in order to explain what he deemed the then exorbitant expenditure of the Government, he said: "Money from the national treasury is continually demanded *to enrich contractors, speculators, and agents*, and the projects are gilded over with every allurement which can be imparted by ingenuity or talent." Let it be remembered that these contractors, speculators, and agents are Democrats, and that the gilding is done by talented leaders of the party, and his explanation becomes perfectly satisfactory why the expenditures have so enormously increased under Democratic rule, and especially during the last six years, under the administration of himself and President Pierce. No men have done more than these two Presidents and their cabinets to fulfill Mr. Buchanan's prophecy, viz., "The corrupting power of money will be felt throughout the length and breadth of the land," and the "public money employed by artful and ambitious demagogues for their own aggrandizement." The corrupting power is already so felt, and the public money so employed. Every one must concur with him that "genuine liberty must soon expire," under such a condition of our national affairs.

Some twenty years ago the Democracy found National and State banks a great power in the land, not under the direct influence or control of the party. To remove this inconvenience it broke down the National Bank, and instituted the notorious pet bank system with a Democratic promise to give the nation a "better currency." In a few years the banks all exploded and the system with them, giving, as the result of that Democratic experiment, the worst currency ever known, and the most wide-spread commercial disaster and ruin ever witnessed. The national loss to traders, manufacturers, and business men of all classes was moderately computed by the hundreds of millions.

The Democracy then told the nation that it must take care of itself in the matter of its currency. That the Democracy would render it no aid but that of a good example. It proclaimed its intention to cut the Government entirely loose from all connection with the nation's business currency, make it a purely hard money Government, which was effectively to restrain undue expansions, and in every event enable the Government to transact its own great business in hard money, and in that alone.

Uninfluenced by the example, no State adopted the experiment, but all made more banks, which, uninfluenced by the panacea, expanded more than they had ever done, and there occurred one of those suspensions which seem to be part of the law of the existence of State banks. After the lapse of a few months, the banks resumed specie payments, and the nation and the State Governments have ever since enjoyed a redeemable currency equal to specie, while the Federal Government has been compelled to resort to a paper circulation of inconvertible treasury notes, which the Secretary of the Treasury tells us must be kept up for two years longer.

This experiment having utterly failed in all its promised advantages, the Democracy promptly steps forward and offers the nation the benefit of still another experiment. It says through its organ, the President, that the States are too lenient toward their banks, and hence their undue expansion; only place them under Democratic control, let them live in salutary fear of inexorable Federal rigor, and there will be no more suspensions. Only give us a bankrupt law against banks and railroads, and you have our assurance that all shall be well; the banks shall cease all undue expansions, and railroads forbear improvidently to incur debts. But should these just expectations fail, should the banks and railroads fail so to act, then they are to have inexorable law, their property and that of their debtors, including the whole trading community, shall be brought under the sacrificing hammer of Federal officials, and thus "the equilibrium restored;" that is, the rapid adjustment of all debts, at whatever sacrifice of property the experiment may require.

The nation has long been fully aware, as much as Mr. Buchanan or his Secretary of the Treasury can make them, that a periodical suspension is one of the unavoidable accompaniments of its State bank system. But great as that evil is, it is not comparable to the evil of making our banks and railroads dependent upon the smiles and frowns of Federal Democratic rulers for a lenient or rigorous enforcement of a bankrupt law. Nor does the evil compare with what would ensue from the honest, rigorous enforcement of such a law at a time of general suspension, in the unavoidable sacrifice of every trader's or business man's property. The nation needs no experiment to tell what would be the result of a sudden enforcement by law of all individual debts. Every one ought to know that an almost universal bankruptcy would be the result. That the Democracy would be sufficiently inexorable in such a crisis, may well be allowed. While the nation was writhing under the effects of the "better currency" experiment, the wail of woe which it sent up to Democratic headquarters was curtly answered with memorable apothegm: "All who trade on credit deserve to break." Put the power in the hands of the Democracy, and it may be relied on to carry out this its maxim. As little will the nation be inclined to confide to the inexorable Democracy the power of needlessly breaking up those very beneficial institutions, our railroads, by a sudden rigorous enforcement of their debts.

7. *It is an Extravagant, Wasteful Party.*

The conclusive proof of this lies in the fact that under its rule the annual expenditures have increased from less than twenty to more than eighty millions.

The single item of five million spent in two congressional terms for public printing, and the waste of six hundred thousand dollars annually in collecting the revenue, as stated in the report of even a Democratic committee, supersede the necessity of any detailed exposure of extravagance.

In the published letter of President Buchanan before referred to, he complained that in 1852 the annual expenditures "*have reached the enormous sum of fifty million*," and predicts that, "unless arrested by the *strong arm of the Democracy*, may in the course of a few years reach a hundred million." "I am convinced our expenditures ought to be considerably reduced below the present standard, not only without detriment, but with advantage to the Government and the people." The "strong arm of the Democracy" has had control of the finances for the last six years, and, instead of arresting waste and extravagance, they have been nearly doubled in amount. Such is the contrast between Democratic performance and its promise while seeking popular favor. Thus Mr. Buchanan, the most competent and reliable witness in such a case, proves the wasteful extravagance of the *honest* Democracy!

The wasteful donation of public lands enabled the directors of a single railroad to use a million of dollars in bribing the passage of the scheme through Congress and the Wisconsin Legislature, as fully proved before a legislative committee. This is one instance out of many that might be adduced to prove how the national treasure and domain are squandered, as Mr. Buchanan says, "to enrich contractors, speculators, and agents."

This summary of only a part of the misrule, shows the necessity of a combined effort of all opponents of the corrupt Democracy to rescue the Government from its evil grasp. The defeat of that party is a great national necessity—the indispensable prerequisite to any reform. That is the only mode by which power can be placed in the hands of honest men, who will—

1. Prevent disunion and check disunion tendencies.
2. Give peace to the nation on the slavery question.
3. Give an honest, economical administration of the Government, and stop spoliations of the treasury and national domain.
4. Not give injurious control to the Federal Government over State banks and railroads, by means of a bankrupt law, as recommended by our Democratic President and Secretary of the Treasury.
5. Not permit the substitution of direct taxation in lieu of duties on imports, to raise revenue for enormous national expenses, as recommended by a Democratic committee.
6. Not permit the transfer of the war-making power to a Presi-

dent, nor allow him to make treaties without the supervising control of the Senate, nor trust him with an enormous secret service corruption fund, to be used either abroad or at home.

7. Not attempt the acquisition of Cuba by any but honorable means.

8. Not permit the importation of foreign felons or paupers.

9. Not squander the national domain in donations to unnaturalized foreigners and pet corporations, but keep it as a sacred trust for all the States, to whom it belongs.

In conclusion, deeming, as we do, the defeat of the Democratic party a great public necessity, for the reasons already stated, and many more, we would rejoice to see patriotic citizens throughout the Union abandoning those unprofitable disputes which have been the main instrument of perpetuating power in the hands of the unscrupulous Democracy, combined together for its overthrow. But co-operation or union, by the Opposition of Kentucky, is, now and forever, utterly undesirable and impossible with any party or persons who seek, by the action of the Federal Government, through any of its departments, to interfere with the institution of slavery; and we declare that we can have no affiliation whatever with disunionists or abolitionists. All others are invited to a cordial affiliation on terms of perfect equality.

CHAPTER XVIII.

THE ISSUES OF THE CAMPAIGN.

Published July, 1859.

The great objects of the Opposition are—*saving the Union, peace on the slave question, and an honest economical administration.*

To this end they propose to proscribe sectional partyism, break up or put down the Democratic and Republican sectional parties by a combination of conservative Union men from all parties.

The necessity for such effort to save the Union arises from the undisputed fact of a conspiracy among most of the Southern Democratic Governors and members of Congress to dissolve the Union by armed violence and civil war if the Republican candidate had been elected President at the last election. Also from the admitted fact that there is a wide-spread and desperate conspiracy at the South to dissolve the Union if a Republican President should be chosen at the next election, a contingency almost certain to occur unless the intervention of a conservative party shall prevent the triumph of either of the sectional parties over the other. Also from the obvious fact that prolonged collision between two such sectional parties must necessarily result in disunion, even if that does not immediately ensue from the election of a Republican President.

By way of permanent peace, ignore the slave question as a party issue, so far as it can be done consistently with the firm and stern maintenance of our constitutional rights as interpreted by the Supreme Court of the United States.

The special reasons for breaking up the Democratic party, over and above its sectionalism and its disunion affinities and tendencies, are mainly these:—

First. Its disorganizing, destructive, usurping tendency. Having destroyed nearly all the conservative elements of our State constitutions, and threatening the same upon the Federal Constitution.

Seeking to establish the pernicious dogma that our constitutions, those sacred safeguards of civil liberty, those protectors of the rights of property, and especially slave property, are always and immediately under the power of a dominant party who may break them up without regard to the mode of alteration, however reasonable, prescribed by the people in those constitutions.

Seeking to put the treaty-making power into the hands of their party chief—the President—freed from a necessary salutary control of the Senate.

Seeking to take from Congress, and give to their party chief, the war-making power, together with the abandonment of the long-cherished national policy of non-interference with the affairs of other nations.

Seeking to give the Federal Government pernicious control over the State banks and railroads, through the instrumentality of a bankrupt law.

Second. Its double-faced duplicity. Having one set of principles and policy for the North and another for the South, and no common cohesive principle but the power of public plunder.

It is a great amalgam of men without regard to principle. Old Federalists and Locofoco Democrats, Nullifiers, Disunionists, Tariffites, Distributioners, Internal Improvement men, Strict Construction States' Right men, Red Republicans, Socialists, Agrarians, Free-Soilers, Slaveholding Nabobs, Ultra Pro-slavery Fire-eaters,—are all mingled with their opposites,—even their President not agreeing as to subjects of great national policy with his own cabinet, nor the members of the cabinet with each other.

Third. Its corruption. Having, according to the indignant avowal of one of its own chiefs, rendered ours "the most corrupt government in the world;" and, according to that of another of its chiefs, fit to be "pitched into the Potomac."

According to the admission, and attempted justification of its principal newspaper organs, levying black mail from all officers and contractors to retain power by corrupting the ballot-box. The enormous amount of the corruption fund thus raised may be judged from the fact that a single contractor, residing in Massachusetts, paid $16,000 toward carrying the Pennsylvania elections in 1856, as was proven before a congressional committee.

Giving the patronage of the navy yards to Democratic members to promote their elections, and filling the yards with useless and incompetent men for the same purpose. Giving contracts to the highest instead of the lowest bidder, and large lucrative contracts without competing bids with the same object. Giving $15,000 a year as compensation to an incompetent coal agent, who did nothing to earn his commissions excepting the making a flagrantly dishonest contract for coal, permitting the seller to be both *weigher and inspector;* the compensation to the agent being so grossly excessive that the President himself required its division among two others of his political pets.

Compelling all persons seeking contracts to buy the influence of leading Democrats, at commissions varying from five to twenty per cent. on the gross amount of the contracts. Such prominent Democrats as the late Chairman of the Committee of Ways and Means, and now Minister to Austria, taking these commissions while a member of Congress. One of these written contracts for pay for influence having been brought under the notice of President Buchanan, he said he saw no objection to it.

Useless offices multiplied and extravagant compensation allowed to increase the power of the party.

Rendering the ballot-box thoroughly corrupt. Bribery, box-stuffing, illegal voting, double, treble, quadruple voting, forged certificates of naturalization, false returns, and all manner of frauds procured by the Democracy, have become the constant mode of carrying every important election.

Reversing the decision of his immediate predecessor, rendered upon the advice of the proper army officers, the present Secretary of War determined to sell the Fort Snelling Reservation without any such advice or consultation. He kept his determination secret except from three or four persons, to whom he made a private sale, at a sacrifice to the Government of certainly not less than $100,000, and, in the opinion of respectable witnesses, a great deal more. One of the persons to whom he made this secret private sale is a New York broker, who had been in the habit of loaning money to the Secretary, and who at the time was $20,000 in advance for him.

Keeping up, for party purposes, the excitement on the slavery question, by pretended extra zeal for the purchase of Cuba, when it is known that Cuba cannot be bought, and clamoring for a repeal of the prohibition of the African slave-trade, when it is known that the repeal cannot be had; and wantonly insulting the North by saying that Kansas had population enough to be admitted as a slave State, but not half enough to be admitted as a free State.

Deciding, at one session, for the purpose of keeping out two Republican Senators, that the rule hereafter, in admitting States, should be to require ninety-three thousand; and then at the next session, for the purpose of admitting two Democratic Senators, disregarding their own rule, and admitting Oregon, with a population of only forty thousand.

Deciding, at one session, after full discussion and deliberation, when the effect was only to reject a Republican Senator, that the continuing assent of a majority of members of each branch of a legislature was requisite to a legal election; and then at the next deciding, for the purpose of retaining two Democratic Senators, that a fraudulent election was valid, though one branch never assented to, but protested against it, when a majority of the members of that branch were not present, and when a constitutional quorum of neither house was present.

Fourth. Its wasteful extravagance. Increasing the public expenditures, for purposes other than the national debt, in six years, from about forty-three to upwards of seventy million.

Making enormous donations of public lands to pet corporations —enabling a corporation in one instance, as proved, to spend a million of dollars in bribing national and State officials.

Attempting to give one hundred and sixty acres of land to every unnaturalized foreigner who would settle on it.

CHAPTER XIX.

DISTRICTING POWER OF CONGRESS.

PREAMBLE AND RESOLUTIONS OF THE LEGISLATURE OF KENTUCKY, MARCH 1, 1844.

WHEREAS, by the sole action of the House of Representatives of the Congress of the United States, the second section of the Act of Congress for the apportionment of representatives among the several States, according to the sixth census, has been declared null and void, we deem it our duty to make the most solemn and formal protest against the recent action of that House on this subject.

The second section of the act which the House of Representatives has thus attempted to annul, provides that representatives in Congress shall be elected by *single* districts, composed of contiguous territory. The necessity for this provision had become not merely obvious, but urgent. Further delay in the exercise of this necessary and important power would have put in peril the permanency of the fundamental structure of the General Government. The whole theory of the Constitution clearly demonstrates that the States, in their aggregate or corporate capacity, were to be represented, *as States*, in the Senate, while the people were to be represented in the other House, *as one nation*, on fair principles of popular representation. What was considered a fair popular representation by the framers of the Constitution, may be learned from the practice in the election of members to the various State legislatures at the period of its adoption, from the election of members of the Colonial legislatures and of the English House of Commons; as also from all contemporaneous exposition and discussion. None of these sources of information authorize the presumption that it was at all within the contemplation of the framers of the Constitution that the principle of a fair popular representation could be secured by a general ticket system, requiring the whole population of a State, amounting to three or four millions, to vote for an entire delegation, consisting of thirty or forty members. On the contrary, they all imply that the principle of fair popular representation requires such a subdivision of the constituent body as will bring the representative as near as may be within the personal acquaintance of those he represents, and subject him to an available accountability. They also all strongly imply that the true principles of republican government require that minorities, among political parties in a State, should have some chance of a voice in the national councils. The wise founders of our institutions did not lack the sagacity to perceive the great importance, as well to the majority as the minority, of having the conduct of those to whom the people's rights were confided watched and reported on by one or more vigilant and interested sentinels from the opposing party.

This equal, just, and truly republican principle of representation had been not merely violated, but that equipoise of the whole constitutional fabric which is based upon it had been put in peril by the action of several of the States. Six of them had already adopted the general ticket system, thereby giving to some of the smaller States more actual strength in the councils of the nation than the largest States. This gross inequality and injustice had justly become the subject of general comment and complaint. It induced, some years back, the serious agitation of the question in our own Legislature, as to the propriety of adopting the general ticket system; and nothing but deference to the sanctity due even to the inferential theory of the Constitution prevented the dominant party from remedying the injustice, as to our State, by seizing the political party advantage which would have ensued from that system. Its adoption by one such State as Kentucky, in the heated temper of the public mind at that time, would have insured its speedy adoption, on plain principles of justifiable self-defense, by every other State in the Union. Once adopted by the large States, all chance for correcting the evil, either by constitutional amendment or congressional legislation, would have been lost forever, and there would have ensued a most pernicious, radical and irremediable revolution in the whole structure of the Government.

In view of this peril, and in avoidance of this national calamity, Congress acted in prescribing the district system. The act received not merely our hearty approval, but we had supposed that, as was its due, it had met with the great sanction of the national approbation. It rested for its validity on the plainest and most indisputable of the undoubted powers of Congress, and on a policy whose wisdom was conceded even by those who opposed the passage of the law. Self-respect, not that which may be supposed to be due to those who are abusing the powers of a co-ordinate department of the Government, induces us to forbear from a full expression of the surprise, the alarm, the indignation we felt at finding a majority of the House of Representatives daring to treat this law as a nullity; so treating it too, under circumstances calculated to induce the suspicion that it is done for the purpose of accomplishing a party advantage, and on reasons so flimsy as not to be worthy of the designation of plausible pretexts.

In seeking for these reasons we have gone to what may be deemed the highest authority, the report of the committee to whom the subject was referred, upon whose recommendation the House acted, and who have, no doubt, brought into requisition, for the purpose of glossing over the proceeding, all the most plausible pretexts that could be invented. The question as to the power of Congress to pass this act, depends on the proper construction of the following clause of the Constitution:—

"The times, places, and manner of holding elections for Senators and Representatives, shall be prescribed in each State, by the legislature thereof; but the Congress may, at any time, by law, make or alter such regulations, except as to the places of choosing Senators." There needs no juster comment on this section than the following, taken from the report of this committee:

"It will be observed that the two clauses of this section differ materially in the tone in which they address the different governments. The one is *commanded* and the other *permitted* to act. The State legislature *shall* prescribe the times, places, and manner of holding elections; Congress *may* make or alter such regulations. An imperative duty rests upon the State legislatures, while a mere privilege is granted to Congress. If the Legislatures of the States fail or refuse to act in the premises, or act in such a manner as will be *subversive of the rights of the people and the principles of the Constitution*, then this conservative power interposes, and, on the principle of self-preservation, authorizes Congress to do that which the State legislatures ought to have done."

Holding, as we do, that the general ticket system is *subversive of the rights of the people and the principles of the Constitution*, the occasion had occurred which called for the exercise of this discretionary power, by Congress, to put an end to that system. This opinion is not controverted by the committee, and cannot be successfully controverted by any one. As the Constitution confers on Congress the power to substitute an entire system of its own, or merely to *alter* that of the States, the inference is irresistible that Congress may, at its own discretion, legislate upon a part only, without engrossing the whole subject. This is so obvious that the committee has not even ventured to deny it, but fully admits it.

Having conceded that Congress may legislate upon a part, without exercising the whole power, by what principle or rule of construction does the committee make the broad and bold assumption, that if Congress assumes the power over one branch of the subject, its legislation must be complete to that extent, so as to execute itself without the intervention of the State legislatures? The Constitution does not say so, but leaves it entirely in the discretion of Congress to exert the whole or any part, however large or small, of the power conferred, and at the same time makes it the imperative *duty* of the State legislatures to supply any deficiencies. "Congress may alter such regulations," says the Constitution. Which regulations? The whole or any. How alter them? In whole or in part. The power wholly to change or abolish must necessarily include the authority to modify in any, the smallest particular. The greater must, in the nature of things, include the less. If Congress be authorized to *alter* the regulations adopted by the States, as the committee is constrained to admit, that authority must of necessity embrace the power to adopt the slightest modifications of those regulations which the wisdom of Congress may suggest. It may *alter* the time in part, the places in part, and the manner in part; either or all. Any such partial alteration necessarily leaves the remainder of the subject to be acted on by State legislation. To prescribe the whole mode of electing representatives is the entirety of the subject, over any and every part of which Congress has discretionary control. In the exercise of that control there is no limitation, it is not confined to any arbitrary classification or subdivision of the whole, as times, places, and manner, but may exert just so much of its authority as it may deem fit. If it touches the subject at all, it is as much bound to carry out the whole subject and leave nothing for State legislation to fill up, as it is to carry out that particular part which it does touch. There is nothing in the language of the Constitution, or the nature of the subject requiring or authorizing a distinction between them. Thus, Congress may say, that all the elections shall be held in the month of November, or in any week of that or any other month, without designating on what particular day of the week or month, or whether the election shall be held on one only or on several days. So it may say, that every voter shall vote in the county in which he resides, without designating at what particular place or places in the county the election shall be held; or that the election shall be held by general ticket or by single districts. Each of these alterations of existing modes is as much within the competency of Congress as either of the others, or any that can be devised; they all alike requiring State legislation to carry them out and make a complete mode of election. Indeed there is no conceivable mode of partial legislation on this subject by Congress, which can "execute itself" in the sense of the committee. With the forced concessions of the committee, it is not even open to dispute that Congress has the power to declare that all the elections shall be held by general ticket. Yet such a law could no more execute itself than the present one. There would still be many necessary provisions which would have to be added by State legislation; such as, by whom the elections should be held, how the votes should be given, what evidence of the qualifications of voters should be admitted, how returns should be made, etc. The States could with as much propriety in the one case as the other say, that as Congress had undertaken to interfere in the matter, let it perfect its own legislation, we will not submit to its mandate to finish by our legislation its incomplete work. The unavoidable concession being made, that Congress may legislate in part, leaving the remainder of the subject untouched, it is worse than ridiculous to contend that it is not necessarily and entirely within its discretion how much shall be left for State legislation, or that there are particular parts of the subject which may be left to such legislation, while there are others that cannot be so left. There being, however, no manner of partial congressional legislation which can "execute itself," the argument of the committee is reduced to the palpable absurdity of admitting a power, but denying that it can be exercised.

So far from there being any incongruity growing out of the nature of the subject in this partial exercise of its power by Congress, leaving the remainder to be exerted by the States, there are a peculiar fitness and propriety in its so acting, which strongly persuade us to believe that such was the intention of the framers of the Constitution. Every principle of justice and equality inculcates that, whatever be the mode, whether by single districts or general ticket, the system should be uniform throughout the Union. Mr. Madison, who, more appropriately than any other man, may be termed the Father of the Constitution, declared in the Virginia Convention, that one of the leading objects of vesting this power in Congress was to produce uniformity in the mode of election. This uniformity, whether by single districts or general ticket, can be produced by congressional legislation only. It cannot be effected by State legislation, because of the improbability, not to say impossibility, of twenty-six different States voluntarily and without concert adopting the same measures. Yet of the two, State legislation is much the most appropriate for laying off the districts. Indeed, except in the case of a State willfully neglecting to form districts for itself, it would be an abuse of this discretionary power for Congress to undertake to form the districts. It is much to be feared that in Congress the formation of districts would be made solely with a view to party advantage, the majority of those making them being free from any direct responsibility to those more particularly affected by them.

Be that, however, as it may, for many obvious reasons the people will never consent, except in cases of absolute necessity, that Congress shall exercise the power of laying off the districts. The power must therefore forever remain a mere dead letter, and never be brought into practical exercise, except in the manner it was used in the last Congress; and, if that mode of its use be surrendered, the general ticket system must become the universal system in a few years.

But, the committee says, Congress has no power to issue a mandamus to the States, commanding what legislation they shall adopt. This truism surely did not need the solemn enunciation of a committee of Congress in the absence of pertinency or application. It being conceded that Congress may not only entirely change, but alter, in part, the modes of the States, surely the States must be bound to conform to the alteration; for, as the committee says, "so much of the power as shall not be embraced in the legislation of Congress, the Constitution makes it the imperative duty of the States to carry into effect." Congress having the right to exercise the power in part, and having exercised it as far as was deemed proper, the mandate for the after legislation of the States comes not from Congress, but from the Constitution.

The committee, in the absence of all argument drawn from the language of the Constitution, attempts to assimilate this to two other cases, to neither of which does it bear the slightest analogy. First, they say that Congress, by partial legislation on the subject of bankruptcy, could not compel the States to legislate on the remainder of that subject. Certainly not, for the Constitution nowhere says that the States *shall* legislate on any part of that subject; but it does say they *shall* legislate on the subject of the times, places, and manner of electing representatives. Second, the committee says that if Congress should pass a law requiring all the elections to be held on one day, without designating that day, such law would be nugatory, because there would be no certain day to which all the States would conform. This is true, and the analogy would be just, if Congress had said there should be one uniform manner without designating that manner, whether by single districts or general ticket. But in the case under consideration, the manner *is* designated and a general rule given, to which the States can as easily conform as they could to a particular day.

There is one and but one completely analogous precedent in the whole complex system of our Government, which, though it could not have escaped its attention, is left wholly unnoticed by the committee. The Constitution, after declaring that each State *shall* appoint Presidential electors in the manner its legislature may direct, goes on to say that "Congress *may* determine the time of choosing the electors." In pursuance of this provision, Congress, in 1792, passed an act, that electors shall be chosen within the thirty-four days next preceding the first Wednesday in December, without designating any particular day or days for holding the elections, but leaving it to each legislature to designate its own day within those limits. This law was passed by the framers of the Constitution, acquiesced in and conformed to by the legislatures of all the States; it is in force to this day, and its validity has never been called in question. Here the Constitution left it discretionary with Congress to determine the time of holding the elections; Congress exercised only a part of the power, and, contrary to the rule laid down by the committee, its legislation was not only not complete, but could not "execute itself without the intervention of the State legislatures," for, if the legislatures had not intervened to fix a certain day, the law would have been a mere nullity from uncertainty. The parallel between the two cases is therefore perfect, and the astutest intellect cannot detect the slightest available distinction between them. That law was as much in the nature of a mandamus from Congress to the States, commanding them to legislate upon the subject so as to supply the omission of a precise day for holding the elections, as this can be for forming the required districts. That case is even stronger than this, for it is not absolutely beyond dispute that Congress had a right there to act only on a part of the subject.

1. *Resolved by the General Assembly of the Commonwealth of Kentucky*, That the adoption, by a majority of the States, of the general ticket system of electing Representatives to Congress, would be subversive of the true republican principle of popular representation, of the theory of the Constitution, and inflict an irremediable national calamity.

2. That at the time of the adoption of the apportionment act of 1842, there was urgent need of the interposition of Congress, by prescribing the district system, to prevent the further spread of a great national evil.

3. That the manner in which Congress did interpose by the second section of that act, was not merely within its undoubted

competency, but was in the only rightful manner in which Congress should ever exercise its discretionary power over that subject, except in the case of a State willfully neglecting to adopt the necessary legislation.

4. That Congress having prescribed the general rule, it is the plain duty of the States, under the imperative mandate of the Constitution, to conform thereto by all needful legislation.

5. That the power in Congress to produce uniformity in the mode of elections, by prescribing the district system as the only mode, is vitally important to the well-being of the republic; and it is the duty of the Senators and Representatives of Kentucky to resist all attempts to annul or abrogate that power, as exercised in the second section of the apportionment act of 1842.

6. That in behalf of the people of this Commonwealth, we do most solemnly *protest* against the recent action of the House of Representatives in Congress, in nullifying that law, as a flagrant abuse of the power of that House, and an outrageous violation of the Constitution and the law.

CHAPTER XX.

THE DRED SCOTT CASE.

REVIEWED MARCH, 1857.

IN reviewing the decision in this case, the subject will be divided into—

1*st*. *The jurisdiction.*

2*d*. *The derivation of congressional power over territories.*

3*d*. *The extent of congressional power over territories.*

4*th*. *The power to prohibit slavery.*

5*th*. *The policy and justice of the Missouri Compromise.*

THE JURISDICTION.

The majority of the Court decided that plaintiff, Scott, being a negro, he could not be a citizen of Missouri; that therefore the Circuit Court had no jurisdiction over the case; and it was accordingly remanded, with directions to be *dismissed for want of jurisdiction.*

Having so decided, the Court should have stopped there, and not attempted to go any further into the case. All beyond that was extra-judicial, and entitled to no further respect than if the judges had expressed the same opinions in a debating club, or had published them in a newspaper for the undisguised purpose of aiding a political party.

There are, no doubt, instances where other judges have extra-judicially expressed opinions on points not properly cognizable in the cases before them; but with good judges such instances have been rare, and they never occur without meeting the serious censure of every judicious member of the bar. They always partake, more or less, of what is most obnoxious to an American lawyer. They are, in fact, *usurpations of power.* The only apology for them, and the only instances where they should be tolerated, is when they afford the means of informing inferior courts of the settled opinion of an appellate court upon matters of practice, or such like minor points, where it is fully as important that they should be settled as that they should be rightly decided. The attempt, thus prematurely and extra-judicially, to reach points involving political or constitutional law, is especially to be deprecated. We all acquire our prepossessions and prejudices on these subjects before attaining the bench, and nothing about poor human nature would warrant a popular belief that the mere putting on of the judicial ermine will always eradicate such preconceived prejudices. The Supreme Court has heretofore been very chary of its power to annul an act of Congress. It has been viewed as a delicate, invidious power, only to be used when absolutely necessary, and even then only with the utmost caution and circumspection. This is believed to be the first instance in which the Court has attempted to annul a long course of congressional legislation upon a matter of much importance.

There are peculiar reasons why the majority of the judges should, in this case, have done nothing extra-judicial to foist upon the country their premature opinions upon the points unnecessarily raised. Those points were among the most prominent issues in the late heated party contest for the Presidency. They still are, and will long continue to be, subjects of the most angry party strife. One of the parties was accused with having, for party ends, wantonly violated a great national compromise, adopted for the sake of peace, and cheerfully acquiesced in for more than thirty years as a great and needful national pacificator. The party was also accused of having at the same time, for like purpose, wantonly violated its most solemn party pledge, not to permit the slavery question to be again agitated in or out of Congress. This rendered the extra-judicial points raised subjects of extreme delicacy, and such as should have induced any judges to manifest reluctance to decide even when properly before them, rather than any undue eagerness to seize hold of and prematurely to decide them. This sort of proper delicacy should have had controlling influence with these judges. They should not have forgotten, they should not for a moment have overlooked the fact, that every man of them owed his elevation to the bench full as much to his affiliation with that offending party as to any presumable superior qualification. They should not have forgotten, that for the foolish—not to say wicked—action of the party upon the main point involved, it had narrowly escaped disastrous overthrow at the last, and fearfully anticipated complete defeat at the next Presidential election. They should not have forgotten, that to declare the Missouri Compromise unconstitutional was to afford their party leaders a justification which few of them had the audacity to allege in their own behalf; and that such a decision was worth to them ten times more than all the apologies they had been able to invent.

Still another reason, on the score of delicacy, for such forbearance. The three judges who did not concur in the opinion may fairly be offset against the three ablest of the six who did. There were then but three, and they the least able judges on the bench, who had to sustain the full weight of this novel opinion, to be thus prematurely and illegally thrust upon the country. Congress had exercised the power, or its equivalent, in various instances, without its constitutionality having been seriously challenged by any man of respectable standing as a constitutional lawyer. It had done so with the sanction of Washington, Adams, Jefferson, Madison, Monroe, J. Q. Adams, and Polk, and, as is believed, with the entire approbation, so far at least as to the mere question of power, of all the very able lawyers and statesmen who composed the cabinets of those Presidents. The power had been exercised with the reiterated direct and indirect sanction of the able judges of appellate courts in at least three slave and at least four free States, while the decision of no appellate court had anywhere impugned the validity of the power. Any three judges, even though they were all Mansfields or Marshalls, should have felt a natural repugnance to the poising their peculiar novel opinion against such a host of able lawyers, judges, and statesmen.

There is still another *legal* reason why these judges should have forborne to express any opinion on the constitutionality of the Missouri Compromise. They decide, or rather say, that the voluntary sojourn of the master with his slave in Illinois, under the influence of its constitution, did not emancipate the slave. They say it is the law of Missouri, and not that of Illinois, which determines his condition, and that, by the law of Missouri, he is still a slave. The same rule applies, and of course determines, the effect of like sojourn in territories under the influence of the act of Congress, even if it be constitutional. As Congress could no more legislate for Missouri on this subject than could the people of Illinois, the law of Missouri will respect the one no more than the other. There was no need, therefore, to go beyond that point. Everything was decided which was necessary to a final decision of the case on its merits, even if there had been any right to look into the merits at all. That point decided against him, the right of the slave to freedom was gone forever. There was no need, then, in any aspect of the case, for one word being said about the constitutionality of the Missouri Compromise. This is an all-sufficient legal reason why no attempt should have been made at an *authoritative* utterance of such word. But as, unfortunately, the members of the Court were divided in opinion on that question, and as, still more unfortunately, the judges were divided according to their party affinities, the Court should have sedulously abstained from any, the slightest intimation of opinion upon the point.

In excuse for the assumption of jurisdiction to decide upon the merits of the case, the Court says that it is the habit of appellate courts, in reviewing judgments at law, not to stop at a single error, but to point out all that occurred in the progress of the cause. This, ordinarily, is true; and it is done for the purpose of preventing similar errors on a new trial. But it is not true that this is done when the judgment is reversed, and the cause remanded, with directions to dismiss for want of jurisdiction. On the contrary, the appellate court stops at that mandate, and looks no further into the cause. The obvious reason for this difference is, that any notice of other errors can do no good, as there can be no recurrence of such errors. Such is the rule and the reason of it, upon principles of mere practice. But it is also based upon much higher and more important principles. Where a court undertakes to decide a cause over which it has no jurisdiction, it acts without authority, and its action is as gross a violation of the Constitution as the most palpably unconstitutional legislative act. The very same reasons that forbade the Circuit Court to decide the cause, equally rendered it illegal and improper in the Supreme Court to pass upon the main question, whether the negro was free. Its jurisdiction for such purpose is but a mere sequence to that of the Circuit Court. There can be no grosser legal absurdity than to contend for its power to pass upon the merits when it decides that the Circuit Court had no such power. All of the appellate power is merely to do, or direct to be done, what the inferior courts should have done in the first instance. Both courts must have power to decide the merits, or neither can have it. The want of jurisdiction is alike fatal to the legitimate action of both.

If the Court had contented itself with its decision upon the plea in abatement, reversed the judgment, and directed the cause to be dismissed for want of jurisdiction, there would have been nothing left by which either party could be prejudiced. They would have stood precisely as though no suit had been brought.

Nor does the Court contradict this. It does not insist that a decision on the merits was at all necessary to either party, as it could give no judgment in favor of either; but insists that such a course was necessary for itself, to prevent its being misconstrued hereafter, as seeming to sanction an error of the Circuit Court by reason of not having noticed that error. This is perfectly disingenuous. There was not the slightest possible danger of any such misconstruction. But even if there had been, it would have been easily obviated in the usual mode, by merely saying the Court had not looked into the merits, because, having no jurisdiction over that part of the cause, its opinion either way could avail nothing to the parties. After deciding that a free negro could not be such a citizen as to give the Court jurisdiction, it was wholly unnecessary, for any purpose, to make a solemn separate decision that a slave could not be such a citizen. It is perfectly preposterous to suppose there was the least danger of any one surmising that the Court thought a slave was such a citizen. Yet upon this shallow pretext, and upon this alone, these judges have plunged into a subject of angry dispute between the great political parties. The question of jurisdiction, and the whole case being sufficiently disposed of by the decision on the plea in abatement, the very fact that the other pretended question of jurisdiction involved an investigation of the merits, was all-sufficient reason against such investigation. Where the Court has no jurisdiction, it is its plain, universally-recognized duty not to express any opinion on the merits, when it can be avoided. To what good end inquire and decide whether the negro was a slave, when the decision upon the case would have been the same even if he had been free?

Derivation of Power over the Territories.

It had heretofore been supposed by jurists and statesmen that this power was derived from the following clause of the Constitution:—

"Congress shall have power to dispose of and make all needful rules and regulations respecting the territory or other property belonging to the United States."

The Court decides that this clause applies only to the territory within the national bounds at the adoption of the Constitution, and not at all to after-acquired territory. This novel distinction, or new reading, it has invented for the undisguised object of getting rid of the legislative and judicial precedents in favor of the power to prohibit slavery in what was formerly the territory northwest of the Ohio. This position would avail the Court nothing, even if its elaborate effort thus to pervert the Constitution had been as successful as it has been utterly unsuccessful. But an exposure of the flimsy reasoning with which it has, at infinite pains, endeavored to make good its position, will expose the undue anxiety of the Court to declare the Missouri Compromise unconstitutional. What was intended for reasoning is in fact little better than a string of loose suggestions, of such flimsy texture that their impalpable character presents the only difficulty in answering them with desired brevity.

Our ablest commentators on the Constitution, Kent and Story, derive the power of Congress over all the territories, old and new, from this clause. Judge Story, (vol. iii. p. 195,) speaking of newly-acquired territory, says: "Until it becomes a State, the territory remains subject to be governed in such manner as Congress shall direct under this clause of the Constitution. No one has ever doubted the power of Congress to erect territorial governments within the territory of the United States, under the general clause 'to make all needful rules and regulations.'"

As to its popular or legislative construction, it would be tedious to refer to all the proof. Let it suffice, in the absence of the known opinion of a single jurist or statesman to the contrary, to refer to the opinions of the two ablest and most brilliant expositors that the Constitution has ever had off the bench—to the opinions of Mr. Webster and Mr. Calhoun. They were the acknowledged heads of the two great opposing schools of constructionists, and when they are found agreeing upon any construction, the fact may well be received for proof that the great mass of both schools are of the same opinion.

In a debate which occurred in the Senate in 1849, in reference to the power of Congress over the territory of California, in which Mr. Webster and Mr. Calhoun took opposite sides, Mr. Webster used the following language: "The whole authority of Congress on this subject is embraced in that very short provision, that Congress shall have power to make all needful rules and regulations respecting the territory of the United States." He afterward said again, during the same debate: "It is under that clause, and that clause only, that the legislation of Congress in respect to the territories has been constructed." To this opinion Mr. Calhoun gave his express and unqualified assent; and in his speech the next year on the compromise bill, in speaking of the power of Congress over newly-acquired foreign territory, he calls it "a power *expressly vested* in Congress *by the Constitution*, as has been fully established."

In 1810, Chief Justice Marshall, in delivering the opinion of the whole Court, (Sere *vs.* Pitot, 6 Cranch, 336,) said: "The power of governing and legislating for a territory is the inevitable consequence of the right to acquire and hold territory. Could this position be contested, the Constitution declares that 'Congress shall have power to dispose of and make all needful rules and regulations repecting the territory or other property belonging to the United States.' Accordingly we find Congress possessing and exercising the absolute and undisputed power of governing and legislating for the territory of Orleans." Again, in 1828, in Canter's case, (1 Peters, 511,) the same learned judge, delivering the unanimous opinion of the bench, said: "In the mean time Florida continues to be a territory of the United States, governed by that clause of the Constitution which empowers Congress 'to make all needful rules and regulations respecting the territory or other property belonging to the United States.' *Per-*

haps the power of governing a territory belonging to the United States, which has not by becoming a State acquired the means of self-government, may result necessarily from the facts, that it is not within the jurisdiction of any particular State, and is within the power and jurisdiction of the United States. The right to govern *may be* the inevitable consequence of the right to acquire territory. Whichever may be the source whence the power may be derived, the possession of it is unquestioned."

Without asking aid from what is said by Judge Story in his Commentary, who no doubt was familiar with the views of the other judges, the just inference from these two cases is, that Judge Marshall and his associates on the bench were inclined to think that the power might, if necessary, be inferred from proprietorship; but they deemed it unnecessary so to decide, because they entertained no doubt that the power to govern newly-acquired territory was expressly conferred by the clause in question. Whatever supposable doubt on this subject might exist in any mind, must be entirely removed by the case of Cross *vs.* Harrison, (16 Howard, 193,) unanimously decided by all the present judges in 1854. The opinion of the Court in that case, delivered by Judge Wayne, speaking of the territory of California, says: "The territory had been ceded as a conquest, and was to be preserved and governed as such until the sovereignty to which it had passed had legislated for it. That sovereignty was the United States *under the Constitution, by which power had been given to Congress* 'to dispose of and make all needful rules and regulations respecting the territory or other property belonging to the United States.'"

In the leading case of McCulloch *vs.* Maryland, (4 Wheaton, 316,) Judge Marshall, speaking for the whole Court, and in 1840, Judge Thompson, delivering its unanimous opinion in U. S. *vs.* Gratiot, (16 Peters, 537,) both refer, without qualification, to this clause, as the true undoubted source of the power over territories.

Here, then, we have five unanimous opinions of the Judges of the Court, delivered at intervals from 1810 to 1854, showing that for forty years they had all treated this clause as the true source of the power, without any intimation of the supposed distinction between new and old territory, or that the clause needed aid from any implied power. We have also the unanimous opinion of all the Judges, as expressed in three of these cases, that the power derived from that clause was not confined to the original, but equally applied to newly-acquired territories. Yet, notwithstanding all this, six of the present judges have the temerity to decide that it applies only to the original territory. What are we to think of this? They could not have forgotten their own decision in Cross *vs.* Harrison. It was too recent for that. Yet they ignore it entirely, as they do three of the other cases, and say not one word about either of them. They quote no authority in support of this newly-invented construction, and cannot call to their aid the opinion of a single respectable lawyer or statesman. The opinion of Judge Johnson, delivered at the Circuit, in Canter's case, and referred to by Judge Taney, will be found on examination to be no such authority. The long course of previous decisions had made its enlarged construction the true and only construction, even if there had been any room for doubt upon the subject originally. Those decisions had made that construction virtually a part of the law of the land. Their present decision is equivalent to a repeal of law and the making of law. This is not adjudication—it is mere usurpation. It is the substitution of mere arbitrary will in the place of the solemn and responsible functions of an impartial judicature.

The Court does not distinctly deny that the language is fairly susceptible of this established construction, but attempts to limit the application of the clause to the original territories—not because new territories would not equally need Federal legislation and governing; not because there was any reason or motive for restricting the power to the old territory—but because it does not say *any* territory, nor *territories* in the plural, instead of *the* territory, which, they say, points only to the territory *then* held. With equal propriety might they contend that the clause which makes the President "commander-in-chief of the army and navy of the United States" does not make him commander of the present army and navy, because it does not say *any* army and navy, nor the *armies and navies* in the plural, but only *the* army and navy, which merely points to the *then* army and navy. The one is not more grossly absurd than the other. The Constitution being made for all time, and the ownership of territory and other property needing Federal government and control being probable for an indefinite time, the phrase, "the territory or other property belonging to the United States," applies to whatever territory and property it may at any time own, as much as the similar expression in the other clause applies to whatever army or navy the nation may happen to have. The language is as appropriate and the reason for the extended application is as strong in the one clause as in the other. The restricted application is only equally ridiculous as to both. This mode of expression is familiar to all our written constitutions, yet this is the first instance in which it has ever been judicially attempted so to confine its meaning by such rigid literal construction.

The Court says, the power to "make rules and regulations respecting the territory" are not the words usually employed by statesmen in giving "supreme power of legislation." Yet the Constitution, by the very same words, gives to Congress its supreme power of legislation over the great subjects of commerce, coinage, and naturalization.

It also says the language is unlike that used to give Congress power of exclusive legislation over the District of Columbia, forts, dock-yards, etc. So it should have been; for, as no territory could lie within the bounds of a State, there could be no concurrent legislation for governmental purposes, and it would have been inappropriate to have designated that of Congress as exclusive.

Why this frivolous carping about the language of the clause? The Court concedes its sufficiency for all the government and legislation exercised over the old territories, and it must be equally adequate for the same purpose as to new territory. The Court cannot mean to aid the clause as to old territory by any power incident to proprietorship; for it declares the new government did not derive any such proprietorship by mere succession from the old confederacy; and there is no clause of the Constitution which makes any direct transfer of proprietorship over the old territory, and none but this that gives Congress any control over it. However grave may appear the doubts as to the correctness of the position, that the new government could not acquire property by succession from the old one, no such doubt can benefit the Court. Its argument must be consistent, or it is worth nothing toward proving the insufficiency of the language of the clause. It is proved by the concession of the Court, if not appropriate, yet to be all-sufficient for the government of any territory; and, therefore, no supposed peculiarity in the language affords a pretext for the restricted construction of the clause contended for by the Court.

It is insinuated by the Court, rather than expressly declared, that the clause in its restricted construction could derive aid from the fact that the old Congress had passed the ordinance containing the prohibition against slavery. Yet it distinctly admits that the old Congress had no power under the articles of confederation to pass the ordinance, and that, upon the change of government, it became a mere "nullity." It furthermore distinctly admits that the new government derived *no power by succession* from the old one. These concessions prove the intimated derivative aid to be a mere absurdity. If there were any force in the insinuated aid, it would have the preposterous effect of cutting the power conveyed by the clause into two parts by a geographical line; that is, it would empower Congress to prohibit slavery north of the Ohio, but not south of that river; the territory north of it being all that was embraced by the ordinance.

It is further intimated, that though the old Congress had no power to pass the ordinance, yet it might have been validated by some supposed agreement of the then States, or their acquiescence. But, unfortunately for the Court, there never was any such agreement, nor does the Court allege a single fact in proof of it; and the time—only two years—was entirely too short to infer a confirmation from mere acquiescence.

It appears, from the thirty-eighth number of the *Federalist*, to have been the better opinion even of that day, that the ordinance was a mere act of necessary usurpation, without any actual legal validity. One of the reasons there earnestly pressed for the adoption is, that it gives power for legally governing the territory, which the old Congress had not. The ordinance bears evidence on its face of the fact, that its authors were conscious of their want of power. It wears the aspect of an intended *quasi* compact with the future settlers of the territory, and contains a formal bill of rights restraining the legislative power of Congress over the territory, which would have been wholly inappropriate, and even absurd, in an act of mere legislation. The intention obviously was, that the ordinance should obtain validity by means of a ratification, to be obtained from the several States. This ratification was never made. It was not done, because all necessity for it was superseded by the Constitution.

The Court says there was no need for any express grant of power to make needful regulations respecting the movable or perishable property which the Government might acquire, because such power would go as a necessary incident to other powers. This is a doubtful proposition, but there is no need for discussing it; for if there was no need for such power as to future acquisition of such property, there certainly was as little or less need for it as to what was then owned; and the same supposed necessity for it as to the one equally required it as to the other also. It may have been intentionally given as to both merely with the view of obviating doubt or dispute; but the better opinion is, that it was intentionally given as to both, because it was deemed necessary. When we recollect that the Convention, not content with a grant of power to declare war and grant letters of marque and reprisal, deemed it necessary also to authorize Congress "to make rules concerning captures on land and water;" and, not content with the power to raise armies and provide a navy, gave Congress power also "to make rules for the government and regulation of the land and naval forces;" and, not content with the power to acquire sites for a seat of government, for forts, arsenals, etc., the Constitution expressly gives, in addition, the power to legislate for or govern those sites—when such necessary and indisputable incidents as these were not left to mere intendment or inference, we can well understand why such intendment or inference was not relied upon for the protection or regulation of the landed or other property of the nation. The Government being one of specified and limited powers, there was the utmost propriety in the obvious intention of leaving as little as possible to mere inference or intendment. It is wholly irrational to suppose that so vastly large a subject as that of the government of the territories, and the regulation of all the other property of the nation, would be left to be discovered and acquiesced in as merely incidental powers.

The Court properly says that the power over the territory and that over other property are so intimately blended in the section, that it must receive the same construction as to both; that is, if it refers to the future acquisitions of the one, it includes those of the other also. Now, it is quite obvious that the Convention could not have deemed it necessary, in addition to the power to "dispose of," also expressly to give power "to make all needful rules and regulations" respecting the small amount of perishable property then owned. Every object that could have been contemplated in regard to this property would have been amply fulfilled by the power to dispose of it. The power to make rules and regulations respecting that description of property must have been given principally, if not solely, with a view to future acquisitions of such property.

Yet the Court says: "No one, it is believed, would think of deriving the power to make rules and regulations in relation to after-acquired property of this kind, from this clause of the Constitution." With due deference, it may be confidently asserted that no intelligent student of the Constitution ever before thought of deriving that power from any other source. Judge Story (v. 3, p. 76) says: "The power is not confined to the territory of the United States, but extends to 'other property belonging to the United States;' so that it may be applied to the due regulation of all other personal or real property belonging to the United States; *and so it has been constantly understood and acted upon.*"

The true meaning of the clause being thus fixed as to the "other property," the Court is tied down by its own concession, that the clause also refers to and includes future acquisitions of territory.

The Court says the intention of the whole clause was merely "to transfer to the new Government the property then held in common by the States, and give power to apply it to the objects for which it was destined." If so, why did not the Convention make a simple transfer, which is nowhere made, in lieu of the mere power actually given—or why not content itself with the mere power "to dispose of" the property?

The conduct of the judges in attempting, for such insufficient reasons, to unsettle the long well-established construction of the clause which they themselves had solemnly affirmed only three years before, cannot be too seriously censured; but the fatuity of their avowed motive for it can excite nothing but ridicule. That motive was to get rid of the legislative and judicial precedents in favor of the power to prohibit slavery in the old territories; not perceiving, what is so obvious to all others, that if their novel construction be conceded, they are in no degree aided thereby. For they do not pretend that the implied power, which they admit Congress has over the newly-acquired territories, can be anything less than a power to "make all needful rules and regulations respecting them;" and it matters not, for their purpose, how the power is derived—whether as an incident or from express grant. Either way the power is equally under the restrictions and reservations contained in the bill of rights. In other words, if Congress has power to make the prohibition under this clause, the bill of rights notwithstanding, it may also do the same under the implied power. The legislative and judicial precedents in favor of the power to prohibit under either mode of derivation, must be equally available as a sanction to its exercise under the other mode also, because they equally prove that the restriction on the legislative power relied on does not prevent Congress from prohibiting slavery in a territory. Under either mode of derivation, it is an exercise of the legislative power of Congress, and the whole of that power is at all times under the restraints imposed by the bill of rights. So that a large portion of their very long and labored opinion has been thrown away in an abortive effort to prove that which, if proved, would really avail them nothing.

Extent of Congressional Power over Territories.

This subject was considered and decided in Canter's case, 1 Peters. It was there unanimously decided that, "in legislating for the territories, Congress exercises the combined powers of the General and of a State Government." That is, according to a familiar, well-established rule of construction as to State constitutions, Congress has all power not expressly prohibited.

This was the main point decided, and the basis of the decision. The Court had to sustain an act of Congress giving judicial power in a territory to a set of judges not instituted pursuant to the Constitution. Conferring judicial power is one of the very highest acts of sovereignty. To show the power in question, it was necessary to decide that Congress had supreme power over a territory, except so far as prohibited. To do this in the most explicit and unambiguous manner, the Court said Congress had the combined powers of the Federal and a State Government. In so saying, the Court did but announce a self-evident proposition. Both sets of powers are indispensable to *complete sovereignty* over a territory, and, as that can exist nowhere else, it must lie in the Federal Government.

Judge Marshall, in thus laying down the proposition in such broad, comprehensive language, did not make any qualification that the legislation must not conflict with the prohibitions of the Constitution, merely because no such qualification was necessary. He knew that no statesman or jurist could ever so far misunderstand the Court, as to imply its sanction to any legislation whatever contrary to those prohibitions. To use the language, "the powers of a State Government," could mislead no one; for everybody knows that all the legislative power of a State is always subject to the restraint of both the State and Federal Constitution. What was meant and all that was meant was, that Congress has complete sovereignty over a territory, except so far as expressly restrained by the Constitution. Yet the present Court fancies that this language of Judge Marshall is attempted to be perverted by somebody into an unrestricted license of all power over a territory. This man of straw, of its own creation, the Court belabors with most successful industry. It expended so much of its energies upon this easy task, that it seems to have had none left for the main point in issue.

Though it gives its full sanction and approval to the decision in Canter's case, yet it withholds its sanction from the expression, "the powers of a State Government," as properly descriptive of those of Congress over a territory. For why? Not because Congress does not really possess all power not expressly prohibited, but because, if you concede to it the power of a State Government,—which has the admitted power to prohibit slavery,—it may be inferred, the Court says, that Congress can do the same as to a territory. Then, to indulge the Court in its caviling, let Judge Marshall's language be qualified so as to read, "the powers of a State Government, except as expressly prohibited by the Federal Constitution," and it will stand admittedly correct. With or without this amendment, the language is not an express authority in favor of the power to prohibit slavery; but, according even to the concession of the Court, it is full authority in favor of the power, unless it be expressly prohibited. It also brings to bear in full force against the Court all the judicial and legislative precedents of the several States which have prohibited the importation of slaves. Let this be remembered when we come to inquire into the sufficiency of the prohibition relied on by the Court.

It may not be amiss, in passing, to remark that the decision in Canter's case is of the most doubtful authority of any ever rendered by Judge Marshall and his associates upon a point of constitutional law, and shows the extreme lengths to which the Court has always heretofore gone in sustaining the validity of congressional legislation. The same course of reasoning by which that decision is sustained would go far to cut loose congressional power over a territory from all constitutional restraint, yet the present Court, notwithstanding all its newly awakened zeal for putting the power under that restraint, has overlooked this bearing of that decision, and unnecessarily and most improvidently given it a direct approval. The Constitution says: "The judicial power of the United States shall be vested in one Supreme Court and in such inferior courts as Congress may from time to time ordain and establish. The judges both of the Supreme and inferior courts shall hold their offices during good behavior." Yet the Court in Canter's case permitted Congress to vest judicial power in courts whose judges were appointed for only a term of years, under the assumption that those courts were merely *legislative* and not constitutional courts. It seems to have been overlooked or disregarded that Congress had no judicial power to confer but that of the nation, and whenever that was attempted to be conferred it must be vested in the manner pointed out by the Constitution. The mandate for pursuing a particular mode is an exclusion of all other modes, and a virtual prohibition of all others. The excuse that these courts were for a territory and not for a State, would equally avail for not bringing any other mode of territorial legislation under the constitutional test. The true rule would seem to be the uniform one, that all legislative and judicial power are derived from the great fundamental articles of the Constitution; and that the exercise of either, in behalf of the nation, must always be in the mode and subject to the restrictions ordained by the Constitution. It cannot be denied that a territorial judge exercises a part of the judicial power of the nation as much as the Supreme Court itself. Properly speaking, there is not and cannot be any such thing as a congressional or territorial judicial power, separate and apart or in any way distinct from the all-comprehending judicial power of the nation. Relying upon Canter's case as a sound precedent, and reasoning upon it by analogy, even such a man as Mr. Webster, on one occasion in the Senate, was seduced into the utterance of much loose talk, little creditable to him as a constitutional lawyer. The present Court would have earned deserved praise if it had annulled the authority of the case as a precedent on that point.

The conclusion on this branch of the subject is, *that Congress has complete sovereignty over a territory except so far as expressly restrained by the Constitution.*

The Power to Prohibit Slavery.

As there were no slaves in any part of the territory upon which the Missouri Compromise operated, the prohibition against slavery therein was a mere mode of prohibiting the importation of slaves. Where the power to prohibit the importation exists, the power to prohibit slavery or to order the emancipation of slaves as a penalty against their importation is a necessary incident, rendering the one power the equivalent of the other, just as the power to forfeit goods is an incident to the power to prohibit their importation. There is, therefore, no need for any separate discussion of the two powers, but both may be considered as involved in the discussion of either.

From the extraordinary and desperate efforts made by the Court to get rid of the legislative and judicial precedents in favor of the power, the inference is, that even in the estimation of the Court itself, those precedents must be of the strongest and most imposing character. So, indeed, they are. The names of legislators and judges who have either exercised or sanctioned the power could be culled by the hundred, every one of whom was fully as competent to form a correct opinion on the subject as either of the six judges who decided this case. The commencement of its exercise may be said to have been anterior to the adoption of the Constitution. It was exercised in the ordinance of 1787, and that, though anterior to the Constitution, is yet a most imposing precedent in favor of the power under the Constitution. For the Court distinctly admits that it was anticipated and intended that the new Congress should either re-enact the ordinance or pass some equivalent law. The clause prohibiting slavery being the most novel and striking feature in the ordinance, it must have been supposed by the framers of the Constitution that they were giving power to prohibit slavery in the territories. Accordingly, one of the first acts of the new Government was to re-enact the ordinance with its prohibitory clause. Since then the same power or its equivalent, the power to prohibit the importation of slaves into a territory, has been exercised by Congress in 1790, 1798, 1800, 1804, 1805, 1809, 1820, 1836, 1838, 1845, 1848, and 1850. This has been done with the sanction of nearly every President we have had, and with that, too, of all the able statesmen and lawyers composing their various cabinets. So far as known, no member of any of those cabinets, no Federal or State judge, has expressed his dissent against the exercise of the power.

In 1790, Congress, not waiting for the time when it could prohibit the importation of slaves into the States, prohibited their importation from abroad into the territory of Mississippi, under penalty of three hundred dollars and emancipation of the slave.

In 1804, under like penalty, it prohibited the introduction into the territory of Orleans of any slave imported into the United States since May, 1798; and further prohibited the introduction of *any slave* into the territory, except by a citizen of the United States removing into the territory for actual settlement.

Nearly all the slave States have, to some extent, prohibited the importation, and this, too, with the entire sanction of their respective courts, and of the Supreme Court itself. Each of these States having, in its constitution, a clause exactly like that relied upon by the Court to prove the non-existence of the power, every one of those many acts of State legislation and adjudication are authoritative precedents in favor of the power, and nearly as much so as if they had occurred under the Federal Government. The Court of Appeals of Kentucky, in affirming the validity of one of these acts said: "We regard it a fundamental principle, which, so far as we know, is denied by no citizen, that each State possesses the unquestionable right of determining for itself, whether, and to what extent, the right of property in the African race shall be recognized within its own territory." The Supreme Court decided in the same way in reference to a statute of Mississippi in Graves *vs.* Slaughter, (15 Peters, 108.) Judge Taney himself there used the following explicit language: "In my opinion the power over this subject is exclusively with the several States, and each of them has a right to decide for itself, whether it will or will not allow persons of this description to be brought within its limits from another State, either for sale or for any other purpose."

This sort of exposition, this reiterated, undisputed exercise of power by both the Federal and State Governments for a series of more than sixty years, is the highest and most authoritative construction that the Constitution can possibly receive. A construction so established, so sanctioned, should probably never be disturbed for any cause. Certainly it should never be attempted by any court at all mindful of its true duty, but for reasons of the *weightiest, clearest, and most indisputable character.* Such reasons the nation has every right to expect the Court to furnish on the present occasion. Let us then see what is its argument to prove the Missouri Compromise unconstitutional. Here is that argument and the whole of it, verbatim:—

"The rights of property are united with the rights of person, and placed on the same ground by the Constitution, which provides that no person shall be deprived of life, liberty, or property, without due process of law. And an act of Congress which deprives a citizen of his liberty or property merely because he came himself or brought his property into a particular territory of the United States and who had committed no offense against the laws, could hardly be dignified with the name of due process of law."

Without the proof before our eyes, it could not be credited that any set of judges would offer this as a sufficient argument in their justification. It is a novel mode of dealing with a grave constitutional question of vast importance. It is a mere naked say-so, without a why or wherefore to prove that the act unconstitutionally deprives any citizen of his property. Yet this is the whole, literally the whole, argument!

If it had not come from so high a source, the intimation that the prohibition *deprived* a slaveowner of his property, within the meaning of the Constitution, would be deemed the excess of absurdity. So long as his slave remains outside the territory, the law does not touch the property. If he brings it within the territory, and thereby subjects the slave to emancipation by operation of law, it is his own voluntary act in *violation of law*, and the consequent loss, whether considered as a penalty or otherwise, is appropriate and just according to the long-established usage of American legislation. It is his voluntary act in connection with the law gives the negro power to have him summoned before a court and get his right condemned by a judgment, just as smuggled goods are condemned. Or the master may sue to recover and get his right adjudged, and in either way he is deprived of his property by *due process of law*, according to any proper interpretation of that technical phrase. This, of course, all rests upon the idea that Congress has power to make the prohibition. Let us inquire into that power.

Sovereignty over the territory must have rested somewhere, and, as it could exist nowhere else, it was in Congress. The power to define what shall or shall not be property and to prohibit importations are among the most indisputable attributes of sovereignty. Congress when legislating for the States can exercise no power that is not *expressly granted*, yet when legislating for a territory it may use any power that is not *expressly prohibited*. Where then is the inhibition, express or implied, against the power to define what shall be property in a territory or to prohibit importations into it? The power to regulate commerce in the territory must be one of the indisputable powers of Congress. Under the power to "regulate commerce," Congress prohibits a citizen from importing his slaves into the Union, and no man contends that he is thereby deprived of his property within the meaning of the Constitution. It was anticipated by the Convention that Congress would exercise this power, and its use therefore was expressly withheld for twenty years. If it had been deemed incompatible with the old cherished principle that "no man shall be deprived of his property but by due course of law," such use of power would have been expressly prohibited. The absence of such prohibition, and the exercise of the power after the adoption of the bill of rights, prove that both the Convention and Congress thought the prohibition was not incompatible with that cherished principle.

It is impossible to ascertain precisely what the prolix and confused opinion means as to the express grant to "make rules and regulations respecting the territory." If it means that Congress could lawfully re-enact the prohibition contained in the ordinance by virtue of that clause, then it concedes away the whole controversy. In making that re-enactment Congress exercised part of its legislative power, and nothing can be plainer than, as contended by the Court, that whenever and howsoever Congress legislates, it must be in subjection to the limitations on that power made by the Constitution. If, then, it was lawful for Congress to make the prohibition as to the old territory, it must be because said prohibition does not "deprive a citizen of his property without due process of law," and the consequence is inevitable, that neither does it so deprive him when the prohibition applies to new territory. Whether the territory be new or old can make no sort of difference as to the true meaning of that part of the bill of rights. It is not within the compass of human ingenuity to invent a plausible reason for any such difference of meaning.

There is an authority on this point which the Court has taken care to forget, but which ought to have had much weight with these judges, however free they may feel to disregard all other authority. It is that of their own recent and unanimous decision in Rhodes *vs.* Bell, (2 Howard, 397.) There the Court, under an old law of Maryland, adopted by Congress, which prohibited the importation of slaves, decided a negro to be free because he had been brought, contrary to the statute, from one into another county of the District of Columbia. If such a law deprived the owner of his property without due process of law, then the legislature of Maryland had no power to pass it, for it violates the Constitution of that State; and Congress had no power to adopt and re-enact the law, because it violated the Constitution of the United States. Here, the point whether such a law was in violation of the Constitution, was directly involved, and the Court in effect unanimously decided that it was not. It may be urged, by way of extenuation, in behalf of the Court, that the point was not expressly raised by counsel; but that is no sufficient apology for the Court, as it was the duty of the judges to notice it, if it be so plain a proposition as they would now have us to believe. They could not have forgotten the Constitution, and that they did not perceive its pretended bearing upon the negro's claim to freedom, only serves to prove that up to that time the idea had never entered the mind of either of these judges that such a law deprived the owner of his property contrary to the Constitution. It is full proof that the idea is a perfectly new invention, gotten up for the first time when they felt such strong necessity for declaring the Missouri Compromise unconstitutional. They quote no authority in support of their novel idea, and it is believed that none whatever exists. Ever since the subject has become a matter of political party contest, the power has been repeatedly discussed in and out of Congress by heated partisans, little careful of their legal reputations; yet it is believed that not one of these disputants ever found sufficient plausibility in the idea to urge it as an objection to the exercise of the power. Thus to invent a misapplication of a great principle, thus to misapply a part of the Constitution without being able to adduce an authority or even an argument in their vindication, is surely a very grave fault, a most serious violation of duty. If a settled construction of more than sixty years, a construction of such transcendently high authority, can be thus disregarded without a reason, the Constitution becomes a flimsy thing to be perverted and misapplied at any moment to serve the purposes of a political party or gratify the caprice of any judge.

What the framers of the Constitution meant is always a proper subject of inquiry. These judges could have gone into history, or even tradition, to have found something to aid them. They had before them a wide field of inquiry. The great principle upon which they rely had been incorporated with the political law of England and this country ever since the days of *Magna Charta*. It is incorporated with all our State constitutions, and is familiar to every lawyer. Where is the authority for the meaning the Court now gives to it? When and where was that or any analogous application of it ever made before?

While the history of the time cotemporaneous with the adoption of the Constitution is barren of any fact, incident, or expressed opinion in support of the Court, that history is rich in material for its condemnation. It is well known that the almost undivided public sentiment of that day was in favor of prohibiting slavery in the then territory. In proof of this, witness the fact that the ordinance containing the prohibition against slavery was almost unanimously passed by the old and re-enacted by the new Congress. Many members of that old and new Congress were also leading and influential members of the Convention. The Court admits the intention to give power to Congress to re-enact the ordinance or pass some equivalent law for the government of the territory. Embodied in the ordinance as originally passed and as re-enacted, is found a *quasi* bill of rights, declaring that no man shall be deprived of his property but by due course of law. This declaration would never have found a place there if the statesmen of that day had thought that the principle conflicted in any degree with the power to abolish slavery, or at least not without the necessary qualification to prevent such conflict. They never would have framed an instrument that was self-contradictory. The first Congress that re-enacted the ordinance, at the same session unanimously proposed the amendment by which the principle was expressly introduced into the Constitution. This they certainly would not have done if they had believed the principle was at all in conflict with the power to abolish slavery, which they had just exercised. They never would have proposed a prohibition on the legislative power, the effect of which would be to nullify what they themselves had so recently done, or prevent the future exercise of a power then so popular and deemed so necessary. If there were any room to doubt the meaning of the members of the Convention, there can be none such as to the intention of the members of Congress who prepared and proposed this amendment. No rational man can believe that they intended it should prevent, or even curtail, the exercise of the power to prohibit slavery in the territories. It may be safely affirmed that the contrary intention stands fully proved.

But why go elsewhere for elucidation when the Constitution itself contains such all-sufficient evidence of the meaning of its makers? They understood that the power to regulate foreign commerce gave full power to prohibit the importation of slaves, and therefore took the precaution to expressly prohibit its exercise for twenty years. The power to "make all needful regulations respecting the territory," necessarily includes the power to regulate its commerce. Under this clause, then, the framers of the Constitution must have intended to give the power of prohibiting the importation of slaves into a territory, just as by the other they gave power to prevent their importation from abroad. This view so narrows and simplifies the subject as to bring it within the ready comprehension of the humblest mind. The only answer that even sophistry can offer against the sufficiency of this argument is, that such prohibition is not a *needful* regulation. The ready reply is, that the old Congress having made so recently such an extended prohibition of that kind, every presumption was that the new Congress would carry out the same policy, and if the prohibition had not been deemed a needful regulation, the power would have been expressly restricted in that particular.

That accurate writer, Judge Curtis, says in his very able dissent, "it is necessarily left to the legislative discretion to *determine* whether a law be *needful.*" This is true when a law is challenged on the score of its mere policy; but it is not true when the law is impugned for alleged breach of any of the great fundamental principles of civil liberty. In that case the judiciary might well intervene, and say that no such law was *needful* within the meaning of the Constitution, as it never intended to confer on Congress power to violate any of those principles. Hence the Constitution was originally framed without a bill of rights; the strict logicians who framed it contending that it was not needed, as no power could ever be implied as *necessary* which was in violation of those principles. If, therefore, the prohibition were really a violation of the principle relied upon by the Court, it could have condemned the prohibition as not *needful*, even though the principle had never been incorporated in the Constitution. It has been sufficiently shown that the prohibition is no violation of the principle as meant by the Constitution, or as understood by jurists; and the action of the old and new Congress in putting the prohibition into the ordinance, fully proves a prohibition against importation into a territory was *needful*, according to the sense in which the word was used by the framers of the Constitution.

Take, in connection with this demonstrated intention, the total insufficiency of the clause in the bill of rights for the purpose of the Court, and the fact that the power has been so repeatedly exercised by Congress and State legislatures for a series of more than sixty years without any judicial denial, but with reiterated judicial sanction, and we have what is more than sufficient to outweigh the opinions of any six or sixty judges, even though every one of them was as brilliant a luminary as ever adorned a bench.

The Policy and Justice of the Missouri Compromise.

If this were merely a judicial opinion, here the discussion should close. But as these judges have dragged their court into the political arena, and have purposely lent the powerful aid of their opinions to foment that prejudice as to the alleged injustice of the compromise so industriously inculcated by modern politicians on Southern people, it will not be amiss to inquire into the grounds of this alleged injustice, and prove how wholly insufficient they are as any excuse for the judges in usurping jurisdiction for the purpose of making such a clearly erroneous decision; in other words, to prove that the compromise was eminently proper, just, and needful; and if not, then that the reverse would afford no extenuation for the conduct of these judges.

The whole history of our National and State legislation proves a universal belief that slave property may be noxious to other property and important public interests, and therefore comes under the sanitary care and restraint of just legislation.

This subject received deliberate investigation upon principle many years ago, from the Court of Appeals of Kentucky, in the case of Jarman *vs.* Patterson, (7 Mon. 644.) The attempt there was, under the Constitution of Kentucky, to prove the invalidity of a statute directing any slave found working for himself, with the permission of his master, to be hired out for the public use. The Court said: "It is true, one of the objects avowed by the Constitution for its own adoption is to secure the enjoyment of property. It is also true that a citizen cannot be deprived of his property unless by the judgment of his peers or the law of the land. But it is equally true that considerable latitude is left to the legislature in controlling property for public purposes and to avoid public injuries. It is also true that the compensation to the owner is required by the Constitution before his property can be applied to public use; but still there is a considerable scope of power uncontrolled by this provision, within which the legislature may regulate the tenure and control the use of property, and *such power is necessary* in all well-regulated governments.

"It is a maxim indispensable to the well-being of society, '*so use your own as not to injure the rights of others;*' and to enforce it, for the protection of individual as well as public rights, belongs to the legislature.

"Hence the power to prohibit and abate nuisances from unhealthy trades," etc.

The Court, then, decides that the nature of slave property peculiarly requires it to be brought within the operation of the principle, and that the act in question impaired no just right of the owner, but only compels him so to use his property as not to injure the rights and repose of others.

Whence the conceded right to prevent a citizen of Kentucky, as well as citizens of other States, from importing his or their slave property into the State, but upon the idea that the legislature has a right to view and treat slave property as noxious to other property and other private rights and interests of her citizens? All the free States and nearly all the slave States have legislated in the same way and upon similar ideas of justice and sound policy. Congress has repeatedly done the same. Upon the same principle nearly all the States exercise the power to prohibit the importation and sale of noxious drugs and of lottery tickets and the circulation of small notes of banks not chartered by the State. The Supreme Court has decided that the power of Congress over a territory is the same as that of a State government over a State. Why, then, may it not legislate in the same way, and make similar prohibitions for the benefit of a territory? If it were conceded that such legislation did, to some small unappreciable extent, impair the value of all slave property, still that would be but an unavoidable incident to the exercise of a power which, according to all analogy and almost universal usage among the States, is recognized as a power necessary to all good government. As expounded by Congressional and State legislation, by Federal and State adjudication and popular opinion, the universal sentiment has heretofore been that slave property might be injurious to other property and other private and public interests, and that such legislation was not only not unjust toward slave-owners, but was eminently just and proper, in view of the permanent well-being of the State. It is not merely presumptuous, but entirely too late, for any three or six judges to act on a contrary hypothesis.

Experience has so conclusively proved the deleterious effects of negro slavery in latitudes not suited to it, like those of Delaware, Maryland, Virginia, Kentucky, and Missouri, that it also proves a power to prohibit it in territories of similar latitude to be a necessary if not an indispensable power of government. We of those five States, though thoroughly convinced that it is an unmixed evil to us, yet are equally convinced that in our time it is an equally unavoidable evil, and one which nothing but the slow hand of time can cure, by the gradual substitution of white for slave labor. If we were now free from the institution, with our present lights, there are but few, very few, intelligent men in those States who would vote for its introduction. Yet, with all this unanimity of opinion against the institution, we are all equally convinced of the impotency of any efforts to get rid of it. This results from the mere fact of its having been permitted to obtain root among us. If once allowed to obtain extensive root in a State it becomes ineradicable. Hence the great necessity for a power to prevent its introduction into territories not suited to it, as the inhabitants must ultimately experience, from the want of such prohibition, all the evils now felt by the people of those five States. The amount of damage to those five States is immense, in a pecuniary point of view alone, while enduring the long procrastination of the transition from black to white labor. In less than half a century it cannot fall short of the full present value of all our land and slaves. No intelligent man doubts that but for negro slavery Virginia would still be the richest and most populous State in the Union. The incipient stage of a territory, when it has few or no inhabitants, is the very time when the question of slavery should be permanently settled. As its proper settlement depends mainly upon climate, the power to settle should be, as it is, a discretionary power.

The Court says that the bill of rights in the Constitution manifests the general intent to protect property as well as personal rights from arbitrary legislation. But conceding that it does, that will not at all tend to prove that prohibiting slavery in a territory where there are no slaves is an arbitrary infringement of the right of property. There can be no infringement of a right that does not exist.

The Court says that "the Constitution gives Congress no greater power over slaves than over any other description of property." This is true; but it is equally true that it restrains the legislative power of Congress in the territories over slave property no more than its power over any other property. It is an incident to all plenary legislative power to define what shall and what shall not be the subject of property. The prohibiting the importation of certain descriptions of property is another of those incidents. The power of Congress to prohibit the importation of horses or cattle into a territory is clearly a part of the supreme power over the territory. So also as to any other description of property, unless slave property be an exception. Why should it be such an exception? It is not pretended that the Constitution makes it so. If not, then that, like all other property, is left to the discretion of Congress to be prohibited or not, as Congress may choose. Under the power to regulate commerce with foreign nations and the Indian tribes, Congress has, as incident thereto, exercised the power to prohibit the importation of slaves and the carrying of whisky into the Indian country. As incident to the power of exclusive legislation over the District of Columbia, it has prohibited the importation of slaves into the District as merchandise. These exercises of power have never been questioned. Yet it is impossible to draw a distinction between these powers and the exclusive power of legislation over the territories, as to their bearing on this subject. If the exclusive power over foreign commerce carries with it the power to prohibit the importation of slaves, surely the exclusive legislative power over a territory must carry with it the power to prohibit the importation of slaves into the territory. The act under consideration is but one mode of declaring and enforcing the prohibition.

The Court fancies there is a distinction, and attempts to point it out by saying that the territories are acquired for the whole nation, and the power over them is a trust to be exercised for the benefit of the whole. This assertion may well be granted, for it is nothing more than the true nature of all the powers of Congress. They are none of them anything else than mere trusts, to be exercised for the joint benefit of the whole nation. If there be any one of those powers which ought to be, in any degree, an exception to this general rule, it is precisely this power over territories. There is a local interest, and it may be a peculiar interest, of the present and future inhabitants of a territory which Congress cannot with justice overlook in legislating for them. If the peculiar local interest be permanent, direct, and vitally important to its present and future inhabitants, while a contrary general interest is small, remote, and indirect, Congress may well permit the former to outweigh the latter. That is, *in foro conscientiæ*, it may well permit such consideration to influence its discretionary power of legislation. This, too, the rather because, when the subject is reduced down or elevated up to the point of pure ethics and the true doctrine of popular sovereignty, Congress is merely acting for and doing in advance for the inhabitants what it is presumed they would do for themselves if in political existence, and if they had themselves the control of the subject.

But, says the Court, such discretionary power in Congress may be abused to the prejudice of one section of the Union. This may be granted, for there is nothing peculiar in that. Such liability to abuse is an incident to every discretionary power held by Congress. The Supreme Court has frequently had occasion to declare it to be false logic to infer the non-existence of a power in government from the mere fact of its liability to abuse.

The Court says that this special exercise of the power is to the prejudice of one and the benefit of another section of the Union. This also *ex gratia* might be conceded, for this also can be proved as the result of the practical exercise of almost every legislative power of Congress. Nearly the whole South is agreed in the opinion that such is the practical result of every tariff on foreign manufactures, whether framed with a view to protection or not. The principal part of the supplies and munitions for the army and navy and the whole of the seamen being procured from the Northern States, the same local inequality attends the expenditure of more than two-thirds of the revenue raised by the legislation of Congress. Even Mr. Calhoun conceded that the alleged unconstitutionality of the tariff could not be judicially got at, because the motive of protection was not emblazoned in plain language upon the face of the act, and the courts could not go behind it to get at the partiality in the motives of its makers, or the partiality manifested in its sectional operation. If he had been more of a practical lawyer he would have known that what he desired would not have aided him in the least. It is an entirely new notion in jurisprudence to attempt to test the existence or non-existence of a discretionary legislative power by prying into either the motive of the legislature or the practical effect of any particular law. These are things with which the judiciary have nothing to do. They are confided by the people to the legislative department exclusively. For abuse of such discretion, legislators are responsible to the people alone. The judiciary holds no such arbitrary revisory discretion over them—and God forbid that it ever should. It would make the judiciary, instead of the people, the real ultimate sovereigns of the nation.

But, taking back the *ex gratia* concession, it may well be denied, *in limine*, that any such prejudice to one and benefit to another section of the Union was the necessary result of the slavery prohibition in the Missouri Compromise. Or if this cannot be made plain to every one's satisfaction, still it can be proven to every intelligent man's conviction, that a failure to exercise the power to prohibit would have resulted in a reverse operation of equal partiality to one and against another section of the Union. That is, that a failure to prohibit would have given the North full as just cause of complaint as the South is supposed to have by reason of the prohibition.

The obvious duty of Congress, in discharge of its trust for the whole nation, was to so legislate for the territory as would most speedily give it the necessary population for becoming a State and most rapidly promote the sale and enhance the value of the Government lands. These were paramount objects, in which the people of every section had a mutual, common interest. To this extent the interests of different sections no way clashed. What Congress did by the prohibition was precisely what, beyond all other things, was best calculated to promote those paramount objects. This is no matter of mere conjectural speculation. It is what every informed man knows to be literally true. The superior growth in wealth and population of the Western free States over that of the Western slave States lying in or near the latitude of Kansas has proved it to a demonstration. Supposing Congress to have acted with a single eye to an honest and impartial discharge of the trust, it did precisely that which it ought to have done, in making the prohibition. The argument *ab inconvenienti* then shifts entirely to the other side, and if it were at all necessary in proving the power, its *existence* could be much more properly inferred from its *necessity* than the *non-existence* can be inferred from the fact of its *possible abuse*.

Experience has also proved that people from the free States and from Europe do not emigrate to and settle in slave States near so willingly or in such large numbers as they do in the free States of the same latitude. In fact, the institution of slavery is a practical though not a legal inhibition against their emigration to such slave States. The institution in a new territory is as much a prejudice to their right to settle there as the want of it is a contrary prejudice to Southern men. Either way, the one side or the other is to be equally prejudiced, indirectly and in the very same way, whichever course of policy Congress adopts. When the indirect injury to the two sections thus stood balanced, what could Congress do but disregard both, and look alone to the local interests of the future inhabitants and to the paramount objects of rapid populating and enhancement of the value of Government lands? So, upon the same sound policy, when it was legislating for the lower latitudes of Louisiana, Arkansas, Mississippi, and Florida, the institution of slavery was permitted to stand, and was promoted as the mode best calculated to secure those great paramount objects. This proves the *necessity* for a discretionary power in Congress over the subject, and, according to the reasoning of the Court, goes far thereby to prove the *existence* of such power.

Besides, two-thirds of the habitable part of the vast acquisition of territory from France had been devoted to the use and propagation of slavery, and it was but equitable that the Northern States should have secured to them an equal chance in settling the other third. In addition to this, then, as now, four-fifths of the people of the slave States were non-slaveholders, and furnish in the same proportion the probable emigrants from the South to such a territory as Kansas. The prohibition, therefore, was full as much for their benefit as for that of the people of the free States, except that, not partaking the Northern prejudice against slavery, its existence would not prevent their settling in the territory. But its presence there would have been to them no allurement. A legislation thus manifestly beneficial to more than nine-tenths of the whole nation, harsh in its bearing upon none, and only incidentally injurious in a slight degree to a species of property confined in its ownership to less than a tenth of the nation, cannot be deemed either partial, unjust, or impolitic.

However, all arguments to prove the wisdom or justice of this particular mode of exercising the plenary power of Congress are mere surplusage. With the wisdom, the justice, or the policy of the act the courts have nothing to do. They never constitute a judicial test of the validity of an act. All that the Court could do was to inquire whether Congress had plenary legislative power, except so far as restrained by the Constitution. This the Court explicitly concedes. What then remained for the Court was to point out the constitutional inhibition against this particular exercise of the power; and this is what it has wholly failed to do.

This notion of the right of an owner to carry his slave property to a territory, is based upon the idea that he has an indefeasible right to go there himself. This is altogether a false assumption; he has no such indefeasible right. There may be what might be termed an *equitable* right of that sort, to a limited extent, but there is no such *legal* right. No such right is guaranteed by the Constitution. Its existence is negatived by the whole course of legislation and adjudication in regard to the territories. Congress has no power to exclude a citizen from any State, for it has no power of legislation over a State for any such purpose. But it has such power in regard to a territory, because it has power of legislation over it for every purpose not prohibited. It accordingly has the power, and has frequently exercised the power, of excluding everybody from the territories until it thought proper to open them for settlement. This power might be used to set apart a territory for the exclusive occupancy of soldiers who had served in the army; or a portion of it for that of a certain class of foreign emigrants, to promote the culture of the olive, the vine, and the mulberry. Such appropriations would be liable to very just exceptions to their wisdom and justice, but the wisdom or justice of an act is no test of its validity. Such a test would annul a large part of our Federal and State legislation. Instead, then, of an indefeasible right to go to a territory in despite of congressional prohibition, no man can rightfully go there except by congressional permission.

As to the treaty of cession with France, it has and can have nothing at all to do with the subject. A treaty can never give judicial control over the legislative power of Congress. A treaty is a part of the law of the land only so long as it remains in force; that is, only so long as Congress permits it to remain in force. The power to abrogate it, in whole or in part, is an indispensable attribute of the national sovereignty, represented by the legislative power of Congress. For its infraction the Government is responsible to the foreign state with which it was made, but not at all to the judiciary. If an act of Congress violates it, it *pro tanto* abrogates the treaty, which to that extent ceases to be a part of the law of the land, and the judiciary have no say in the matter. If there was any vested individual right secured by the treaty, and which by any possibility could be affected by this act of Congress, it must be that of one who was a colonial inhabitant of Louisiana at the time of the treaty, in reference to a slave then held, or the descendant of such slave. Neither of these conditions is fulfilled by the owner or the slave in this case, and, therefore, no question under the treaty could rise out of the case. It is needless, therefore, to prove, as could easily be done, that the clause of the treaty relied on is not susceptible of a construction which would even tend to control the equitable discretion, much less the power of Congress, over the subject.

Conclusion.

The inference from the whole is, that these judges, in thus attempting to overrule former decisions and thwart a course of legislation of more than sixty years' standing, are endeavoring to deprive Congress, and thereby the inhabitants of a territory, of a proper, beneficial power, indispensably necessary to the permanent well-being of the territory. Such a result should never be attempted but upon compulsion, and for reasons of the clearest and most indisputable sufficiency. Such is not at all the character of the reasons upon which these judges have ventured to base their opinions. On the contrary, no lawyer will feel that he hazards anything in characterizing them as about the flimsiest and least satisfactory that ever influenced the opinion of any respectable tribunal upon an important question. As to the nation acquiescing in such an opinion, the idea is preposterous. Instead of quieting the subject, it will only serve still further to inflame the controversy, by stimulating the already too highly excited jealousy of Northern people against the imputed undue influence of the slaveholding power.

What degree of national censure is due to these judges, each citizen must determine for himself.

That they deserve a solemn rebuke, by way of protest, from Congress, no dispassionate and discreet lawyer can doubt; but that they will receive such rebuke, no man can believe. They themselves present the spectacle of six men not more venerable for their age than for the perfect purity of their private lives, inaccessible to the approach of any of the baser motives of corruption, and holding the most exalted and independent position in the Government, yielding to the suggestions of party sympathy so far as to bring upon themselves the sad reproach of having rendered a *political and sectional instead of judicial decision.* Their powers of reasoning and judgment, though they may not be of the highest order, yet are abundantly sufficient to have forewarned them that they were doing what there was great danger of being received as a gross insult to the intelligence of the whole nation, and more particularly to the intelligence of the American bar. Having dared and defied this danger, they cannot complain while receiving the only retribution which can reach them, the indignant censure of an independent bar and an independent press. By this single act they have done more to lower the moral tone and standing of our judiciary than anything that has ever occurred. They have brought the purity, from party bias, of our highest court under just popular suspicion. They have shaken the stability of all law, by destroying that of our highest law. The Constitution is, and must always be, in effect, what practical construction makes it. They have taught the lesson that its construction is never to be considered as settled, but ever to remain a changeable, fluctuating thing, and always be what the party passions and party exigencies of the hour may require.

Should any honest, intelligent reader be disposed to impute an undue severity to these strictures, he is requested to ask himself the question: If the opinions of these judges were as much calculated to do their party injury as they are to do it a benefit, *do you, on your conscience, believe that those opinions ever would have been delivered?* If he answer in the negative, then he will recognize the duty of every good citizen to lend his aid toward teaching these judges, as a warning to all others, that no station, however exalted or apparently irresponsible, affords exemption or shelter against a properly evoked national censure.

Finally, it may be claimed to have been proved:

First. That the Court had no jurisdiction or lawful authority to decide or intimate an opinion on any point, except that a negro cannot be a citizen; and the attempted apology for so doing is so destitute of even plausibility as to betray a reckless purpose, for some unavowed reason, to reach and decide the constitutionality of the Missouri Compromise.

Second. That the clause of the Constitution giving power to "make all needful regulations respecting the territory" is the true source of the power to govern territories; the language being sufficient, and it being contrary to principle to resort to any implied power when there is an ample express grant. That in denying this, and attempting to restrict the application of the clause to old territory, the Court willfully violates the settled construction of sixty years' duration, as manifested by the writings of our ablest commentators, the debates of our most eminent statesmen, and the repeated decisions of the Supreme Court, that of the present judges included. That the attempted apology for so doing is so unsatisfactory and so badly sustained by the reasoning of the Court as to betray an improper anxiety to get rid of the legislative and judicial precedents against them.

Third. That the power of Congress over a territory extends to all needful legislation *not expressly prohibited*, as proved by a reiterated course of unchallenged legislation during near seventy years, under the direct sanction of express decisions of the Supreme Court, and in accordance with the plain language of the Constitution.

Fourth. That the power to prohibit slavery in, or to prohibit the importation of slaves into, a territory, is a needful power, as proved by practical experience, together with the repeated action of Congress and the legislation of every State in the Union. That this power belongs to Congress because it is not expressly denied, being an indisputable part of unrestricted sovereignty, and because the Constitution itself bears full proof of the intention to confer the power, the Constitution saying, as it does, that the power to *regulate foreign commerce* carries the power to prohibit importation of slaves; and the power to make *all needful regulations* respecting a territory necessarily including the power to regulate its commerce, must also include the power to prohibit the introduction of slaves into a territory, according to the plain intention of the Constitution. That the novel assertion of the Court, that such prohibition deprives a man of his property without due course of law, within the meaning of the Constitution, is sustained by no one reason that the Court could invent, nor by any authority that it could find, but is opposed by cotemporaneous exposition of the meaning of the framers of the Constitution and a host of legislative and judicial precedents both State and Federal.

Fifth. That the prohibition made by the Missouri Compromise was just and politic, even if viewed solely in reference to the white population of the slave States themselves, at least four-fifths of them being non-slaveowners, and furnishing from their class nine-tenths of the probable emigrants from the slave States to such a territory as Kansas.

END OF VOL. II.

www.ingramcontent.com/pod-product-compliance
Lightning Source LLC
LaVergne TN
LVHW050525100826
845148LV00002B/443

* 9 7 8 1 4 2 5 5 1 9 4 9 0 *